EUGENE FIELD'S CREATIVE YEARS

With every affectionate regard to Mr. and Mrs. Dennis.

Eugene Field.

March, 1895.

EUGENE FIELD'S CREATIVE YEARS

BY
CHARLES H. DENNIS

GARDEN CITY   NEW YORK
DOUBLEDAY, PAGE & COMPANY
1924

If I should seem now and then to trifle upon the road, or should sometimes put on a fool's cap with a bell to it for a moment or two as we pass along, don't fly off, but rather courteously give me credit for a little more wisdom than appears on my outside.

—TRISTRAM SHANDY.

Study hard, and with a little favour and good lucke, when a man least thinkes of it, hee shall have a Rod of Justice in his hand, or a Miter upon his head.

—DON QUIXOTE, Shelton's Translation.

CONTENTS

iii CONTENTS

EUGENE FIELD'S CREATIVE YEARS

EUGENE FIELD'S CREATIVE YEARS

I

YORICK AND A GREATER

I

TWELVE years of intimate association with Eugene Field, a master of the art of friendship, has left me a store of rich memories. These come thronging as I take up the long-delayed task of endeavouring to present a true and adequate picture of that remarkable man. His rare qualities should be better known than they are to the many admirers of his genius. Because of the undue prominence given by writers in the past to the lighter aspects of his mind, Field to many has become in a sense a legendary character—a sort of Eulenspiegel— very different from the true Field. This, perhaps, is not surprising, despite its extreme injustice, in view of the abounding whimsicality of his character. Even many who knew him well have been prone to exalt his extraordinary feats of clowning while almost wholly ignoring the many beautiful manifestations of his deeper nature.

The poet Stedman, a good friend of Field's, called him Yorick and went far in the direction of establishing the fitness of the name. And Field was indeed Yorick, but with more than a dash of Ariel—when he was not Mercutio. Stedman himself, in coining for the witty Westerner—who to Stedman seemed so very Western—the name Eugenio, recognized something finer in the mediæval

1

quality of Field's intellectual roystering than anything
that went to the making of a king's jester.   Rather was
Field the merry comrade of him who ruled the court, one
ready to cross rapiers with the best.   If at times he be-
laboured opponents with blown bladders of broad farce it
was because to level at them his irony's point would have
bestowed upon them a dignity they did not deserve.

But it is idle to liken the whimsy-ridden Field—whimsy
is a word from Field's own special magazine of things
worth while—to people out of Shakespeare or out of
history.   He was first and foremost emphatically himself—Grand Old Field, according to his own frequent mock
heroic characterization, the "Chicago Dante," the

> .   .   .   .   bard
> Of pork and lard.

Critics have called him "the children's laureate," "the
children's Shakespeare," sometimes "the children's Chaucer."   Striking terms these; labour-saving devices, if you
please.   But the man Field who lived so merrily and yet
so broodingly; who faced fate so light-heartedly and
courageously; who combated his natural loneliness so persistently and wrought with his pen so brilliantly and often
so sympathetically, so understandingly, deserves a more discriminating analysis of his methods of thought and his philosophy of work than ordinarily has been accorded him.

My present efforts to picture Field as he was in his
creative years—the results of which efforts must be sadly
imperfect in many respects—will be notably reinforced by
numerous bits of self-revelation from Field's own pen,
not a few of them singularly fascinating.

II

It is mid-afternoon of a day in the early '90's.   The
quiet of the editorial rooms of the newspaper office affords

a striking contrast to the confused movement and noise of the earlier hours and those of the hours that are to follow. From the remoter end of the narrow hall, the protrusive elbow of which gives it the form of a carpenter's square, comes the sound of an elevator door opening and shutting. There follows one staccato yelp, short and sharp and surcharged with agony. Another yelp and then another. They come nearer; they grow louder. Footsteps approach, peculiar footsteps, indicating a sort of loping gait, footsteps punctuated with the thudding ferrule of a cane. The yelps increase in volume and their note of suffering becomes heartrending. Then a tall thin man, smooth-shaven, cadaverous, enters my little work-room and drops into a chair at the side of my desk, writhing as if in intense pain, one fist pressed desperately against the small of his back. But I am not alarmed and my sympathies are in no degree aroused by these signs of suffering.

The visitor is Field. He is calling—informally, as always—upon his managing editor, and his demeanour is quite as usual on such occasions. The formula never varies.

A bit of conversation is a part of the game. It runs somewhat like this:

"Hello, old man. Back's bad to-day, I see."

"Oh! Oh!" from Field. "Oh! Oh! It's killing me. I felt it as soon as I stepped off the elevator. I can't stand it much longer. Oh! Oh!"

"Yes, isn't it terrible? But I endure the ordeal, as you see, with my usual philosophy. I have been in excruciating pain for the last five minutes, so I knew you were approaching."

By this time the show is over. Field is chatting normally, his sham agony forgotten.

Some years previously, when Field and I worked together in a little room only large enough to contain our two selves, our desks, and an extra chair for any visitor, we each had been accustomed humorously to put the other in his place at odd moments by telling him how grievous was the backache induced by that other's presence. This feeble joke persisted throughout all our later association, so that the yelps and agonized writhings became a sort of ritual to be performed whenever one dropped in to see the other. Even in the crowded street on more than one occasion I have discovered Field standing at the edge of the sidewalk giving his vivid imitation of one suddenly stricken with great pain, he having seen my approach before my eyes lighted on him. The mischievous grin that overspread his face in response to my appreciative laughter showed how thoroughly he enjoyed his own absurdities. Exchanges by mail or messenger of backache remedies, ranging from liver pads to bottles of horse liniment, constituted one aspect of the ridiculous joke. Witness also this pathetic note:

DEAR DENNIS:

An occasional thought of you gives me severe pain in the lumbar region. As I write this, there are dull throbbings just back of my pancreas. Oh! ough!

Yours in physical torment,

St. Louis, June 7th, 1888.   EUGENE FIELD.

Such methods of showing regard for a friend are, to say the least, unusual. Yet this horse-play vividly recalled to each of us our old intimate associations in the days of "Culture's Garland" and "Little Boy Blue" and in the succeeding delightful creative days and nights of the Horace paraphrases, of the Red Horse Mountain poems, of "Wynken, Blynken and Nod" and the whole cycle of lullabies.

III

Days and nights. For most of Field's poems in that period were written in bed, very late at night, or rather very early in the morning. This was a practice that originally grew out of Field's dual rôles of editorial executive and writer of humorous prose and verse, first on the Kansas City *Times* and later on the Denver *Tribune*, both morning newspapers. Because of his other work, Field in those years found opportunities for writing only after midnight in his office and in his home before his midday hour of arising. The habit of reading and writing in bed clung to him through the years when he no longer had a sufficient excuse for indulging it, habitually robbed him of sleep, and probably shortened his life.

The trivialities by which I have here attempted to illustrate one of Field's most characteristic traits—his habit of dramatizing his friendships—may serve also to indicate why he was so greatly beloved by those who not only knew but understood him. The exchange of some conventional word of greeting with one who had his regard would not have satisfied his affectionate nature any more than it would have appeased his harlequin fancy. So he built up legends about each person whom he enriched with his sympathetic companionship. It pleased him to represent such friends to their faces as shedding a baleful influence upon him, as seeking by their malign presence to wither the white flower of his blameless life. Consequently there was much mock serious recrimination, and Field's laugh was never more hearty than when in these merry exchanges he himself received a palpable hit. Monumental virtue and Edenic innocence were characteristics with which at such times he modestly endowed himself, whereas the sinfulness of the friend or friends then present ostensibly grieved him exceedingly. His weighty words of admonition, delivered in his deepest bass tones and excruciatingly funny in their substance, had all the outward seeming of words spoken by a Daniel come to judgment.

These adventures in make-believe were, of course, mere passing gusts of fun. They constituted but one of innumerable manifestations of his imagination's infinite variety. Hopeless indeed would be any effort to catalogue his pranks. These were as natural to him as breathing and required as little effort. Being mere surface ebullitions of a joyous spirit and a creative nature seldom surpassed in readiness and richness, they have received far too much attention from writers who have tried to picture the true Field. To reduce them to their proper relationship with his really significant qualities, one may liken them to the games that children play when school lessons are done. Ambition, Field's exacting schoolmaster, saw to it that the pupil made progress steadily despite that pupil's inextinguishable playfulness. Meanwhile his games gave Field mental refreshment, they exercised his imagination and helped to give him such expertness in literary balancing feats as was a source of continual astonishment to readers of his daily newspaper column.

For Field was, first of all, a journalist. Those who have pictured him as a captive Samson toiling at the mill of the Philistines did not really know the man. Even long after his bibliomania had developed in full force, even after he had achieved fame throughout the English-speaking world, he maintained his keen interest in public affairs and his comments on men and measures were as admirably conceived and as incisive as ever. As an example of the strong professional interest he took at all times in the work of making a newspaper, I quote the following which appeared in his column a little more than a year before his death, at the time of a great and menacing strike of railroad workers:

The Chicago press is covering the strike admirably. It is a business involving labour, danger, patience, discretion, discrimination, ingenuity, skill, and expeditiousness. The qualities answering these demands are being exhibited to a degree by the Chicago newspaper reporters at this time; the excellence of their work has been sustained through a period of exceptional excitement and fatigue. Never before have reporters responded with such promptness to the demands of duty and never before have such even and well-sustained results been wrought out amid confusion, tumult, and danger. We have always been proud of our Chicago reporters; as a class they are a manly, dutiful, ambitious, courageous, keen lot of fellows. We are prouder of them now than ever before. We hope that no evil will befall them in these trying times and that there will soon come a suspension of this terrific strain upon their energies.

IV

But it is Field the poet of childhood in whom the world is mainly interested; for he it is whom the world loves. Many of the schools of the United States annually celebrate "Eugene Field Day" with recitations and songs from his poems. He is the poet of happy children and especially of children who dream in their waking hours. He is also the consoler of parents who have lost a precious little one. And he is more. He brings into the lives of imaginative small folk glimpses of such wonderful things as serve to reinforce their rational belief in fairies and all the other strange but admirable dwellers in the Land of Nowhere.

The extent to which Field's child poems enter into the training of children in schools and homes is really extraordinary. Mary E. Burt, in her preface to "The Eugene Field Book," a volume intended for use in schools, writes that while in Liverpool in the year before Field's death she "was first impressed with the great value of Eugene Field as a poet for the schoolroom." In that city, while looking for new methods of effectively training the child mind, she was taken to one of the several schools "most approved in advanced thought and method." In one of its classrooms which she visited "about one hundred boys of an average age of ten or eleven years were reciting 'The Rock-a-By Lady' with great spirit. Afterward," she continues, "at a brilliant poetry contest at Carnegie Hall, New York, 'Seein' Things at Night,' recited by a twelve-year-old boy, receiving a tremendous encore from a crowded house of scholarly people, I was reassured that a new poet had come to share the laurels so generously bestowed by the American public on Whittier, Longfellow, Lowell, and Holmes.   But it is in my own schoolroom and among my own pupils that the most genuine realization of Eugene Field's genius has come to me." Similar testimony will be given readily by many another experienced teacher.

It was Field's special desire that his poems should contribute to the emancipation of children's imaginations from the drab surroundings of every day.   His life was a constant rebellion against that deadly matter-of-factness which so soon throttles the child's beautiful habit of wondering, the habit that makes of it a fearless adventurer questing after all manner of mysteries. Living and thinking by rule was in his view a frightful obstruction to intellectual growth.   He had intense and well-considered opinions on this subject.   In the eyes of little children he saw a reflection of his own longing to discover hidden things, to respond to the spirit of high adventure.   He sought to give them in beautiful words and in lilting rhyme inspiration for independent research among the fascinating unrealities that are so very real to truly imaginative childhood.   That the resulting achievement is something fine, in that it helps to satisfy a real hunger in the souls of little folk, is clear to those who are aware of the peculiar affection that children have for the verses Field wrote for them.

How Field came to possess the power to interpret the child mind is no mystery.   All his life he studied the books of writers for children of many lands. He was a master of fairy lore. Legends and folk tales he collected with tireless persistence. He studied children themselves at every opportunity. He knew how to set them to wondering and he delighted in their quaint and illuminating ways of expressing their thoughts. In this specialized knowledge of childhood as in other important respects his whole career was a growth. He constantly made intellectual progress and he worked year after year to develop his mental powers through the help of books and plays and music and the conversation of notable men. With it all he continually practised the art of friendship. He loved his kind and lavished the wealth of his comradeship upon those who gave in return the poor payment of appreciation for his sincerity, his genius, and his desire to make of life something finer than mere animal existence.

Stagnation he abhorred. He was in turn newspaper executive, unsparing satirist, humorist, poet. He was notably successful in each of these rôles. But success with him was not satisfying success until it had been built upon pure and tender thoughts that are cherished by human hearts. So he became in his later years the children's poet; and the simplicity and imaginative power of the child mind had for him the strongest appeal of all.

II

A Blend of West and East

I

THERE are in existence two short autobiographical sketches of Field. One, the well known "Auto-Analysis," is especially interesting because in it Field summed up briefly, about a year before his death, the points in his career that seemed to him of special significance. The other sketch was written about seven years earlier, when Field was still at the threshold of his fame. Brief as it is, it sets forth better than have been set forth elsewhere the principal events of his life up to the time he joined the editorial staff of the Chicago *Daily News*. The sketch was prepared for Andreas's History of Chicago. Of it Field wrote humorously to B. H. Ticknor, his first publisher, in 1888, when "Culture's Garland" was in the making and Stedman had declined to write a preface for the book:

Mr. Stedman need not be ashamed to write a preface for me. I'd have him know that a biographical sketch of myself appeared last winter in A. T. Andreas & Co.'s Pictorial Chicago, Vol. III. It would have had my portrait, too, if I'd been willing to pay $50 for the book.

Here is Field's own brief story of his early career:

Eugene Field was born in St. Louis September 2, 1850. His mother dying before he was quite six years old, he was taken to Amherst, Massachusetts, and reared by his cousin, Miss Mary Field French. Travelled in Europe 1872–73. Began his newspaper career in June, 1873, as a reporter on the St. Louis *Evening Journal*, of which paper later in the year he became city editor. In May, 1875, he went to St. Joseph as city editor of the St. Joseph *Gazette*, where he remained

10

about a year and a half, when he returned to St. Louis as editorial paragraphist on the *Journal* and *Times-Journal*, where his work attracted a good deal of attention.   During 1880–81 he was managing editor of the Kansas City *Times*.   In the latter year he went to Denver as managing editor of the *Tribune*.   In August, 1883, he came to Chicago.

Wrote his first verse in 1879, his first story in 1884.   For two years he was corresponding secretary of the Missouri Press Association. He was married at St. Joseph, October 16, 1873, to Miss Julia S. Comstock.

In this little sketch Field erroneously gave September 2d as his birthday.   His poem, "Thirty-Nine," bears the date September 2, 1889, as if that were the "hapless," the "wretched" day apostrophized by him.   Until his last years Field thought that the date of his birth, but he finally discovered from family records that his birthday actually was September 3d.   The rest of the autobiographical sketch is accurate and it constitutes one of the remarkably few bits of reliable information published about Field in his lifetime.   So little, indeed, had appeared about him in print that on his sudden and untimely death the newspapers found themselves possessed of but scanty biographical material.   They were forced to depend largely upon a brief article that I had written for a literary journal at Field's request two or three years before.   By way of expressing his appreciation of the article at the time of its publication Field gave me a framed and autographed portrait of himself.

Though not quite thirty-three years of age when he began his service on the *Daily News* he already had been ten years in the newspaper harness.   In that time he had won distinction both as a writer for the press and as the executive head of newspaper staffs.   Yet after his death so experienced a journalist as Julian Ralph wrote of Field:

He was rather a literary man on a journal; a wit, an essayist, a rhymester upon a newspaper, if you please, but not a journalist.   He always talked to me about the work of practical and genuine journalists as if what they did was partially incomprehensible to him— and wholly strange and wonderful.

This leads me to suspect that the canny Field took pains to draw Ralph out and made rather a thorough job of it. Indeed, at the time Ralph visited Chicago and made Field's acquaintance, "Sharps and Flats," Field's famous column, contained a succession of stories that Field had gleaned from Ralph. Field's supposed lack of knowledge in regard to the business of making a newspaper apparently proved excellent bait for the accomplishment of Field's purpose—that of getting Ralph to tell all he knew.

II

What sort of newspaper man was Field, viewed from the side of practical service?

James McCarthy, a writer widely known through the West under his pen-name "Fitz-Mac," wrote after Field's death:

Field was managing editor of the illustrious old Denver *Tribune* thirteen years ago, when I came out from the East to be its news editor. He was therefore my immediate superior and the duties of my place required me to be in constant intercourse with him, asking his advice and receiving his instructions in the gathering and handling of the telegraphic news. He was himself a very complete journalist —the swiftest and easiest in handling his work that I have ever known—while I was far from being the most capable or experienced of news editors. It was thus in his power, if he had possessed a mean spirit, to have made my job unpleasant for me. But his sweet patience, his brotherly forbearance and helpfulness, made my relations with him one of the pleasant memories of my life. Thus he won my gratitude and affection.

In later years Field spoke affectionately to me of "young McCarthy," and he encouraged McCarthy to persevere in making paraphrases of Persian poems done somewhat after the manner of Field's own playful rendering of Horace.   These indications of his continuing regard for his former associate are illuminated by McCarthy's testimony.   McCarthy wrote of Field:

We were like two lovers together, each anxious to be seen by the other only at his best, and therefore carefully avoiding familiarity while cultivating a delightful intimacy.   My intimacies with dear old Field occurred late at night after the forms had been sent down to press.   We were both in delicate health and the night work was killing.   When it was over we were too dead fagged to join the rest of the staff in the usual refreshment of sandwiches with beer or coffee, too tired also to go home and sleep; so we often went out and walked together in the morning air to refresh ourselves, walked for hours sometimes until the head weariness became leg weariness, and we could go home and sleep.

Those hours are beautiful memories to me.   It was spring, and the hours before dawn had a tender soothing melancholy in them, with a tinge of mystery which no doubt gave the tone to our conversations.   We talked a great deal, I remember, of death.   Neither of us expected to live twelve years.   Both of us had almost a curiosity to turn the sealed page and penetrate the mysteries of the beyond. Our talks were not dreary nor depressing, but seemed to cheer and refresh us.   We sometimes walked out on Capitol Hill, where the fragrance of hyacinths and lilacs filled the cool morning air, and gazed off through the dim light across the valley to the snowy range whose crest was distinguishable by a rim of amber-greenish light. We walked like two boys, hand in hand.

This, then, was the Field whom McCarthy knew, and this was the Field whom I knew, except that Field when I knew him had grown confident of his coming fame and of his ripening power, confident of his ability to write beautiful things worthy of the world's applause.   Both McCarthy and I were years younger than he and so he accorded to us a kindly support and an elder-brotherly regard.

III

Field's early childhood was passed in St. Louis, the city in which he was born and where his father, Roswell M. Field, was a distinguished lawyer.   The hatred of Negro slavery which had induced the elder Field to undertake, without hope of monetary reward, the defence of Dred Scott, the slave, for whom he fought a long and brilliant legal battle, made him a strong supporter of the Union when rebel sympathizers sought to win Missouri to their cause.   But young Field and his brother Roswell knew little of the struggle of the border loyalists, for they were then under the care of their well-beloved cousin, Mary Field French, in Amherst, Massachusetts.   However, the war spirit as he felt it in New England and manifestations of which he beheld all about him impressed the boy deeply.   In my last conversation with him, in August, 1895, Field told me in some detail his plans for a book which he contemplated writing and which was to bear the title, "A New England Boy in Wartime."   In that book he intended to relate his experiences and impressions during the war years, sketching also the actions of the fervent men and women whom he saw determinedly holding the lines behind the Union armies.   His love for the rugged Yankee character would have made the writing of this book a delight to him.   I have no doubt that its humorous and pathetic scenes, framed in his boy's wonder, would have proved very effective not only in a literary sense but also as a cross-section of human emotion in a time of great strain.   Field told me that he would attempt to show how the long and desperate conflict affected individual men and women, what they said and did, how their strong characters reacted to the shocks of lost battles and to their grief over slain sons.

He related one incident that he intended to incorporate in the volume.   With two or three other boys he was walking one day along a country road not far from Amherst, when they saw some distance away an old horse and carryall.   "It is Deacon Spencer's," they told one another, "but there's nobody driving."   To think of the deacon's old horse going anywhere of his own accord severely taxed their young imaginations. But as they stood staring they discovered that a man was in the carryall, a man who leaned far forward, his head below the top of the dashboard. The strange drooping apparition startled them. Soon, however, they recognized in it a familiar figure despite the unfamiliar attitude. "It's the deacon," they said. The wonder grew. At last the boldest of the boys ventured to pronounce this tremendous verdict: "The deacon's been drinking!"

The old horse ambled steadily forward. The scandalized boys stood in their tracks. When the carryall came opposite them the deacon slowly lifted his head and the boys saw that his gray and weatherbeaten face was streaming with tears. The deacon halted his horse and said to them brokenly: "Boys, our beloved President, Mr. Lincoln, has been assassinated."

IV

How deep was the impress, both mental and spiritual, that Field took from his boyhood surroundings in New England is continually manifest in his writings. Yet his schooling, like the other elements in his early career, was a curious mingling of East and West. After their preliminary instruction in Amherst, under the eyes of Miss Mary Field French, Field and his brother were sent to an excellent boarding school for boys at Monson, Massachusetts, kept by a worthy minister, the Rev. James Tufts, and his wife. That was in the fall of 1865. The Rev. Mr. Tufts said years later that Eugene was a very mischievous boy whose mind had been little developed. There, as one of six boys under the minister's care, he was drilled in Latin and he learned some Greek. Thus he plodded through Cicero and Virgil and made forays upon Homer. Even in that day he loved declamation. Mr. Tufts is authority for the statement that the boy was "by nature and training respectful toward religion." This indeed is not surprising in view of the Puritan surroundings in which he had been reared at the home of Miss French and at his father's boyhood home in Newfane, Vermont, where his stately Congregational grandmother still resided. However, fellow pupils of Field's have recorded some of the many pranks played by him in the three years that he was under the guardianship of Mr. Tufts, and they were of a sort to indicate that he did not trouble himself to be respectful toward any secular thing.

Finally the long-suffering master of the school deemed Field ready for college. He was received at Williams College in the fall of 1868. His scholarly father required him to write all his letters to the elder Field in Latin, and indeed he had made respectable progress in that language, of which he remained fond throughout his life. One of his classmates in Williams was Isaac Henderson, with whom years later he renewed acquaintance in London, Henderson in the meantime having become a well-known novelist. Field recorded gracefully in his verses, "The Boltons, 22," his pleasant London associations with his old college mate.

Before the end of his freshman year the serious-minded faculty at Williams decided that Field had too little love for learning and too great fondness for mischief to be a desirable student, so he was gently sent back to the patient minister-schoolmaster at Monson. But then his father died and Professor John Burgess of Knox College became his guardian. Very soon after his nineteenth birthday he entered Knox, at Galesburg, Illinois, to be under the eyes of his guardian. Knox also found in him an exceedingly lively acquisition to the student ranks. Field took up his residence at the leading hotel, where he lived amid surroundings that quite dazzled his fellow students, with whom he became immediately popular, despite what they called his "Eastern notions." The very considerable size of the library that Field owned was a wonder to them. However, the hotel burned and Field's books burned, too. Another loss which Field suffered through this fire he never ceased to regret. It was the loss of all the letters his father had written him from the time he was taken away from his St. Louis home after his mother's death.

One of Field's associates at Knox long afterward recalled how Field looked as he sat in his hotel room, carelessly dressed and wearing his hair rather long, smoking a cob pipe and surrounded by youths who listened delightedly to his droll stories. His love for newspaper work manifested itself in his frequent contributions, mainly on college topics, to the Galesburg *Register*. A common question about the college was: "Have you read what Field had in the *Register* to-day?" Though his mischievous doings were innumerable, the professors and instructors were fond of him, since there was nothing ill-natured or demoralizing in his fun.

v

Field once related to me a curious incident of his life at Knox. His head, he told me, was full of romantic ideas and he had a very special desire to emulate the example of his greatly admired father by winning renown as an ardent lover. For the elder Field, as a budding lawyer in his native town of Newfane, had suddenly taken captive the heart of a young girl and the two had been hastily united by a clandestine marriage, though the bride at the time was engaged to be married to another man who had the approval of her parents. The girl's incensed relatives immediately brought about the separation of the runaway couple and soon induced the girl to marry illegally the man of their choice. Field carried the matter into court, demanding that his wife be restored to him, and by a series of remarkable suits which he conducted brilliantly and relentlessly he made the case celebrated throughout New England. Finally a court decision, delivered apparently in the interest of the innocent offspring of the inconstant young woman and her second mate, pronounced their illegal marriage legal. Thereupon Field removed to St. Louis and he later married happily there.

The admiring son of Roswell Field, while a student in Knox College, thinking to prove his own romantic fervour, began to make violent love to the very young daughter of a Knox professor. The startled maiden promptly told her parents, who as promptly shut her up at home and warned the ardent young Romeo off the premises. Thus was Field's experimental romance effectually squelched in its preliminary stage. There being plenty of other mischief to engage his attention, he surrendered to adverse fate without more ado.

Field wrote, long afterward, an amusing little article about Galesburg, into which intrudes a tantalizing hint of mystery. He started out by denying, with a fine show of indignation, a report ostensibly published by a Buffalo newspaper that there were "no dress suits in Galesburg." He objected particularly to the flippant tone that characterized the offensive article. "To say anything about Galesburg," he declared, "without having first bared the head and assumed a reverential attitude as well as a solemn tone is simple and unadulterated sacrilege." Further, it was false to affirm that there were no dress suits in Galesburg. "Colonel Clark E. Carr has one," Field testified. "We saw the Honorable Hank Evans wear it at a reception in Springfield one evening." Yet Field conceded that Galesburg was not a dress-suit town. "Galesburg," he said, "takes life seriously and with imposing solemnity. She abhors and eschews every worldly vanity, and the only excess in which she indulges is the planting and cultivation of rose bushes." Then Field proceeded to develop the theme in this wise:

Rose bushes everywhere—in the streets, over the lawns, all through the gardens, climbing over the porticoes, on the window sills, in the houses—everywhere rose bushes and roses, fragrant and beautiful. If ever a scandal invades this delectable community it is kept strictly sub-rosa, and all things carnal, spiritual, temporal, and eternal are glinted and tinted with couleur de rose. These rose bushes and these roses lend their characteristics to the community itself, so that however fragrant may be the memory one has of Galesburg it is always *a thorn that pins that memory to the heart.*

The italics are mine. When those last words were written Field perhaps had in mind the loss of his beloved father's letters.

VI

Field's brother Roswell had entered the University of Missouri at Columbia about the time Eugene entered Knox. In the autumn of 1870 Eugene joined his brother in the Missouri institution, entering as a junior. A son of Field's roommate at Columbia has told me that, according to his father's testimony, Field had a passion for social diversions at that time and was far too busy with all manner of distracting occupations to do much studying. On one occasion, when Field had been instructed to hand in an essay the next day, he chose to go to a dance instead of writing the essay. His roommate, at Field's request, wrote it for him and the next morning Field copied it— and I fancy he materially improved it in the process. Then Field took the essay to class and was highly commended by the professor because of its literary quality.

To a fellow student at Columbia, Edgar Comstock, Field became attached. Young Comstock's sister Ida came to visit him and saw much of Field, whose extraordinary mirth-making methods impressed her greatly. She found that he was a special favourite among the girls, to whom he showed many attentions.   At some entertainment of the students he was to sing "Comin' Thro' the Rye" or, rather, a special version of that song made by himself.   "For this occasion," Ida—then Mrs. Below— wrote years afterward, "I drove five miles with him to get an old-fashioned hoopskirt; and imagine my consternation when, entering the principal street of the little town, he donned that obsolete adjunct of feminine attire! The more I begged him to take it off the faster he drove."

That visit of Miss Ida's was fateful indeed, for it led to Field's being invited to visit young Comstock's family in St. Joseph.   There he found a houseful of fair young daughters and among them a dainty miss in short dresses, Julia Comstock.   Field fell in love with fourteen-year-old Julia at sight and speedily won her affections, to the alarm of the mother, who insisted that her little Julia was much too young to think of marriage.   However, Field agreed to wait.   So he went back to Columbia.   At the end of his junior year he collected what was left of his small patrimony—about $8,000—and went to Europe, taking along the brother of his lady love, whose expenses he paid. After six hilarious months in England, Ireland, France, and Italy, the money was spent to the last dollar and the travellers returned as best they could, mainly through the kindly aid of Field's unfailing friend and second father, the executor of his father's estate, Melvin L. Gray of St. Louis.

"I came home broke," Field once said to me.   "So I got married."

VII

His young sweetheart had reached the age of sixteen when they were wedded.   She was his good angel through-

out the rest of his life.   Indeed Field never doubted that
his Julia, his "dear girl with velvet eyes," was by far the
greatest blessing ever bestowed upon him by a kindly
fate.   Her love for and her pride in him were joined with
extraordinary good judgment, fine intelligence, marked
gentleness, and an uncomplaining spirit.   She pre-
sided over his household with graciousness and dignity
and despite straitened circumstances kept things going
in decency and comfort.   And she bore him eight children.
Field had the good sense to make her the family treasurer,
so that she had the handling of the incoming funds to the
extent that he could deny himself the luxury of spending
money for books and for a multitude of other things that
appealed to his fancy. James Whitcomb Riley said
soon after Field's death:

His wife is as remarkable a woman as he was a man. She is
strikingly handsome and yet with a face of force and strength of
character suggesting to me that Field was in no small degree indebted to her for the inspiration that had led him on to success.

If he was not indebted to his wife for inspiration at
least he was very deeply indebted to her for the unfailing
comfort of his home, for sympathetic companionship and
encouragement, and for the steadying influence that
enabled him to prepare himself systematically through the
years for the literary work that brought him fame.   Field
was proud of her and on all occasions she accepted his
jokes at her expense with a serenity that was not to be
shaken.   By way of illustrating his method of enjoying
himself regardless of his wife's embarrassment I give this
typical example:

One evening as the two were starting to call at a friend's
house Mrs. Field chanced to remark that she wished she
had put on a better dress.   A moment or two later they
boarded a street car.   While Field stopped at the door to

pay the fares Mrs. Field moved to the front of the car and sat down.   Field fumbled in his pocket for a coin, found it, drew it forth and, as he handed it to the conductor, said in his deepest voice, so that his words were plainly audible to all the occupants of the car: "I wish to pay the fare not only of myself but of that beautiful lady in the exquisite and costly gown whom you see sitting yonder." Having thus drawn all eyes critically to the dress which Mrs. Field wished she had not worn, Field was perfectly happy.

One of Field's favourite stories—a story usually told with much elaboration and never twice in precisely the same way—related how in a dream he died and went to heaven, where he encountered many interesting people of past ages.   The conversations he had with them were surprising enough, but the one of chief interest was with that amiable but sorely tried patriarch, Job.   After a little improving exchange of ideas Field complimented his ancient companion upon his long-established and well-deserved reputation for patience.   Thereupon the venerable spirit heaved a profound sigh.   "It is true," said Job, "that for a very long time I enjoyed quite a reputation for being patient, but now I have had to take a back seat. You see, there's a woman in Chicago—name's Mrs. Eugene Field—who has proved herself to be a lot patienter than I."

III

With Valley Folk and Mountain Men

I

MARRIED men find it necessary to take a serious view of life. Field, who was married soon after reaching the age of twenty-three, had been working since the preceding June as a reporter on the St. Louis *Evening Journal*. In that city he made a home for his young wife. Before the end of the year his ability won promotion for him and he was made the city editor of the newspaper. His first assignment as a newspaper man had been to write a criticism of a performance of "Romeo and Juliet" by a dramatic company in a local theatre. His humorous instinct led him to build the criticism around the ill-fitting wig of the Mercutio of the cast. He thought he had produced a particularly effective piece of criticism, but to his chagrin when it appeared in print all references to Mercutio's comic wig had been edited out of it.

In the second year of his newspaper service Field made a tour of Missouri with Carl Schurz, then a United States senator from that state. Schurz, who was seeking re-election, made political addresses wherever he went and Field reported the meetings for his newspaper, incidentally perpetrating countless jokes. One of these jokes has become famous and various versions of it have found their way into print. I had the story from Field's own lips and so tell it as he told it to me.

When Schurz and his party had arrived at one town where he had been advertised to speak, the local celebrity

to whom had been assigned the task of introducing him
failed to appear.   The crowd had assembled and was growing impatient, the orator of the occasion was on the platform, but still the absence of the chairman of the meeting
prolonged the awkward wait.   Schurz expressed his
annoyance to those seated near him.   Field thereupon
jumped up from his chair, saying, "I'll introduce you,
Senator," and, knowing that Schurz would suspect a
trick, advanced to the front of the platform before Schurz
could demur.   Then Field made the introduction sub-
stantially as follows:

"Ladees und chentlemens, h'm, h'm!"   (He coughed
hoarsely.)   "I recret it dot I haf a fery bad coldt."   (More
coughing.)   "I am so sorry to say it, but I gannot make
dot speech.   Howeffer, it gifs me creat bleasure to introduce to you mine tear friendt, dot prilliant chournalist,
Meester Euchene Fieldt"—turning and waving his hand
toward the amazed and indignant Schurz—"who will
now attress you."   Then he sat down.

Field's lively verses, "The St. Jo Gazette," presents a
very good picture of the work of a "lokil editor" in a city
of the size of St. Joseph back in 1875, in the spring of
which year Field removed thither.   Something of his
mettle as a gatherer of news is indicated by a story he told
me one time with a considerable show of satisfaction.   On
an afternoon in the early summer of 1876 he called on the
railroad station agent, as was his daily practice, seeking
some bit of information for the columns of the *Gazette*.
He found the agent disturbed and puzzled.

"I heard a message going over the wires a little while
ago," the agent told him.   "I didn't hear much of it—
only enough to learn that there has been serious trouble
somewhere and that a lot of men were killed.   There was
fighting or something like that."

Field was deeply interested at once. He tried to solve the mystery by a system of deduction hastily improvised. He knew that General Crook was in pursuit of Sitting Bull's rebellious Sioux warriors somewhere in Wyoming and that General Custer and his forces were particularly active in the chase. So he took a chance. With such information as he could gather from recent reports of the movement of the troops in the northwest he wrote the story of a battle that might very well have been fought. He thought he was making the conflict reasonably sanguinary, but he did not make it sufficiently so fully to conform to the facts. However, it was a first-class fighting story. The *Gazette* published it with suitable headlines and so that newspaper was able to boast when authentic reports of the disaster to Custer and his men were received that it had given the world the first news of the massacre on the Little Big Horn. Field was particularly happy because his deductions had been so nearly right that his story stood up unashamed in the face of the official dispatches.

II

It was after his return to St. Louis late in 1876 that he began to win more than local fame. The year before he left that city to become the managing editor of the Kansas City *Times* he wrote his first poem, "Christmas Treasures." In Kansas City he found himself in a whirl of stormy journalism, for the fiery editor of the *Times*, Dr. Morrison Munford, a Southerner and an ex-Confederate soldier, was a true son of battle. The year that he passed amid these surroundings closed his considerable term of active newspaper service in Missouri, a state which he had come to know thoroughly in all its aspects. The Missourians always had a fascination for him. He wrote much of them, and his knowledge of their public men was intimate. Because of his habit of assailing those whom he particularly liked, his innumerable attacks on "poor old Mizzoora," as he habitually called his native state, and upon those dwelling within its borders, may indicate that they ranked high in his affections. As a typical example of Field's treatment of the commonwealth and its inhabitants I quote an article written by him not long before the opening of the World's Fair in Chicago in 1893:

It is understood that Mr. Adam Forepaugh, the popular showman, is asking for a concession to make a Missouri exhibit during the World's Fair. The matter is to come before the Board of Control as soon as the concessions for the Borneo, Arkansas, Patagonia, Fiji, Guinea, and Lapland exhibits have been granted. It seems settled that no Missouri exhibit shall be made except as a private enterprise and there are few who have the information and the money to engage in a scheme involving such hazards.

Mr. Forepaugh, as an experienced and fearless collector, is perhaps better qualified for the delicate and arduous task than any other American citizen. He has travelled extensively in Missouri and is on friendly terms with most of the native tribes. It would be his endeavour to get together an imposing array of the natural wonders of that part of our republic, which at this time is, as it were, a sealed book to the rest of the country. Among other curiosities there would be a cage of tailed men that run wild in Clay County, a race unseen of but not unknown to Darwin, and by that famous investigator regarded as the much-talked-of "missing link."

Then again there would be the tree-dwellers of Calloway County, an insectivorous race that, spending their lives swinging from limb to limb in the scrub oaks and cottonwoods of central Missouri, have not infrequently been mistaken and shot by careless hunters for possums and coons.

There will be pigmies from the Ozark Mountains and genuine mermaids from the Osage River. The latter are most eccentric amphibians that come ashore regularly once every four years to vote the Democratic ticket. Another curiosity which Mr. Forepaugh will seek to obtain is the famous yellow dog of Boone County, which precocious quadruped voted for Buchanan in 1856 and subsequently was elected a justice of the peace in Blackfoot township.

There will be numerous cages of web-footed men from the swamp districts and hairy men and ringed snakes and singing mice and tattooed men and cave-dwellers and lizard-eaters, etc., etc.; there will be a complete collection of the fauna of Missouri, including the species of mossbacks found only in St. Louis; in short, neither pains nor expense will be spared to bring together such an exhibition of the natural, social, and intellectual resources of Missouri as shall give the beholder a fair knowledge of that singular part of the North American continent.

Throughout his adult years in Missouri, Field had been trying to find himself intellectually. He had a great longing to go upon the stage when he was through with college—he never got beyond his junior year—and he was restrained with difficulty from doing so by Mr. Gray. At one time he consulted Edwin Forrest on the subject, but the tragedian advised him in picturesque terms to give up the idea. Still, Field and a few stagestruck companions actually organized a dramatic company and went barnstorming in a few Missouri towns. Apparently the venture was a sorry failure, for Field never cared to talk upon the subject. Later, while he was in Kansas City, he appeared in a private entertainment as Madam Jarley and displayed a choice collection of imitation waxworks in a manner that gave the audience huge delight. And at all times Field, with his deep, flexible, and entirely wonderful voice, the extraordinary mask which was his face but which he could instantly transform into any one of an endless variety of other faces, and his inimitable gift of mimicry, was prepared to give strikingly good imitations of actors with whose leading parts he was familiar. He was particularly fond of imitating Sol Smith Russell and Henry Irving. Friends who were aware of his dramatic gifts, including not a few of his many actor friends, were convinced that he might have won notable success upon the stage in comedy parts. But when Field discovered the joy of doing creative work with his pen he had no further thought of deserting journalism and abandoning his hopes of successful authorship to take up the circumscribed profession of play-acting.

Whether his memories of laborious and unappreciated beginnings, of misunderstood endeavours, of ambitious efforts ill requited, caused him so persistently in after years to lampoon Missourians, or whether his lampooning was indeed a veiled expresson of affection for the people whose unprogressive politics and whose peculiar philosophy of life, a heritage from the old South, vastly amused him, is a question that I cannot answer. However, I believe that his familiarity with their customs, their speech, and their modes of thought—all so different from those he had known in New England—caused him to regard them whimsically at all times, as if they were a race apart. To evoke laughter at their expense, however, was in a sense to turn the laugh upon himself, a Missourian.

III

Writing, in 1892, of the death of his former editorial superior on the Kansas City *Times*, Dr. Morrison Munford, Field set down some of the memories of his years of newspaper work in Missouri. Of the period of his service there he wrote:

With the death of Doctor Munford ends an epoch in the history of Missouri Valley journalism—a period remarkable for turbulence, excitement, vicissitudes, and development. Beginning shortly after the close of the Civil War, it witnessed the enactment of scenes which only the times of war would seem to warrant; life and property were held of slight consequence, violence obtained to a preposterous degree, crime actually ran riot, and there appeared to be no such thing as observing temperance or moderation in action, speech, or thought. In the rapid, uncouth, wild, irresponsible drama humankind played in that valley in those times was our friend Munford a conspicuous character, and it is of him and of his associates that we would speak a little now—not by way of panegyric, for we seek neither to bury nor to praise anyone, but in the line of reminiscence, of casual tribute to men and to times of which we often think proudly and tenderly.

After giving his estimate of the leaders of Missouri journalism in his day, Field proceeded:

He who writes these lines remembers—oh, so distinctly!—how many, many times he used to pause in the midst of the toil of those days and nights out yonder in the farther West and wonder to himself whether ever he should think pleasantly of those times. For they were grinding days, and they wore upon the impatient, restless spirit. Ah, how sweet is this recompense which time has brought! The race is not yet run, nor the battle ended; but from the higher ground it is to look back upon those places where clouds once rolled and the storms seemed relentless, and now—lo! now they are pleasant pastures, rejoicing in the bridal with still waters, and the vision is delectable.

Field's Yankee blood and training and his inherited hatred for the "lost cause" of the Confederacy put him out of tune with the prevailing social and political institutions of Missouri in the years following the Civil War. However, his youthful search for a political party of progress caused him to consider casting his first vote for the presidential candidate approved by the Democratic Party after the candidate's selection by Republicans who opposed the reëlection of Grant in 1872. So he made a hopeful pilgrimage to the national convention of the Democratic Party. His observations there merely served to confirm him in the Republican faith of his father. Years afterward Field wrote:

The first national convention attended by the writer of these lines was that of the Democrats in Baltimore in 1872. There was a small number of delegates and the convention was held in a hall of meager proportions and of wretched appearance. The proceedings were short; at the time the writer received the impression that everything must have been fixed beforehand, for the programme was pushed at a two-forty rate. There were two incidents of a notable nature. When Delaware was called upon to record her vote a small, sickly looking gentleman arose in the body of the delegates and began to speak in a voice so feeble that he could hardly be heard. There were calls for him to take the platform and he did so amid general applause. Standing in this conspicuous wise, his emaciation and physical weakness were all the more apparent, but this condition and the exceeding pallor of his face, the luster of his eyes, and the weird carelessness with which his long, black, bushy hair was tossed about his head gave the man a certain distinct fascination. He was Thomas F. Bayard, who had arisen from a bed of sickness to protest solemnly against the stultification which the Democratic Party contemplated. He pleaded earnestly and eloquently, but in vain; his auditors listened respectfully and applauded him heartily; they even extended his time, but they voted against him.

When New York was called Governor Hoffman answered, and as he stood up his splendid figure and handsome face and noble bearing electrified every beholder. He said little, but what he did say was delivered with rhetorical art and grace; he had a deep, persuasive voice and an ingratiating manner. The convention seemed to go wild with enthusiasm when, with dramatic effect, he cast the fifty votes of New York for Horace Greeley and B. Gratz Brown. And at that instant a large silk banner bearing upon it a portrait of Greeley was swung out from the gallery in which the spectators sat, whereupon the delegates sprung to their feet, faced the banner, and cheered lustily.

A large number of heelers had come over from Philadelphia to give the independent, or "liberal," movement their moral support. The writer accompanied them to Philadelphia that night upon one of the wretched boats that ply between that city and Baltimore. As he lay awake that hot, miserable night hearing the curses and blasphemies of the drunken mob, he made up his mind that his maiden vote should and would be cast for the nominees of the political party that was happily free from the moral support of this brutal element of humanity.

IV

"Wrote his first verse in 1879," records Field's autobiographical sketch which I have quoted. And in his "Auto-Analysis" Field says:

I wrote and published my first bit of verse in 1879. It was entitled "Christmas Treasures." Just ten years later I began suddenly to write verses very frequently.

This of course does not mean that Field had not written much verse before 1889. It means merely that he did not burst into full song until that year, though "Little

Boy Blue" and other beautiful poems already stood to his credit.

Field always had a special fondness for "Christmas Treasures." He regarded this first of his poems—he had written much doggerel and other humorous verse previously—as an important milestone on the road to literary distinction. From it he dated his attainment of the intellectual stature of a poet. One day nearly a decade later I expostulated with him for devoting so much of his time to imitations of old English ballads, of the improving verses of Dr. Isaac Watts, and other bizarrerie instead of undertaking serious creative work. "I enjoy doing these things," Field replied, "and besides I am not yet ready to do my best writing. My mind develops slowly. I wrote no poetry at all until I was nearly thirty years old." So "Christmas Treasures," which Field once called "the first piece of serious work that I ever wrote," always was dear to him because it had given him, years in advance of any other bit of writing, tangible proof that he was capable of real poetic expression.

I think these verses have another claim to the consideration of admirers of Field's genius. To me they appear to contain the germ of "Little Boy Blue." And the poem is about a little child and about Christmas—themes that particularly appealed to Field from the beginning to the end of his literary career.

Certain verses of a very different sort composed by Field before he left Missouri won enormous popularity, it is difficult to understand why. "The Little Peach," written while he was on the staff of the Kansas City *Times* and first published in that newspaper, was copied everywhere. I recall that as editor of a college publication I copied and parodied that doleful ditty, as did many other would-be humourists. Somehow Field's diabolically fascinating lines made the tragic fate of Johnny Jones and his sister Sue screamingly funny. They were recited on the stage night after night. Lugubrious music was written for them and they were sung through innumerable noses. Francis Wilson has related that he first encountered the verses in London. He had no knowledge as to their origin, but he saw possibilities in them, so he brought them back to the United States and employed John Braham to set the words to dance music. Then Wilson used "The Little Peach" with great success in "Nadjy." In short, the verses brought reputation and no money to their author. Bad as they are, he gave them a place in his "A Little Book of Western Verse." In 1900 he wrote from London:

The awful song of "The Little Peach" has been put upon the market here by rival music publishers. A local poet has injected into the soulful poem this stanza:

"Said Johnny Jones his sis unto:
  'I fear it's more than I can do,
  But get that peach I must for you—
    For you.'
He thought the way to climb he knew—
His foot got caught, off came his shoe,
His jacket torn, his trousers too,
    Right through!"

Field undoubtedly was proud of the popularity of "The Little Peach." He frequently recited it to friends, always calling it hard names and always making it extremely amusing by loading it down with bathos, causing his voice to break here and there and descend into fathomless depths of clownish emotion. He once wrote of the verses:

Appeared in the Kansas City *Times* first. Sung by Henry E. Dixey, Sol Smith Russell, and almost every other comic singer of note in the country. Popular, but rotten.

V

At last Field found his way out of the Missouri Valley. The mountains of the West claimed him. Into the exhilarating life of Denver he threw himself wholeheartedly. The Denver *Tribune* management, through its efficient editor, Ottomar H. Rothaker, had selected Field for the newspaper's managing editor with a deliberate purpose. Field's consummate audacity and his ability to write scathingly were qualities that the management coveted, for it was making a strong fight to achieve first place in Colorado journalism. And Field gave the *Tribune* notable service.

One of the stories told of Field relates to his preparations to depart from Kansas City to take up his new work in Denver. The chief characters in the story, Field and George Gaston, who kept a bar and café not far from the *Times* office, told me the story in collaboration one day when Gaston called on Field in Chicago. In going over old times they laughingly related for my edification the version of the story here set down.

Field had been a frequenter of Gaston's place all the time he lived in Kansas City. Gaston regarded him with the greatest admiration and Field enjoyed unlimited credit there in consequence. When he was about to depart for Denver, Field paid a farewell visit to Gaston, accompanied by Rothaker, who had come to hasten Field's departure. There were also a number of others in the party. Gaston took occasion to say to Field: "Gene, when are you going to pay me what you owe me?"

"How much do I owe you, George?" asked Field.

Gaston named a substantial sum.

"Do I get a discount for cash?" Field demanded.

"Yes."

"How much?"

"Here, I'll tell you what I'll do," said Gaston, who knew that Field had no money.   "Pay me a dollar and I'll give you a receipt in full."

Field turned to Rothaker and said: "Lend me a dollar."

A silver dollar was placed in his hand and Field immediately transferred it to Gaston, who thereupon gave Field a written receipt covering his total indebtedness.

"Now, George," said Field, "you know that when a customer pays his account in full, as I have done, the proprietor is expected to stand treat."

"That's right," returned Gaston, highly amused. "What are you going to have?"

"Champagne for the party," replied Field.

Gaston at Field's request told me another story that had greatly amused Field when he first heard it.   "I am a Democrat," said Gaston.   "I voted in turn for McClellan and Seymour and Greeley and Tilden and Hancock and all of them were defeated.   In the political campaign of 1884 I was in bad health and thought I wasn't going to live very long, so I said to myself: 'Before I die I want to be able to say that I voted for one man who was elected President.'   So I voted for Blaine and Blaine was defeated.   Then in 1888 I said to myself: 'I'll not be fooled again into voting against my party.'   So I voted for Cleveland and Cleveland was defeated."   Gaston told me this story in 1889, and I cannot say whether or not he stuck by Cleveland again in 1892 and so finally voted for a winner.

VI

Field did much to build up the circulation of the Denver *Tribune*.   Besides directing the editorial staff he daily wrote paragraphs and verses that appeared on the editorial page under the heading, "Nonpareil Column."   The contents of the column created much comment and other

newspapers quoted liberally from it.   Later Field gave his
contributions the heading, "Odd Gossip."   He also wrote
theatrical and musical notes and reviews of plays.   An
inveterate theatre-goer, his characterizations of stage
productions were as brilliant as they were unique.

Mr. Willard S. Morse of Seaford, Delaware, who has
one of the most complete collections of Fieldiana in existence, was treasurer and later manager of the Tabor
Grand Opera House while Field was in Denver.   Mr.
Morse has written for me these memories:

Field was constantly at the Tabor and met many of his theatrical
friends there.   I remember particularly Helena Modjeska (see Field's
"Modjesky as Cameel," in which he mentions me), Marie Jansen,
Emma Abbott, Lawrence Barrett, and John McCulloch.   There was a
host of others.   Denver at that time was a good theatrical town on
account of its splendid opera house, and it was a regular stopping
place for a week's stand of all the large shows on their way to San
Francisco.   Field wrote, I think, all the theatrical articles that appeared in the *Tribune;* at any rate he certainly wrote many of them
and he would often come to me to obtain data.

Field was rather wild while he was in Denver, but I never knew of
his drinking.   However, he could go out with a crowd and get just as
"full" as the others were without drinking anything himself.   He
was always getting up jokes on people, but the time and the conditions that existed permitted almost anything to be done, for nothing
was taken seriously.

Mr. Morse's observation that Field could get as
"full"—that is to say as hilarious—as his bibulous companions without drinking at all explains much.   In this
matter-of-fact world Field in his earlier years found
among men who were engaged in drinking the lively comradeship that matched his mood; his high spirits and his
riotous imagination too commonly made sober men stare
and frown.   Their sense of personal dignity raised its
awful front to rebuke Field's merriment.   In a raw civilization where drinking was a part of the ordinary citizen's
every-day experience, Field not infrequently was sus-

pected of intoxication not only because of the condition of his companions but because his normal flow of spirits induced him to act somewhat as young men were expected to act after they had "liquored up." Surely drink could have had little attraction for one who was so full of mirth in any company merely because the sparkling wine of existence habitually went to his head. He would have nothing to do with liquor at any time during his years in Chicago. Neither did he associate with drinking men.

It was in Denver that Field in one of his dramatic criticisms wrote that a certain actor "played the king as if he was afraid somebody would play the ace." And it was in Denver that he wrote in ponderous iambics a description of a concert by Theodore Thomas and his orchestra. It began:

> O Theodore! of all musicians
> Thou art the boss, with a long primer B.

How the orchestra went into action was thus described:

> Then thou dost swing with more
> Vivacity thy little club, and all
> The other boys keep chipping in, as when
> To ope the jack-pot's sturdy bands we strive,
> And of the holding two tenspots are found
> To be the upmost hand. But after while
> Dost thou the circumambient atmosphere
> Like thunder pound and opened is the pot,
> And every one comes in, and chips pile up;
> With anxious zeal the fiddlers chase their bows
> Across the desiccated bowels of
> The feline lately gone beyond the range;
> Like a high-pressure engine flies the arm
> Of him who the seductive trombone works;
> And all the while the rooster with the big
> French horn doth blow th'internal revenue
> From out its sheeny convolutions deep.

The following typical paragraph written by Field for the *Tribune* serves well to illustrate the searing quality of his pen—that fateful instrument which branded so many victims:

Colonel G. K. Cooper went swimming in the hot water pool at Manitou last Sunday afternoon, and the place was used as a skating rink in the evening.

A parody which Field wrote on a well-known poem by Sidney Lanier, then newly published, was a product of that time and its remarkable run through the newspaper press seems to justify its partial reproduction here:

> Over the monstrous, swashing sea,
>   Over the Balderdash sea,
> The jayhawk wings his fluttering flight,
> The pelican greets the morning light——
>   Antonio, where is he?
>
> Over the gruesome, gruntling sea,
>   Over the Brobdingnag sea,
> Antonio came in the dead of night——
> Came like a jabberwock in his flight——
>   And borrowed four dollars of me.

Something should be said here of the "Tribune Primer," that slight pamphlet which has been republished so many times. There were forty-eight pages within its blue paper cover and the pages were four by six inches in size. The number of copies published is variously estimated at fifty up to two hundred. The very few existing copies of the original edition of Field's first publication are prized by collectors and command high prices. The absurd little primer lessons that make up its contents were originally published in the *Tribune* and were copied everywhere and soon were generally imitated by other newspaper humorists. Indeed, Field once said that he stopped writing them because everybody else had begun to do so. The reader of to-day is likely to pronounce the contents of the "Tribune Primer" sorry stuff. The following sample should suffice to indicate the character of the "lessons," many of which seem to have been conceived in a spirit of elfish mischief:

THE BABY

Here we have a Baby. It is composed of a Bald Head and a Pair of Lungs. One of the Lungs takes a Rest while the Other runs the Shop. One of them is always On Deck all of the Time. The Baby is a Bigger Man than his Mother. He likes to Walk around with his Father at Night. The Father does Most of the Walking and All of the Swearing. Little Girls, you will Never know what it is to be a Father.

Another production of that time was a lullaby of no particular merit which Field attributed to Henry Ward Beecher when he printed it in the *Tribune*. But in the midst of all this fooling he wrote his beautiful poem, "The Wanderer," to which he signed the name of Helena Modjeska and which was speedily republished far and near and universally credited to the gifted Polish actress, then at the height of her fame. Madame Modjeska once said of Field:

I knew him from the time I made my first American tour in 1879, when I met him in St. Louis. We were good friends ever after. He wrote much about me, some of it very funny. He once wrote a poem and signed it "Helena Modjeska." I think he wrote it only to have me deny its authorship, which I did. But it was a beautiful little poem.

Field indeed wrote much about Madame Modjeska, for whom he had a high regard. Consequently he made her the victim of many preposterous stories. The following is a mild example:

It is rumoured that the popular Paderewski is not the spring chicken that his business managers would fain have us believe him to be. We learn from a credible source that he was a suitor for Helena Modjeska's heart and hand as far back as 1864, at which time he was a professor of piano playing in the conservatory at Cracow.

But he was cut out by Count Charles Bozenta Chlapowski, political editor of the Cracow *Daily Polander*. It is furthermore narrated that the constant practice of eating lemons has given Paderewski's hair the peculiar tint and the still more peculiar willowiness which make it so remarkable a feature of the artist.

In her "Memories and Impressions," Madame Modjeska wrote, describing her first American tour:

In St. Louis I saw Mr. Eugene Field, another of the dear friends I gained in America. I admired him for his genuine poetic talent, his originality and almost childlike simplicity, as much as for his great heart. He had indeed a many-sided and rich nature—most domestic in his family relations, a delightful host by his own fireside, and yet a perfect Bohemian in artistic circles. The author of exquisitely dainty poems, and withal a brilliant and witty humorist, he was equally lovable in all these various characters.

VII

Field's long hours of work and his irregular habits threatened to break down his health. His family was growing, he was poor—his salary was forty dollars a week—and he had become weary of his hilarious companions in Denver. He determined to seek his fortune in some city farther east. Then chance threw him and Melville E. Stone, editor of the Chicago *Daily News*, together. The two had met some years before in St. Louis and Stone had taken a liking to the brilliant young man. He now offered Field a position as a special writer on his newspaper at fifty dollars a week, with the prospect of a higher salary as a reward for effective service. Equally enticing was the promise that he should be permitted to write precisely what he pleased, subject to reasonable editorial censorship. Stone himself was a young man, not much older than Field, and he was capable of appreciating the fine qualities of the scintillant Westerner. Field's ambition was to be a writer exclusively, and here was a chance not only to give up executive work but to increase his income and at the same time broaden his field of opportunity.   So Field resigned his position on the *Tribune* and removed to Chicago.

Stone wrote of Field in his "Fifty Years a Journalist": "When I met him the *Tribune* was about ready to quit. To this end he had contributed his full share." But Denver friends of Field's insist that the decline of the *Tribune* followed the departure of its versatile managing editor and was due to its inability to retain the sparkle that Field had imparted to it.   In any event, some months after Field went to Chicago the *Tribune* was absorbed by its rival, the *Republican.*

In order to discharge his debts and pay the expense of establishing a new home in Chicago, Field announced to his Denver friends that he would give an entertainment. He sold tickets in such numbers that he is said to have cleared about $2,000 in this manner.   When the entertainment was held the hall was crowded.   Field was the sole attraction.   He played the piano, sang, recited, and gave imitations of popular actors.   The audience pronounced the affair a complete success.   It was followed by a rousing farewell dinner to Field.

When he departed from Denver he was regarded there merely as an eccentric newspaper man and a good fellow. But after his death Denver was the first city to erect a public memorial in his honour.   In its monument depicting the adventure of those bold voyagers, Wynken, Blynken, and Nod, the city has shown its love for and pride in the poet.

IV

FIELD'S EARLY DAYS IN CHICAGO

I

THERE have been many newspaper columnists, so-called, but the greatest of them all was Eugene Field. He had made a specialty of this form of writing in St. Louis, in Kansas City, in Denver. In spectacular ways he had demonstrated his ability to interest and amuse newspaper readers. His endless drolleries and his breath-taking audacities had attracted the amused attention of the whole country. He took employment on the Chicago *Daily News* to give his whole time to this kind of writing. It was an opportunity such as he long had craved.

A few words about Chicago as it existed in that day should not be out of place here, since social conditions in the city where he laboured necessarily were reflected in Field's daily grist of satirical comment.

Chicago then boasted a population of a little more than 500,000. Its continued rapid growth and its abounding prosperity had made the citizens too generally satisfied with mere money-getting. Its relatively few very wealthy men aspired to be leaders in social and intellectual as well as in business activities. Field's resentment at the rule of the dollar in art as in abattoirs is disclosed in much that he wrote about Chicago. The effect of his satire was wholesome, but at first it was neither understood nor relished by the general public. However, it was seized upon with avidity in other cities; the newspapers of the country, particularly those of New York, displayed it prominently. And it was extremely funny. Those Chicagoans who saw the beneficial purpose that inspired it were not slow in showing their appreciation.

The city of the early '80's extended only from Fullerton Avenue on the north to Thirty-Ninth Street on the south, vast open spaces lying beyond those thoroughfares, which now are miles inside the city's boundaries. Lake View, the suburb to the north, which in recent years has become a densely populated part of Chicago, was then mainly given over to cemeteries and celery farms. Hyde Park, to the south, was distinguished for little else than its magnificent distances, though its great pleasure grounds and its boulevards already were taking form. Lincoln Park, in the northern part of the city, was still in part a cemetery as well as a place of recreation, and one who chose to do so might go there for meditation amid the tombs. The river was crowded with lumber hookers and the flimsy wooden bridges were swung open every few minutes to let two-masted stacks of pine shingles go through in the wake of furiously smoking tugs. The water in the river was as black as ink, with an imperceptible flow lakeward, and with persistent malevolence it discharged typhoid germs into the source of the city's drinking water. The central business district was ragged with vacant lots, on many of which remained piles of smoke-blackened bricks and other débris, relics of the great fire of 1871.

Standing at Monroe and La Salle streets and facing south, one saw along the west side of that thoroughfare not a single building all the way to Van Buren Street except a little wooden shanty on stilts in the heart of the present banking district, where were on sale at all hours prehistoric sandwiches and slabs of petrified pie. There was nowhere else that we night workers could go for our midnight meals except Billy Boyle's, in "Gamblers' Alley," where wonderful steaks and chops were always to be had at prices that staggered us poorly paid beginners in newspaper reporting. At Billy's, however, the social atmosphere was truly remarkable. There mingled our most eminent journalists, our most impressive police officials, our most popular politicians, and our most prosperous gamblers. There one might learn who had met with great winnings or heavy losses that night in our leading gambling houses in Clark Street or in our select and exclusive roulette and poker parlours in Monroe and Jackson streets.

At least a dozen such resorts, well known to everybody, existed within a radius of three or four blocks. Nobody did anything about it. There were leading business men of that day who said—and many more who thought—that wide-open gambling was an excellent thing for the city, that it "put money into circulation." So when a well-to-do customer came to town to buy a stock of goods, and some live business man—after selling him the goods—took him around to see the city, and the customer lost heavily at a poker table or a roulette wheel, the live business man felt like a philanthropist—he had "put money into circulation" in his dear old home town.

But we had other forms of innocent amusement in that day. Our league baseball games were played downtown in what is now Grant Park, and there stood also our Exposition building, where was held every form of entertainment from bench shows to national political conventions. In that rambling old structure were nominated three or four presidents of the United States. There were held the famous Theodore Thomas summer night concerts, where music lovers might enjoy the best works of the great composers while sitting around little foam-flecked tables drinking beer.

The boisterous and well-contented town was governed

from a two-story shack having the architectural charm of an icehouse or a livery stable.   It stood at the southeast corner of La Salle and Adams streets and was well named the Rookery—a name that is preserved to the present day by the skyscraper standing on the site of the old municipal structure.   One walking across the rickety floor of that weird seat of government made a noise like the clatter of horse hoofs.   Yet there His Honour the Mayor, Carter Harrison the First, had his office and there the various city departments functioned.   And there we police reporters had a spacious room which the city council shared with us on Monday nights.   And there a reporter on a rival newspaper one day removed a cigar from between his teeth, held it up for my inspection and said: "A *Daily News* man gave me this. Eugene Field. Nice fellow. I used to know him in St. Louis."

II

Thus I learned that Field had arrived in Chicago.   We at the *Daily News* office had been awaiting his coming with a good deal of curiosity, for we had heard many stories about his drolleries, and we were familiar with his "The Little Peach" and his "Tribune Primer."   When we met Field he proved to be tall and slender and pale, with large eyes of light blue sunk in cavernous depths and with scanty yellow hair that gave signs of coming baldness, a wide mouth of wonderful mobility, and a straight thin nose with high-arched, sensitive nostrils.   He had also a good aggressive chin and a searching, comprehensive glance.   His voice was a magnificent deep bass and capable of many shades of expression.   Though our expectations had been keyed up to a high pitch we were not disappointed in him in any respect.   Indeed his approachableness and his unfailing good nature were a revelation.   Here was a man already famous who mingled

with us cubs of the local room on terms of complete
equality. True, he humorously called us "deckhands"
and "galley slaves" and affected to treat us with scorn if
we interrupted him when he was busy; but there was always merriment in his big blue eyes, even when he sug-
gestively plied a small bellows—a machine which he
kept on his desk to repel bores—as if to annihilate us like
other vermin with a deadly blast of insect powder. That
was the extreme penalty for entering his room unbidden
and interrupting the steady progress of his pen.

We found Field to be a surprising paradox—a merciless
satirist who loved his fellow men. His deep, mellow
voice, his singular alertness despite the habitual slouch
of his tall figure—Field himself would have called his
lank frame "gangling"—and his inexhaustible flow of
spirits, spiced with drollery, made him the idol of the
staff. In his amazing working costume he looked like
a scarecrow, but his mind was racing all the time and
"copy" grew under his hand at a rate that would almost
put to shame the modern adept at the typewriter. Not-
withstanding his chronic attitude of devil-may-care, his
working system was admirable in its efficiency. He used
a pen with an excruciatingly fine point and he wrote on
unruled paper with a sheet ruled in black lines below it to
guide his writing straight across. He would invariably
place on three half sheets of large letter paper in his
microscopic handwriting—almost as legible as print
despite its minuteness, provided one's eyes were good—an
abundant supply of paragraphs for the lean types to devour. I have read hundreds of columns of Field's manuscript—"fodder" he called his daily product—and all
of it was almost incredibly neat. An erasure was so
great a rarity that such a blemish practically never was
found, though interlineations were not infrequent, these
showing where Field had gone back to develop an idea still

further or to enrich a sentence with apposite words from
his extremely copious vocabulary. Two hours of uninterrupted work were commonly sufficient to enable him to
complete his daily stint.

Field would arrive at the office about eleven o'clock
each day, would remove his coat, get out a rusty pair of
scissors and an old cigar box, take them to the exchange
editor's room, and there prowl through his favourite
newspapers. These always included Dana's New York
Sun, McCullagh's St. Louis *Globe-Democrat*, McLean's
Cincinnati *Enquirer*, Halstead's Cincinnati *Commercial
Gazette*, Watterson's Louisville *Courier-Journal*, Whitelaw
Reid's New York *Tribune* and some lesser sheets in which
he took a special interest. He would run his eyes over
them column by column. As he went along he would
gouge the pages with his scissors, snipping out articles or
bits of articles, a headline, a printed name, or some other
fragment that might suggest a paragraph to him. All
these gleanings would be deposited in the cigar box.

In the meantime Field every little while would burst
into laughter as he skimmed the *Sun's* satirical editorials
or the editorial paragraphs written by McCullagh for the
Globe-Democrat—"pointed as a tack," he called them in
his verses, "Little Mack," verses which inspired Mc-
Cullagh to send Field a heavy gold watch and chain,
which, according to a tradition in the *Globe-Democrat*
office, cost $300—or when some freakish idea of his own
flashed through his mind. When he thought he had
accumulated a sufficient quantity of topics for his use he
would carry his loot to his own room and then would
go out to lunch with some member or members of the
staff. An hour later he would return and settle down to
work.

Getting ready to write was with Field a sort of ceremony. He took off his coat and relieved his shoulders of

the weight of his suspenders. If the weather was cold
and the office chilly he donned a shapeless old baggy garment, but usually he wrote in his shirt sleeves. He took
off his shoes and put on a pair of disreputable slippers
which dangled from his toes when he elevated his feet—
as he invariably did—to the top of his desk. His trousers
he rolled high above his ankles. Then he seated himself
sideways and threw his legs over the corner of his desk
so that he sat on his spine. Taking an oblong of stiff
cardboard, he placed upon it a sheet of paper with ruled
black lines and a blank sheet of paper over that. These
he sometimes held on his knees while he wrote and sometimes he rested them upon the edge of his desk. He kept
at hand a collection of coloured inks and generally he
would begin his work by constructing an elaborate initial
letter, all red and blue and gold, or otherwise strikingly
illuminated. Because of the beauty and clearness of his
manuscripts photographic reproductions of them make
satisfactory books, as some publishers have demonstrated.

If on any day the cigar box ran dry of suggestions before
the bottom of the third sheet was reached Field resorted
to an effective system of his own to make good the de-
ficiency. He explained it to me on one occasion. "I begin to repeat to myself the names of the states," he said.
"First comes Maine. Some well-known person who
lives in Maine pops into my mind and I write a paragraph
about him. Then I pass on to New Hampshire. Long
before I have exhausted the possibilities of this method of
scaring up ideas I have all the paragraphs I need." This
device is typical of Field's own particular efficiency system
which enabled him to do his work expeditiously. That
system, evolved by himself, explains how he could do so
much writing and yet devote many hours daily to the
multitude of quaint avocations that continually enticed
him.

November 28, 1886, evidently was a day on which ideas were lamentably scarce, for the next morning the following appeared in his column:

"Tell me, O Aristarchus, tell me by the shield of Pallas Athene, what find you in the exchanges this day that you briskly apply your never-to-be-satiated and ever-devouring shears?"

"Of a truth, O Mnesthenes, the times go hard, for neither on the all-thundering editorial pages nor in the columns of the Argus-eyed local reporters, nor yet even in the from-everywhere-selected miscellany can I find matter worthy to be culled for our all-pervading sheet. And by the gods immortal I do esteem it to be cruel fortune that at this time, when news is scarce and advertising slow, it is required of me to bring to the altar of the remorseless printers fresh and plenteous hecatombs of reprint."

"You speak true things, O Aristarchus, wielder of the nimble scissors! But, by the dog, how hardly shall it go with *me* who, when these papers bear me no word-provoking pointers, am forced to sit me down to gaze at the four walls and to invoke of mendacious Hermes the aid which he alone with his inventive arts can bring!"

III

Field began his work on the *Daily News* August 15, 1883. His first column of paragraphs appeared in the next day's issue under the innocuous heading "Current Gossip." It was not until August 31st that the title of the column was changed to "Sharps and Flats," which continued to be its title up to Field's death. Field may have consciously borrowed the name from a comedy in which his friends Robson and Crane were then playing. Slason Thompson, who soon afterward joined the staff of the *Daily News* and became a close friend of Field's, was one of the two authors of the play. Field, however, once told Hamlin Garland that he called the column "Sharps and Flats" because "I told Stone I'd write a good deal about musical matters and the name seemed appropriate."

By way of making a start Field had taken over, heading

and all, a column that had already been established to
present miscellaneous bits of information.   Readers who
had been accustomed to find there notes on the wool clip
of Australia and similar unexciting matters must have
rubbed their eyes in astonishment on that fateful August
morning when they read there such "current gossip" as
this:

The Vanderbilts have invited Henry Irving and Christine Nilsson
to put up at their ranch during their New York season.   It is amazing
to contemplate the bother some folks will put themselves to in order
to get a pass to a show.

If readers thought there was some mistake about the
Vanderbilt paragraph their perplexity must have been
increased when they read:

Minnie Palmer's dramatic success in Great Britain is said to be
largely due to the enterprise of her husband, who has made the press
and public believe he is the original John Rogers who was burned at
the stake "followed thither by his wife and nine small children."

Readers of that first column also were told:

The dark waltz squeeze is a saltatory divertissement which appears to be achieving lamentable popularity among social circles of
the giddier class.   It is supposed to be a cross between the Alhambra
mazurka and the Castilian fandango—two foreign varieties which
Hannibal Hamlin is said to have brought back with him from the
effete court of Spain.

It was typical of Field that he represented the septua-
genarian statesman who had been elected Vice-president
of the United States on the ticket with Lincoln in 1860 as
having interested himself in frivolous foreign dances.   For
there is much that one might write of Field's humorous
views on the gayeties and perplexities of old age and of his
absurd plans for his own diversions and avocations at the
advanced age which he was never to attain.   In his merry

moments Field always spoke of himself as "Old Field" or
"Grand Old Field." He would sometimes give imitations
of himself at the age of ninety. In one of these bits of
acting, which may have been imitated from Irving's
manner in "A Story of Waterloo," he would be seen sitting, very much bowed, leaning on a cane and staring with
vacuous eyes at nothing. This was supposed to be the way
he would look when, his writing days over, he would be
displayed as a grand old relic in a front window of the
Daily News office.

IV

My friendship with Field began in a somewhat novel
way. One night, as usual, a group of us, our work completed, was standing about the big-bellied stove which
occupied the centre of the local room and was the only
source of heat for the entire editorial department in that
primitive time. Field was telling stories and giving
imitations of actors, much to our delight. Suddenly he
inquired where he could obtain a veritable sandbag, such
as the old-fashioned footpads then carried for professional
use. He needed the weapon, it seemed, in order that he
might perpetrate a joke. There was an estimable young
woman journalist in St. Louis of the name of Miss Fanny
Bagby. Field had published a number of playful paragraphs about her. One of them, as I recall, told how Miss
Bagby had attended a prize fight and there had performed
prodigies of reporting, besides capturing the manly affections of one of the pugilists. For his various sins of
this general nature against Miss Bagby, Field desired to
make amends by sending the lady an appropriate gift.
Because of her name Field thought a sandbag would be
especially fitting. When he inquired where he could get
one I spoke up from among the "deckhands" and offered
to supply his need.

Accordingly the next day I applied to a police captain whom I knew well and he, with a regretful sigh, selected from among his professional souvenirs a beautiful new sandbag which he had taken from a yegg not many days before.   It was of clean white canvas, about fifteen inches long, as thick as a man's wrist at the larger end and tapered slightly throughout its length, being tightly stuffed with buckshot.   The weapon was well suited to the work of felling a man approached from behind.   It was supposed merely to stun the victim without doing him any permanent injury.   I presented the sandbag to Field, who received it with manifest satisfaction, and it was speedily on its way to Miss Bagby, sweetly decorated with bows of blue ribbon.

From that time forward I found myself accepted as one of the company of martyrs deemed worthy by Field to be objects of his friendship and his sport.   Thereafter, until the joke wore thin, upon approaching me he would begin to sing loudly through his nose the old hymn tune of "Dennis"—probably learned in the days when as a little boy he escorted to church his pious grandmother, relict of General Martin Field of Newfane.

Not very long afterward, much to my surprise, I was pitchforked into the position of dramatic critic, largely, I believe, through Field's recommendation.   This was more than a little embarrassing to me, for I had paid no particular attention to the drama.   However, I did my best under serious disadvantages, for the city editor continued to demand my services as a reporter throughout each afternoon and part of each evening.   When I finally found an opportunity to give thought to the new plays, the theatre into which I catapulted myself was well along with its evening performance, so that my efforts to obtain material for an intelligent criticism of the play and the acting were characterized by the frenzy of desperation.

To add to my embarrassment I would usually behold, enthroned in a proscenium box, Stone, the editor, Ballantyne, the managing editor, and Field. "What will they think of the rubbish I am going to write about this play when they see it in print to-morrow?" was my despairing thought at such times. However, I got along somehow until a new city editor commandeered me as his assistant—a job with hours of service extending over a large majority of the twenty-four.

One memory of my hectic experiences as a dramatic critic relates to the exceedingly intimate account given nightly by Field to the assembled members of the editorial force—given out of his own efficient imagination—of the alleged passionate courtship of myself by a mature and somewhat ponderous foreign actress then appearing in Chicago in tragedy rôles. According to Field, the deeply smitten lady each day confided her tender emotions to him and the two took long and earnest counsel together concerning ways of overcoming my coldness. To the shrieking delight of the staff—while I stood by grinning foolishly—Field in very broken English repeated in full the impassioned remarks of the fair victim of my manly charms. They were liberally interspersed with fervid cries of "I lofe him! I lofe him!" The unimportant detail that the gifted lady was wholly unaware of my existence did not, of course, detract in any degree from the realistic quality of Field's nightly revelations.

v

The most numerous of Field's callers in those early days were of the tramp printer or tramp reporter type. The shifty Cantell Whoppers of Field's "Mr. Dana of the New York *Sun*" serves well as a specimen of the tribe. They all called him "Gene," and they had known him in St. Louis or some other Western city. They greeted him

with almost tearful affection and each struck him for a
"loan"—and got it. Even if Field had to borrow the
money from some other member of the staff, as not un-
commonly was the case, he invariably "grubstaked" the
frowsy, jobless, and shiftless old acquaintance who made
the distress sign and who called him "Gene." Thus the
term, "Field's friends," came to have a very special
meaning to Field's fellow workers.

It was a joyous moment for those fellow workers when
one day the amiable Field lost his temper in dealing with a
tipsy derelict who had drifted in and demanded financial
assistance without taking the trouble to identify himself as
an authentic old timer of Field's acquaintance. Relations
between the two finally became so strained that Field
pulled off his coat and prepared to throw out the pest.
However, to the disappointment of the staff, the startled
stranger hastened to make it known that he was some
Bill or Joe whom Field had met in Denver. Thereupon
Field bestowed upon him a silver coin instead of a black
eye.

Field also had friends of another distinctive type—
breezy Westerners who wore broad-brimmed slouch hats
and overcoats of fur. Of this type was Billy Buskett,
then a Montana ranchman, but formerly an associate of
Field's in St. Louis. Buskett—"Penn Yan Bill"—taught
Field to sing the few lines of "Ossian's Serenade" that
Buskett remembered from having heard his father sing
them. The song delighted Field, who was particularly
captivated by the sporting and athletic feats with which
the lover sought to win his lady. For weeks Field went
about the office roaring:

> "I'll chase the antelope over the pla-ain,
> The tiger's cub I'll bind with a cha-ain,
> The wild gazelle with its silvery fee-eet
> I'll give to thee as a pla-aymate sweet."

The verses that Field afterward wrote of Penn Yan
Bill's wooing surely repaid his friend many times over for
teaching him "Ossian's Serenade":

> He came from old Montana and he rode a broncho mare,
> He had a rather howd'y'do and rough-and-tumble air;
> His trousers were of buckskin and his coat of furry stuff—
> His hat was drab of colour and its brim was wide enough;
> Upon each leg a stalwart boot reached just above the knee,
> And in the belt about his waist his weapons carried he;
> A rather strapping lover for our little Susie—still,
> She was his choice and he was hers, was Penn Yan Bill.

Field's somewhat famous quest for the words of the
song of which Buskett knew only the chorus perhaps has
sufficient interest to warrant a short account of it.   One
of the attractions of Field's column, by the way, was the
discussions of odd subjects that he frequently carried on
there.   On November 12, 1888, he published a letter by
himself to himself, though ostensibly written by a mythical John Gifford, saying:

> I am very anxious to get a copy of the words of a song that was ex-
> ceedingly popular twenty or thirty years ago.   The song was entitled
> "The Burmese Lover."

The letter also quoted a garbled version of the chorus.
    Two days later Field wrote:

> From the answers with which we have been overwhelmed we gather
> that the song which Mr. Gifford calls "The Burmese Lover" is more
> commonly known as "Ossian's Serenade"; that it was sung (and per-
> haps composed) by Ossian E. Dodge, and that under the latter title it
> can be obtained in sheet form in any music store.

He added that he had been supplied with numerous
versions of the song.   The version which he selected for
publication proved to be not only the "Serenade" but
also two stanzas of four lines each from a song by Nour-
mahal in "Lalla Rookh."   One of the stanzas was that

beginning, "Our sands are bare, but down the slope," and the other was that having for its first line, "Come if the love thou hast for me." The plagiarism Field pointed out on November 17th, saying: "This is an interesting affair; we ask the assistance of our readers in exploiting it." He also remarked upon the great number of letters he had received bearing upon the published version of the song. On November 20th he presented a long communication from a correspondent who sought to trace "Ossian's Serenade" to Marlowe's "Come with Me and Be My Love." Field's comment was:

Candour compels us to confess that we see in the twain no more likeness than exists between Bill Smith and Tom Brown, who are simply brothers in Adam.

Many years after Field's death a member of the staff of the Boston *Transcript* wrote in that newspaper that Field when once on a visit to Boston called on him at the *Transcript* office and asked him to start an inquiry about "Ossian's Serenade." According to the *Transcript* writer, "the inquiry was published, though not with Field's name or initials, and it brought out the origin, authorship, and history and the words of the piece." This is very curious, for Field's visit to the *Transcript* office probably was in the fall or winter of 1887, when he passed a number of months in the East. If he was made aware of the results of the *Transcript's* inquiry, when he started his own inquiry nearly or quite a year later he possessed full information on the subject of "Ossian's Serenade." Yet I well remember the interest he took in the correspondence which grew out of his "John Gifford" letter and his pleasure on obtaining the full text of the song.

V

Relations with Actor Folk

I

ALL his life Field was an inveterate theatregoer. He liked the people of the stage and they liked him. When he began his work in Chicago he already numbered many leading actors and actresses among his warm friends. Whenever any of these theatrical favourites of his were in the city he was much in their company and he would attend their performances night after night. They furnished him with many interesting stories and he invented countless extravagant yarns about them. They found the publicity useful and so his fancy was licensed to take its most daring flights when it dealt with his stage friends.

Here is one of his grotesque inventions which appeared in his column only a few days after he began writing for the *Daily News*:

Minnie Maddern begins her season in Chicago next week. She is now fifteen years old. [She was in fact eighteen, but she became a star at fifteen.] Cincinnati papers say she has grown a couple of inches taller during the summer vacation. Minnie's husband has also matured in appearance, and he recently celebrated his sixteenth birthday by having his face shaved for the first time in his life. The kind old nurse, Aunt Martha Billings, who looked after the young couple last year, will accompany them this season and see that no harm comes to them on their travels. Between Ogden and Cheyenne last spring little Minnie fell out of her berth and sprained her ankle very badly. She lay kicking and screaming on the floor of the car till Aunt Martha came and put her back to bed again. Minnie and her husband often quarrel, like other children, over the candy kind

friends send them.   Once in a while Aunt Martha has to spank them
both very severely before quiet is restored.

That Field came fully to appreciate the worth of the
sterling actress of whom he wrote so amusingly in her
early years on the stage is shown by the following, written in the last summer of his life:

We are glad to hear that Minnie Maddern Fiske is to return to the
stage.   Her retirement six years ago was very generally regretted by
the public, for her distinct genius was just beginning to be recognized.
Her delineations of the tenderer feminine characteristics were unique
in points of fidelity, delicacy, subtlety, and sweetness, and it is gratifying to feel that in the return of this admirable young artist to the
profession she always adorned and ennobled we are to have a ful-
filment of the brilliant promise of her girlhood.

Field's special comrades among his many actor friends
were Sol Smith Russell and Francis Wilson.   For these
he had a brotherly affection and they responded with
equal regard.   Though Field was accustomed to give
imitations of many actors he was especially happy in
reproducing Russell's voice and manner.   He wrote much
about these good comrades of his.   What he thought
of Russell as a man and an artist is well expressed in the
following:

Said Mr. Henry Irving on one occasion last winter: "Every time I
have been in America I have kept on the alert in the hope of discovering a distinct American type—some American combining and illustrating the foibles and the beauties of American character as distinct
from the English-speaking cousin across the ocean.   Such an illustration I have found in Sol Smith Russell, and the discovery has given
me more pleasure and brought me nearer to a knowledge of the
American people than all the other experiences I have had in this
country."
Mr. Russell's humour is many-sided, and it is always so gracious
that we know not which phase most pleases us.   He is best in his
lighter moods—so we think when we see and hear him then; but, on
the other hand, he is best, too, in those pathetic passages with which
he tempers and shades his art.   His work is—if we may be indulged

in the metaphor—a bouquet of fresh and brilliant posies, beautified and vivified by dewdrops sprinkled here and there, as though they were tears wrung from the flowers themselves.

Russell was not only a close friend but a fellow dyspeptic, so Field used to tell a story to the effect that one midnight, after giving a performance in an Eastern city, Russell went into a restaurant to get something to eat. While partaking sparingly of bread and milk he saw an old-time actor of the name of Parsons attacking with marvelous gusto a plateful of corned beef and cabbage.

"Merciful heavens, Parsons!" cried Russell. "How dare you fill yourself with such victuals at this time of night?"

"Oh, I can stand it," replied Parsons, happily.

"But, my dear fellow," expostulated Russell, "do you know how long it takes corned beef and cabbage to digest?"

"No, I haven't the remotest idea," said Parsons.

"Well, I happen to know," said Russell; "it takes five hours—five solid hours."

"Oh, that's all right," said Parsons. "I've got just about that much time to devote to it."

A somewhat similar story of J. L. Toole was told to Field in London. Dropping in at the Garrick Club one evening, Toole found Irving eating a Welsh rarebit. After gazing fixedly at the concoction, Toole shook hands with Irving and said solemnly: "Give my love to dear old Charles Matthews." Then he turned and walked away. Matthews had been dead three years.

Of another good actor friend of his Field told this story:

John T. Raymond always stopped off at Virginia City and always had a bad house. He complained to the manager of the theatre. The latter said that Raymond ought to come at a suitable time, suggesting that he was certain to have a crowded house if he came when there was to be a hanging.

"Well, you let me know," said Raymond, "when the next hanging will occur and if I can get here I will."

The manager told Raymond there was to be a hanging a fortnight from the following Friday. By cancelling certain other dates and making a tedious journey Raymond was able to bring his company back to Virginia City at that time. Surely enough, the town was full of people—they had come in from all the territory round about—thousands of them, all with plenty of money and all crazy to see the hanging. Raymond was overjoyed. "At last!" he cried, with a sigh of relief.

In order to accommodate the crowds expected at the theatre that night, benches and chairs were hired and brought in. "Spare no expense," said Raymond, gleefully. "Let us make hay while the sun shines."

But at two o'clock that afternoon a telegram came from the governor reprieving the criminal and by six o'clock the camp was as deserted as a last year's bird's nest.

Field's best known piece of humour written about Francis Wilson is that in which he tells of Wilson's versatile legs:

They are twins, yet totally unlike, reminding one of a well-mated man and wife, who are so very different that we speak of them as well matched. The left leg is apparently of a serious turn, as may be observed on all occasions requiring a portrayal of those emotions which bespeak elevated thought and philosophic tendencies. The right leg is mercurial, ubiquitous, passionate to a marked degree, whimsical, fantastic, and grotesque. The contrast between the two gives us a comedy in itself which is very pleasing; for the constant struggle between the perennial levity of the right leg and the melancholy demeanour of the left leg is funnier by far than most of the horse-play which passes for comedy in these times.

Now the most extraordinary thing about this extraordinary piece of criticism is that it quite satisfactorily describes the dramatic qualities of the Wilson legs. And the criticism calls to mind Field's one-time famous review of the many Hamlets he had seen on the stage, ranging from emaciated princes of Denmark to "stout models" in melancholy Danes, a review which characterized the players by their respective pairs of legs, such as the highly educated extremities of Booth, Irving's eccentric underpinning, and the well-rounded but not well-schooled occupants of the trunk hose of Miss Anna Dickinson.

II

Of Robson and Crane, Field made all manner of sport. He even invented a precocious child, Stuart Robson Crane, and for months he recorded in his column the many ingenuous remarks alleged to have been made by that engaging, though nonexistent, young prodigy. Of these many stories I choose one that is manifestly modelled upon certain immortal mendacities of the sainted Parson Weems. Field wrote:

Mr. Lawrence Barrett, who is an authority whom no one can doubt, tells an entirely new story about Master Stuart Robson Crane, the precocious five-year-old son of Mr. William H. Crane, the popular comedian. "My summer home is at Cohasset," says Mr. Barrett, "and it is there, too, that Mr. and Mrs. Crane, with their interesting child, seek rest and refreshment during the summer months. Our cottages are not more than a stone's throw apart, and the closest intimacy subsists between our two families—an intimacy which, pray heaven, may not be interrupted save by the pale hand of death. For little Stuart Crane, upon whom his parents have lavished the wealth of their generous affections, I conceived the most cordial attachment last summer; the amiability of the child, no less than his marvellous precocity, attracted me to him and ere long I found— not to my dismay—that the tendrils of my heart had stretched out, so to speak, and had twined themselves about the little fellow. Every morning it was his custom to come over to my cottage, and I took pleasure in sitting with him on the front porch reciting passages from George Boker's plays and telling him stories suited to his childish tastes. I formed, as I say, a sincere attachment for the boy, and it pleased me to discover in his character a sturdy moral foundation, which he seemed to inherit from the maternal side of his family. Well, it was last July, as I remember, that his uncle, Squire Eleazor Crane of Bangor, Maine, came down to Cohasset to visit the Crane family. Among other gifts for the little boy he brought a chest of carpenter's tools—just such a present as every boy delights in. For the next week young Stuart busied himself at sawing, hammering, and hacking away at everything he could lay hands to, and at last one morning I saw him out in his father's back orchard chopping wildly at one of the cherry trees—a splendid specimen of the oxheart variety, which Mr. Crane especially valued because he had once dislocated his wrist while attempting to climb it (the tree) for a wager. Well-nigh overcome with horror, I called to the child to desist, and when he came to me and asked me what harm there could be in his practising on the trees with his hatchet, I represented that the wanton destruction of any of God's beautiful creations was very, very wicked.

"While we were still talking upon the subject I saw Mr. Crane come out of his cottage and saunter through the orchard in our direction. Presently his eyes fell upon the lacerated trunk of the favourite cherry tree. From those rude scars that the child's hatchet had made exuded sap and gum, as if, in sooth, the proud tree were shedding tears over its irremediable misfortune. Then I saw that Mr. Crane was very indignant. He came toward us with flame upon his cheeks and anger in his eyes.

" 'Young man,' said Mr. Crane, addressing the child, who still retained in his grasp the instrument with which he had wrought havoc in the orchard, 'young man, who cut my cherry tree?'

" 'Father,' said the child, slipping the hatchet under his bib and looking calmly up into his parent's stern face, 'Father, I cannot tell a lie—it was Mr. Robson.'

" 'Unhappy child!' cried now the thoroughly infuriated father, 'why this futile tergiversation? You say that Mr. Robson cut this cherry tree, yet he went down to Boston last night.'

" 'Nay, chide me not, Father,' remonstrated the child; 'that is why he went.' "

Of Robson, Field once told a tremendous story of certain alleged experiences in Alaska, where Robson, according to Field, once taught a class in Sunday school. One winter day he took the dear little children out riding in a sled. When far from civilization they were pursued by a pack of ferocious wolves. With rare presence of mind the resourceful Robson, while whipping his horses to their utmost speed, threw out one child after another to the terrible beasts, which stopped long enough to devour each child in turn. Very properly, he threw out first the wicked little boy who never had dropped any pennies into the plate at Sunday school.   After the last child had been thrown to the wolves, the good Mr. Robson reached town in safety.   Robson's friendship for Field even survived the publication of this yarn.

Here is another of Field's stories about Robson:

"About two years ago last summer," said Robson, "a young man called at my cottage in Cohasset, bringing a letter of introduction from a friend in New York.   I was as cordial as I could be and the fellow kept calling off and on all summer.   He did not interest me particularly, but he was harmless.   One day he said to me: 'Mr. Robson, that Miss Barrett is a charming girl.'

"'Ah, and so you have met the Barretts, have you?' says I.

"'I have,' says he, 'and I regard Miss Barrett as one of the most charming young ladies I ever saw.'

"'She is, my boy, she is,' says I.   'Pitch in and win her and the day you wed her I'll give you $5,000.   And here's a dollar to bind the bargain.'   . . .

"About two months ago that young man turned up at my cottage again, wearing a particularly triumphant smile.

"'Mr. Robson,' said he, 'I've done it.'

"'Done what?' says I.

"'Proposed to her,' says he.

"'Proposed to whom?' says I.

"'Why, to Miss Barrett,' says he, 'and I'm going to marry her.'

"'The ——— you are!' says I, for the news fairly knocked the wind out of me.

"'I am indeed,' says he, and then he reminded me of the promise I had given him about the check.

"'My boy,' says I, as amiably as I could, 'Stuart Robson never forgets and he never violates a pledge or a promise.'

"The morning of the wedding I was feeling too indisposed to leave my bed.   I had been sitting up late the night before with a sick friend. So I called my daughter to me.

"'Alicia,' said I, 'are you going to the wedding?'

"'Yes, Father.'

"'Then take this check with you,' said I.   'Be careful not to lose it, and after the wedding hand it to the groom.   But, mind you, Alicia, do not give it to him until after the minister pronounces them man and wife; for he might drop dead in the meantime.'

"When my daughter returned that afternoon I said: 'Alicia, is it all over?'

"'Yes, Father.'

"'And did you give him the check for $5,000?'

"'Yes, Father.'

"'What did he say when you gave it to him?'

"'Father, he cried.'

"I was gratified, I will admit, that my trifling benefaction had touched his heart. Yet I was anxious to know the full extent of his appreciation.

"'He cried, did he?' said I. 'How long did he cry?'

"'Father, I am not sure, but I should say about a minute.'

"'A minute! A minute!' said I. 'Why, I cried an hour before I signed that check!'"

III

Of Denman Thompson's "The Old Homestead" Field wrote thus beautifully, recalling memories of his own boyhood in New England:

There are some, we are told, who are blind to the truth which this quiet play illustrates; some who call it unreal and strained and false. We pity such folk; it seems to us that they have missed a large share of the beauty and sweetness of life. To us—and we rejoice in having lived many years in the heart of New England—to us "The Old Homestead" is a most realistic representation of Yankee life and Yankee character. We recognize in Uncle Josh and Cy Prime and Aunt 'Tilda certain dear old friends of ours—old friends whom we knew a long time ago under different names, perhaps, but the very same in heart and manners and speech. And in the Ganzey boy we seem to see an old acquaintance; surely we used to know him away back in the '60s—yes, and we have been fishing with him, too; he was the very boy who caught the big pickerel in Baker's pond—the all-fired big pickerel that got away. And the other boys and girls who frisk before us in this dear old play, they are the companions of our youthful days. How have they kept so young? The years have passed them over; old Time has not dealt with them as he, alas! has dealt with some of us. Yet with those comrades of our childhood we renew the heartiness and carelessness of youth; the wrinkles go, the heart beats high again, care is forgotten, the frost of winter melts away, and all about us and in our hearts it is spring once more— radiant, hopeful, joyous spring.

Perhaps the most striking of all the many hundreds of articles written by Field about player folk is the following, a product of his full powers and displaying the sweetness and the vision that came to him in the closing years of his life:

We find this bit of gossip floating the rounds of the press: "Clara Morris used to be a chambermaid in the house next to my father's," says a Cleveland woman. "We saw her daily—brushing, sweeping, and dusting, as is the habit of that craft. After a while we heard that she had gone upon the stage, and later that she was meeting with some success. We knew her then as Miss Heriot. It was not until Ellsler took her in hand that she developed into anything remarkable, however. I wonder if she would remember me if I should make myself known to her."

Possibly she would, madam; yes, probably. We advise you to call upon her at the first opportunity and pay her that tribute which is due to genius which has triumphed over seemingly insuperable obstacles. She would like to talk with you of her earlier days when, amid dust and dirt and drudgery, her soul looked confidently up to higher, better, nobler things. She has a good account to render of herself.

And how is it with you, madam? To what extent have *you* improved by the means with which the Creator possessed you? How have *you* wrought by the light within you? Have you, too, struggled upward and onward, or are you still where you were when, many years ago, you watched that chambermaid at her daily toil?

Go, by all means, and call upon Clara Morris, and bless her, in the name of her sex, for her patience, her purposes, her endeavour, her accomplishments, and her valour.

Another stage favourite of Field's day inspired him on one occasion thus to rhapsodize in a manner unusual for him:

What a splendid creature is Miss Lillian Russell! It is delectable and beneficial simply to sit and look at her, for a finer specimen of feminine health and beauty is not to be found elsewhere. In the contemplation of her noble physique one forgets—or at least does not care to recall—that Miss Russell is unquestionably the best soprano upon our lyric stage; it is enough to look upon her beauty, which is a magnificent combination of vigour, colour, grace, and delicacy.

Nothing else in this beautiful world of ours is half so beautiful as a beautiful woman. And the distinct and supreme advantage which

man has over the other sex lies, we think, in this: That it is his in-
alienable prerogative to court the sweet creatures who constitute
pretty much all there is in human life worth living for.

IV

The conquest of beautiful women by the power of
passionate devotion was a favourite topic of Field's in
private conversation. He would say that no man was
worthy of the love of a good and beautiful woman, but
that any such woman was to be won by any sincere man
who was reasonably presentable, because all women responded to persistent proofs of a man's love for them.
Indeed, he held that the man's devotion, not the man
himself, commonly made the irresistible appeal to the
woman whom he won.   In setting forth this theory to me
one day he expressed the wish that it might be submitted
to a convincing test.   He added that if he were not a
married man he would be tempted to enter upon the
adventure himself.

"Take, for example," he said, "a young unmarried
woman, beautiful, gifted, famous, and universally admired.   Why should she marry and thus in a measure
sink her individuality in that of a man?   Why should she
surrender the admiration and the love of all the world to
become the possession of a husband?   Take, if you please,
Mary Anderson, since I think at this time of no other
woman who so well meets the conditions I have mentioned.
Yet, if my theory be correct, any decent, intelligent young
man who should succeed in convincing Mary Anderson or
any other famous and beautiful unmarried woman of his
overmastering love for her would win her by the very
power of his devotion."

This conversation took place in the early '80's, when
Mary Anderson was at the height of her success upon
the stage.   And I think I discover an echo of Field's re-

marks to me in these words, written by Field about that time:

It is a trifle hasty of Mary Anderson to telegraph all the way from England that she is "wedded to her profession alone and will always remain Mary Anderson." This sounds heroic and romantic enough, but it lacks probability. The lady has arrived at an age when it is not hard to predict her future. She will marry, of course, but not a titled man. Her husband will be a plain, practical business man; he will wear a slouch hat and chin whiskers and will be somewhat below the medium height. He will be addicted to cheap cigars and the European hotel system; he will wear arctic overshoes in cold weather and a brown linen ulster in August; he will probably be a crank on the subject of farming or stock raising and will utilize Mary's earnings toward purchasing and conducting a farm or a ranch. He will be Mary's business manager and, no matter how homely and inefficient he may be, Mary will dote on him just as every female of advancing years dotes on the novelty of a husband.

This brief quotation may serve to indicate some of Field's antipathies among stage folk:

We have seen Tom Keene in "Richard III" and George Edgar in "King Lear" and the Rev. Miln in "Macbeth." Once upon a time Katie Putnam played Juliet for three nights in Cheyenne, and at another time on the Omaha circuit we saw Jane Coombs as Ophelia. We are not sure about it, but we think we shall never forget Charles Pope's performance of Othello, and Lawrence Barrett's eleven Irishmen as the Roman populace in the tragedy of "Julius Cæsar" constitute a spectacle always to be remembered.

Yes, we can truthfully say that we have not found life a mere bed of roses, and we do not regard it as any particular stretch of fortitude when we add that we think we are prepared for M. Sully and his French Hamlet.

Greatly respecting and admiring Joseph Jefferson, Field was proud of possessing the friendship of that sterling actor. He related many stories of Jefferson, including the following, which was told him in London by B. L. Farjeon, the novelist, Jefferson's son-in-law:

The Farjeon children write plays for their grandfather. Very thrilling plays they are, too. Grandfather Jefferson enjoys them hugely, but one day, while reading one of these productions, he stopped and asked: "Frank, what do all these blanks mean? There doesn't seem to be any sense at all." "That's where you are to swear, grandpa," explained the child. "We left it blank because we knew you could do it better than we could."

V

Something should be said of Field's relations with Henry Irving and Ellen Terry. He became a close friend of theirs and he had unbounded admiration for their genius. His imitations of Irving's Hamlet and other characters were extraordinarily good and were a source of vast amusement to Irving and particularly to Miss Terry, who was accustomed to demand that Field "do" Irving whenever they met. At the time Field began his work on the *Daily News*, Irving was making preparations for his first American tour. Field then was wont to bristle at every mention of the name of the eminent English actor, being quick to suspect that Irving would take a condescending attitude toward his American audiences. All Field's paragraphs dealing with the coming visit of Irving and his company expressed incipient hostility. Yet Field's surrender was instant and complete when he saw the English players act and beheld the admirable stage settings of their plays. From that time forward he was unstinted in his praise of the artistry of the actors and the conspicuous worth of their productions. Even Irving's curious mannerisms, which Field imitated so amusingly, he accepted with no very special protest. As an example of his comments on the Lyceum productions I present the following, written by Field in London in October, 1890:

On Saturday night Herman Merivale's dramatization of "The Bride of Lammermoor" was produced by Mr. Irving's company at the Lyceum theatre.

Ravenswood is, I think, one of Mr. Irving's most impressive

delineations; it is wholly imbued with that sombre weirdness which is Irving's most powerful charm.   Picturesque to a degree, it is full of feeling—now passionate, now overbearing, and again tender and chivalric; never were discordant qualities more artistically or more powerfully portrayed.   Ellen Terry's Lucy is, as you would suppose, a marvellously effective presentation, inexpressibly sweet, graceful and tender in its womanliness.   .   .   .

As for the mounting of the play, it is beautiful, as close to nature and to history as art will admit of.   Mr. Irving remarked recently: "I am not a slave to accuracy.   I remember once that in a certain scene in 'Much Ado About Nothing' I put what I called a cedar walk on the stage, and some gentleman wrote to say that cedars had not been introduced into Messina until fifty years after Shakespeare's time.   To be artistic and well within one's bounds is one thing; to be hopelessly geographically and historically incorrect is another."

Field's artistic and literary education he owed in no small degree to the stage.   To him it was a wonderland of unfailing delight.   The study of emotions as depicted by the best actors of his time gave him an insight into the stirrings of the human heart such as his reading of quaint and fantastic books never could have given him.

VI

PLAYMATES AND PASTIMES

I

A FEW weeks after Field joined the staff of the *Daily News* there came an explosion in the editorial department of its rival, the Chicago *Herald*, due to a change in editorial management that was resented by certain temperamental sub-editors and reporters, who walked out. All of them, in number seven or eight, were promptly added to his staff by the enterprising Stone. Being experienced newspaper workers, they constituted an important addition to the force. Of the new arrivals, John Ballantyne was made managing editor of the morning edition of the *Daily News*, and David Henderson, later a well-known theatrical manager, became managing editor of the evening editions. Slason Thompson became chief editorial writer for the morning edition. The other newcomers were provided with less prominent places on the staff.

Thus was Field thrown into close contact with two men who for some years remained close friends and companions of his. Ballantyne married a sister of Field's wife, the sister being a member of Field's household, so that family ties united them. Ballantyne was tall, serious, slow-spoken. Field, who saw humour in everything, commonly spoke of Ballantyne as "my Scotch brother-in-law." In his newspaper work as well as in his leisure hours Ballantyne was always accompanied by his stubby black pipe and his dog Snip. That devoted animal went everywhere with her master and lay under his desk while the master performed his tasks. Ballantyne died two years before Field, having passed out of newspaper work some years earlier. A year after her master's death Snip died—Snip, "the only dog Field ever thoroughly detested," according to Thompson in his biography of Field. And yet Field placed Snip among the dog immortals by writing this tribute to her memory:

Old Snip is dead. Presumably you did not know her; yet, if you are a lover of dogs, you will like to hear tell of her. For many years she belonged to our old friend John F. Ballantyne, the journalist. It is proper that we should say a few words about our old friend's faithful dumb servant.

Snip was born away out in Iowa in the neighbourhood of Spirit Lake. That is a charming locality, for there are stretches of prairie on either side, here and there are patches of timber, prosperous farms spread out their broad acres, and amid it all lies a large, tranquil blue lake, at one time the haunt of spirits (as it is said), but now abounding only in fish and wild fowl. In this ideal spot Snip was born; her father was a setter and her mother was a spaniel, so rightfully enough Snip came by those instincts and qualities which made her famed for amphibian prowess. Amid pleasant rural scenes Snip grew from puppyhood to mature years, gladdening the heart of her master with her precocity and her exploits by land and water; for there is famous hunting in the Spirit Lake country, and Snip was equally expert in detecting the wary prairie chicken and retrieving the stricken duck. She was in her prime when our friend Ballantyne made her acquaintance. She impressed him favourably—somewhat under size, perhaps, but nicely muscled and moved well, had a fine coat and colour, splendid brush, good head and ears, kind eyes, stanch feet, was well broke, game and docile. Mr. Ballantyne was an enthusiastic huntsman and he loved a fine dog. It was his good fortune to become Snip's owner, and that was certainly good fortune for Snip. For eight years the two were fast friends. All who were associated with Mr. Ballantyne in newspaper work recall the shaggy brown dog that used to lie under her master's desk and wag her tail hospitably whenever a caller entered the office. And it is pleasant, very pleasant, to associate in our thoughts now the unaffected, straightforward, loyal personality of the master and the kindly honesty of his shaggy pet. . . .

But all the time Snip was growing old; then, too, she developed rheumatism and with it an inclination to walk upon three legs and to groan whenever she turned herself over before the fire. In spirit, however, she was the same good-natured Snip, and she cheerfully submitted to every manner of personal indignity at the chubby hands of the children of the neighbourhood and never was she known to exhibit the slightest symptom of vindictiveness except upon the rare occasions when, more in playfulness than wrath, she treed a strange cat or disapproved of the monkey that accompanied the organ grinder who paid occasional visits to Orchard Street. Some folk suggested that Snip had survived her usefulness and that it would be a mercy to her to put her out of the way—as if the poor, faithful creature ever *was* in the way! Our friend Ballantyne knew better than that. Old Snip lived on and her age was peaceful.

One time—it was just about a year ago—old Snip was vastly troubled. The master did not come. The others hurried in and out of the house and many were in tears, and the home was distraught, and still the master did not come. Old Snip was vastly troubled, and she hobbled to and fro, and in and out of doors, and looked up and down the street, and waited for one who did not come. She must have known; for that night the poor old creature could not sleep, but wandered about the house and listened and waited. They said her suffering "was almost human."

One day at last when he *did* come home, old Snip seemed to understand; she lay near the mound of white flowers in which he slept the wakeless sleep, guarding that beloved master to the very last.

The most pitiful time of it all was when, after the funeral, they came to breaking up housekeeping and moving the things. It seemed as if old Snip knew what was going on and as if she rebelled against leaving that home. Then she could not be found and for three days they thought her lost. In her grief she had crawled under the front steps, preferring to die there than to live away from the house that had sheltered her so long. They found her there, nearly dead of thirst and hunger; they called, they coaxed, they threatened, and all in vain. At last the children dragged her out, for she always let the children do their will with her.

For the last ten months old Snip has been in the country. She loved the country, you know, with its quiet and its freedom, and so it seemed right that she should end her life amid those pleasant, peaceful scenes. She grew old very fast and most of the time she slept. Once or twice a day she would hobble into the yard, and, from force of instinct or of habit, come to a point at a harmless robin or a pert sparrow; sometimes she would sit in the doorway with drooping eyelids, as if she were thinking of the old days. But, as we have said, she slept most of the time, and it was evident that in dreams she renewed the delights of the past, and oftentimes she started from those dreams and roused up and raised her head and opened her honest eyes hungrily and eagerly, as though in response to a call she thought she heard.

Old Snip sleeps now in the prairie on which she delighted to disport. Her end was as peaceful and gentle and sweet as her nature had always been. Maybe she was glad to go; for who knows but that, at the last, of a sudden she heard the voice she longed to hear and felt once again the caress of the hand she loved?

II

In Field's early years in Chicago his favourite companion was Slason Thompson. That sturdy, combative New Brunswicker was a year or two older than Field, a bachelor with literary tastes and a moderately well-filled purse that was always at the disposal of the impecunious Field. Better yet, he was always ready to engage in the rough-and-tumble humour in which Field delighted in those days. Thus Field and "Nompy," as he called Thompson, were much together until Thompson married and left the staff of the *Daily News* to assist in establishing a weekly literary journal which struggled against fate for a few years and then perished.

"I am Nompy's only bad habit," Field would say and then would redouble his jests at Thompson's expense. Frequently he would revile his friend because Thompson's ancestors had deserted the American colonies when the colonies gained their independence from the British crown. Particularly did he deride Thompson for adhering to the Mugwump articles of faith at the time of the Blaine-Cleveland presidential campaign. Thompson with his good-natured truculence would thrust out his chin, clench his teeth, and force through them his favourite war-cry, "By doggies!" as he prepared his retort to the effect that Field was forming his literary style and his personal code of ethics on the Mulligan letters or made some rejoinder equally withering. Thompson's forcefulness was especially amusing to Field, who once said of his friend, "Even when he hunts flies he hunts them with a club."

Field's implacable pursuit of the Mugwumps—as Republicans who supported Cleveland in his various presidential campaigns were called—continued up to the time of Cleveland's second election to the presidency in 1892. On July 22d of that year he wrote:

The Mugwump party of Chicago held its regular mass meeting yesterday. At roll-call the following signified their presence: A. C. McClurg and Slason Thompson. Half an hour later M. E. Stone came in and that made three. . . .

From the special committee on Franklin MacVeagh, General Mc-Clurg reported that not a word had been received directly from Mr. MacVeagh in the last week. He had heard, however, from another source that on the Fourth of July Mr. MacVeagh was seen in the restaurant of the Hotel des Grandes Hommes, in the Boulevard des Independents, eating peas with a fork. (Loud applause.) He gathered from this that in spite of his membership in the Iroquois club Mr. MacVeagh was at heart a Mugwump. (Cheers.)

On October 3d Field wrote this final account of the fortunes of the Mugwump party:

When General McClurg gets back to Chicago he will find the Mugwump party in a demoralized condition. Mr. Slason Thompson, one of the pioneer Mugwumps and heretofore a yowling Clevelandite, has changed front and now announces his determination to vote for Harrison. Another Mugwump who has gone back on Cleveland is Mr. Franklin H. Head. One of the original Mugwumps was Franklin MacVeagh; he has gone over to the Democrats, body and soul, and so has Lawyer John W. Ela—both these gentlemen having recently joined the Iroquois club. A count of professional Mugwumps at the present time would reveal but two—General McClurg and M. E. Stone. The latter may not be a Mugwump on election day, for, in his capacity of vice-president of the Globe National Bank, he is being disciplined by President Wetherell, Cashier Moulton, and Director Harper, and these Republican veterans express confidence in their ability to bring the prodigal home, with his belly full of husks and contrition. So, taking one consideration with another, the prospects are that on election day the once powerful Mugwump party of six will be reduced to one, which unit will stand at the polls in all the isolated grandeur of an obelisk in the sands of Egypt.

There were in those early days other interesting members of the *Daily News* staff besides the persons already mentioned.   A tall and youthful Vermonter came to us after a few months of reporting news from rural villages for the Springfield *Republican*.   He called himself George B. McClellan Harvey and his droll stories of Vermont village life tickled Field immensely.   His favourite oath, reminiscent of his farmer friends of the Vermont hills, was "B'gosh t'Lmighty!"   After some months of brilliant service as a reporter, the death of his father called him back to New England and then he took up journalism in New York.   When I met him again he was American ambassador at the court of St. James's.

Another member of the staff was Harry B. Smith, who wrote humorous verse and did music criticisms.   Soon he formed a working arrangement with a young Chicago composer, Reginald de Koven, which led to the production by them of a number of successful light operas.   Smith's later career as a writer for the stage is well known.

III

Field's habit of using the late night hours for his writing remained with him almost to the end of his career.   Having written his column in the afternoon, for a period of months he was accustomed to return to the *Daily News* office after the theatre and then he would write letters or putter over some humorous verses to send to a friend or compose poems in archaic English.   If he found that Editor Stone had wrought destruction among his paragraphs he would write more to fill up his column.   His verses, "The Ahkoond of Swat," written late one night to fill a hole made by Stone's inexorable blue pencil, expressed his annoyance at the censorship to which his work was subjected:

> When the writer has written with all of his might
>   Of Blaine and of Cleveland a column or more,
> And the editor happens along in the night
>   (As he generally does between midnight and four)
> And kills all the stuff that the writer has writ,
>   And calls for more copy at once, on the spot,
> There is none for the writer to turn on and hit
>   But that distant old party, the Ahkoond of Swat.

After the first year or two Field gave up killing time at the office late at night after the theatre. Instead he went home, went to bed, and there read and wrote until long after midnight.

One of the numerous manuscripts of Field's that are in my possession bears marks of revision that caused special heartburnings to its author. The story of it serves to illustrate how sensitive Field was to any changes made in his articles or verses.

After the execution of the anarchists condemned to death for complicity in the fatal Haymarket riot in Chicago there was a funeral parade of thousands through the city streets as a protest against the hangings. An old soldier of the Civil War, one Howell Trogden, much to the disgust of the marchers, insisted upon marching ahead of the parade bearing aloft a large American flag. Field wrote a poem on the incident. Late on the evening of the day before its publication he came to me in a state of very unusual indignation. There had been, he said, an "Indian war dance" around the tortured body of his poem. Stone and Thompson had participated in the horrid ceremony and had mutilated his verses barbarously, according to Field's view of the matter—so barbarously that Field declined to acknowledge them as his literary offspring.   Therefore he insisted upon their being published outside of his column and he attached to them the initials "S. T. F." They appeared in the issue of November 14, 1887.

Field gave me the manuscript of the poem next day.   I thought then and I think now that the changes made in it against Field's protests were useless or worse.   The alterations appear on the manuscript in Stone's handwriting, but Field held Thompson to blame for some of them.

Here is Field's poem as Field wrote it:

OLD MAN TROGDEN

Down the broad street with solemn tread
Came the funeral train of the lawless dead;

Ten thousand comrades in the cause
Of Justice scorned and of outraged laws.

No banner floated at their head,
But on their breasts they wore the Red,

And in their eyes there flamed that day
The rage of tameless beasts at bay.

Then one old battered soldier said:
"Why floats no flag at the column's head?

"Where is our symbol?   It should fly,
Mauger the threats of anarchy!

"Give me that flag; these arms have oft
Lifted its glorious folds aloft!

"Shame on these men that they deride
The flag for which our heroes died!

"And shame on me if I should fear
To own that love I hold most dear!"

Up the broad street with solemn tread
Went the funeral train of the lawless dead,

And, waving his banner in their van,
Stubbornly trudged that brave old man.

Ten thousand comrades in the cause
Of Justice scorned and of outraged laws;

And in their eyes there burned that day
The fury of tameless beasts at bay!

But what was their rage to this hero grim——
What were their curses and threats to him?

Over the bloody carmine pall,
Over the vengeful hearts and all

Floated the flag, and none so bold
To wrench that flag from the old man's hold!

Teach us, old man, that we may know
The patriot valour of long ago;

Teach us that we may feel no fear
When viprous enemies appear;

And teach us how sweet 'twould be to die
Under the flag you raised on high!

IV

Field's love for old English and the jargon of knight
errantry clung to him from boyhood until he was weaned
away from such affectations by the success of his simple
child poems. As schoolboys he and his brother Roswell
had read Sir Thomas Mallory and had played at being
Sir Launcelot and the rest, coming out strong with
knightly speech. I have seen in a manuscript volume,
abundantly illustrated with excellent original drawings by
a young artist friend, a long and supposedly humorous
narrative in verse entitled "The Duke of Cahokia,"
writted by Roswell Field soon after he left college, probably while Eugene was on his European trip. The whole
was done in archaic English and liberally larded with

knightly phrases.   So it is reasonably clear that the writing of bad verse in obsolete words was a family failing. It has always seemed to me extraordinary that a man of the force, the originality, the broad experience, and the keen sense of humour possessed by Eugene Field should have been obsessed with a fondness for the stilted ancient forms of speech until he was nearly forty years of age.

In spite of all his avocations and pastimes, however, Field was continually planning or writing or rewriting some fanciful story into which he endeavoured to put the best work he found himself capable of doing.   It was usually a fairy story or a highly imaginative tale on some theme associated with Christmas.   Field all his life had for that great Christian festival the love and enthusiasm of a little child.   With the approach of December he was always busy in his spare hours on a Christmas story or a Christmas poem or both.   These had to be worked out with the greatest care and then rewritten and continually revised until they conformed to the high standards he set for himself.   Then there were the many gifts for friends to be planned and purchased.   He was quite unselfish in these gifts.   They were not expected to bring gifts in return.   They were usually books and commonly they were inscribed, "With Eugene Field's love"—which was to him no empty grouping of words.   Friendship was his very life and no friendship satisfied him that was not, as one may say, a "going concern."   With his friends he discussed freely any work that he had in hand, asking their advice and repeating incidents or special passages and inviting criticism.   He always knew the precise effect he wished to get, so that his shaping and reshaping of his material in the end brought the results he desired.

In this manner he wrought slowly and painstakingly a number of beautiful or whimsical stories.   These in his earlier years he relied upon to bring him fame.   Even after their publication in the *Daily News* he laid them aside for further revision, never deeming them completed so long as they were not wholly satisfactory to him in every phrase and every word. His poems, too, were wrought with great care, but not with the laborious effort that went to perfect his stories. Indeed, many of his poems sung themselves, but they also had to be put aside for a time after the delightful creative effort that brought them into existence. He would lay them by for perhaps a day, perhaps a month, a year, or several years; when he took them up again it was with a considerable degree of mental detachment, almost as if they were the work of another. Then he would give them the finishing touches that cold reason prescribed.

Even after he began to try earnestly to do his best work with his pen the curse of the grotesque was heavy upon him. In his hours of relaxation archaic ballads continued to take up his time and claim his thoughts. Some of these weird products were transcribed by their author on huge sheets of parchment at heavy cost of time and labour. He illuminated them with elaborate capital letters in coloured inks and otherwise embellished them. Then the parchments had to be given a look of age with coffee stains or by the laborious application of soot and grime. As a whole they were intended to furnish material for a ponderous literary joke. The product was named "The Shadwell Folio" and an elaborate tale of their alleged discovery was concocted by Field with no happy flow of imagination. Months of labour at odd hours went into this arid diversion. The poems of the "folio" were finally published in Thompson's weekly journal, *America*. They fell flat.

v

I have two of the parchments before me as I write. One contains "Madge: Ye Hoyden," written on a skin eighteen

by twenty-four inches in size.   After Field had carefully
lettered it, he made many changes in the verses, and these
changes appear on the parchment.   They brought the
poem into the form in which it was finally published.
The title is in red ink, as are also the Roman numerals
before each stanza.   Running down the side of the poem
is this summary or argument, written in red ink:

The hoyden is chided by proper housewives, but she cares not, for
she is merry at heart and neither thinks nor does any evil thing.
When Sir Thomas tempts her she says that she is promised to Robin.
This vexes Sir Thomas. Robin and the hoyden are wed. Robin
falls sick and the hoyden earns their daily bread.   Sir Thomas tempts
the hoyden a second time. She slams the door. The hoyden toils
and never makes any complaint. The devil tempts Robin and makes
a compact with him. All of a sudden Robin gets well. The devil
claims his allegiance and Robin runs away with Sir Thomas's young
wife.   Sir Thomas asks the hoyden to come and live with him, but the
hoyden saith that she will stay at home and pray for Robin's return.
She prays. Robin returns and the hoyden dies. God help us all!

The parchment also contains this waggish final stanza
which, having been intended only for the eyes of friends,
never saw print:

Godde graunt us everech such a wiffe
    as madge ye hoyden staunch & trew
& graunt us grace to do in liffe
    ye whych yt wiffe wolde have us doe;
& tho all helle assailed olde ffield
    hee wolde defye yt feenly crewe
nor wolde not neuer yeeld!

The companion to this ballad is "Ye Diuell & Ye Miller
Hys Wiffe," done on small parchment sheets and bearing
the date, July 10, 1887.   It also has its summary, written
in red ink down the right-hand margin of the sheets:

The devil comes to the miller's cottage and tempts Hodge, who is
dazzled by the devil's promises. But Mawk, his wife, is not fooled.

She sees that he is the devil and she tells him to go away and leave her husband alone. "He is mine," says the devil. "We'll see about that," says the wife. She attacks the devil with a knife and they wrestle around and fight savagely. She cuts off his tail and beats him till he is black and blue. Then he begs for mercy. The devil goes away and never bothers them any more. "Go to bed without your supper," Mawk says to Hodge; "I'll run the mill to-day myself."

These spirited stanzas, thirteen in number, do not appear in Field's collected works. Here are the first two:

> A feenly diuell of renowne
> Upp on ye earth ffor euill strode,
> & roaming upp & rooring down
> he came per chaunce unto ye towne
> Where Hodge ye miller bode.

> Hee knockit att yt man hys doore——
> sais, "Hodge, giff you will gang with mee
> to do my seruice evermoore,
> no longer shall you be soe pore
> Nor meeke as now you bee."

There follows the battle royal between Hodge's wife and the devil, which ends in the devil's complete discomfiture.

> Withouten tale bot glad enow
> Yt hee had scapen with his liffe,
> Yt diuell backe to hell did goe
> nor neuer came yt way no mo
> to worrit Hodge hys wiffe.

Other manuscripts of the same period in my collection are the Chicago effusion, "Ye Lost Schooner," and this pathetic ballad:

Ye Crewel Sassinger Mill

All uppe & downe ye riuer & upon ye sandy shore
Ye yemen ben a moning & ye women shrike ffull shrill,
&, like a praroor ffire, ye news are spred from doore to doore
Yt Sawney leesed a finger in ye sassinger mill.

O Sawneys hande is ben as ffaire as euer dole a pack
  Or drawed a pair of ten spotts on ye aces for to ffill;
None bolder hande nor Sawneys never whoppit up ye jack—
  Bote now it leesed a finger in ye sassinger mill.

His fayther slew a barrow on a Moneday afternoone—
  Ys morning, whiles yt Sawney did ye hopper all to-fill,
His euill sister Betty gaue ye cranke a turn too soone,
  & Sawney leesed a ffinger in ye sassinger mill!

Such sorry stuff in time fortunately lost its attractions
for Field.   However, after he began to harvest his dreams
by writing real poetry he was beset with fantastic ideas
that gave him no very propitious start toward true poetic
expression.   For a considerable time he was haunted with
a desire to compose a mass of Alaskan balladry.   The
somewhat vague idea of "Krinken" came to him and he
hummed and recited lines around which he planned to
write the poem.   Finally "Krinken" was written and
it encouraged its author to continue to cultivate that
particular sort of poem.   I recall urging him at this time
to write poems about real human beings of whom he knew
something and stop trying to write about Eskimo babies
and Eskimo sea gods, or whatever they were.   Field took
such advice good-naturedly enough, but he kept on trying
to hammer out Alaskan balladry.   The adventure did not
greatly prosper.

During this period Field was receiving, as they were
delivered to subscribers, the paper-bound parts of Professor Francis James Child's "The English and Scottish
Popular Ballads," and this work gave him great pleasure.
He was also reading assiduously a large number of books,
particularly books published in Bohn editions.   For new
books or books by standard authors he cared little.

VII

A Humorist's Views of Public Men

I

FOR two or three years after Field began his work for the *Daily News* he was apparently content to fill his column with many brief paragraphs consisting of terse comment on well-known persons, mainly political comment, or amusing misrepresentations of theatrical folk. That he was a paragrapher of the first order was universally conceded at that time. He meant the biting humour of his paragraphs to be a sort of Ithuriel's spear to expose at a touch hypocrisy and pretense in political and social life. At the same time, well-known persons for whom he had a special regard he was particularly likely to make the victims of his sportive fancy. The satisfying proof of their worthiness was their willingness to take these misrepresentations in good part; the unpardonable sin was to resent them. There was one eminent lawyer in Chicago whom Field greatly admired because of his exceptional services in a high and laborious office. So admiring him, Field, of course, wrote extravagant, though playful and harmless, untruths about him. Soon the lawyer sent Field a brief and formal note requesting Field never again to mention his name in print. Field was more than a little hurt by his friend's lack of that spirit so much admired in the glorious company of martyrs, and in complying with the request he eliminated the sensitive gentleman from his list of acquaintances.

At times Field dropped into verse by way of making his extremely personal comments especially striking. Witness the following sample stanzas from a long effusion:

BAILEY DAWSON

This hoary sage
Of unknown age
(In counsel most prolific)
Is wont to dwell
In that hotel
Known as the Grand Pacific.

He is in height
A goodly sight,
His embonpoint is portly;
In manner he
Can haughty be,
Tho' commonly he's courtly.

His eyes are blue
And twinkling, too—
In Latin, *res delecti*—
His whiskers flow
Like driven snow
Below his jowls and necktie.

'Tis by his nose,
Couleur de rose,
That you'd most likely know him—
But we've no time
To put in rhyme
What is itself a poem.

With all his wit and incisiveness in dealing with politicians Field did not shine as a political prophet. However, the following paragraph, written in 1892, was indeed prophetic:

About four years hence Major McKinley will find the country ready for him and his presidential candidacy. This year there are other fish to fry and the little fish must be disposed of before the big fish can be attended to. Four years hence this country of ours will be bigger than it is now—bigger in wisdom and in its capacity to appreciate wisdom.

Another paragraph that Field wrote on the same day is worth reproducing because it recalls to mind one of the most humorous convention portraits ever perpetrated:

Mr. Depew is certain of Mr. Harrison's renomination at Minneapolis next week, but this proves nothing except that Mr. Depew is one of Mr. Harrison's most optimistic advocates. Four years ago Mr. Depew was certain of his own nomination, but he came no nearer to it than Beasley did to Bagdad. Do you remember the large campaign lithographs which Mr. Depew brought with him to Chicago? They were admirable portraits. The lines of type, one above and the other beneath the portrait, announced Mr. Depew as "the farmer's friend" and "the granger's choice." We have one of those lithographs; it is appropriately framed and it hangs on the wall opposite to us as we write. We value that relic highly; it is one of our choicest souvenirs.

II

In the months preceding the national conventions of 1884 Field, being strong in the Republican faith, was considerably wrought up over the outlook. The elections of the preceding autumn were mainly Democratic triumphs. The results in Ohio and elsewhere were duly recorded by Field in his column with signs of pain and apprehension. Meantime a certain Democratic governor of New York, one Grover Cleveland, frequently drew his fire. If there was nothing else to say about him on some particular day, one was reasonably certain to find a paragraph by Field commenting upon the completeness of Governor Cleveland's disappearance from public view. Cleveland's entire lack of significance in the political affairs of the country was a favourite theme of Field's at that time.

So the weeks passed and the national conventions of

1884 came on. The *Daily News*, which was independent in politics, was earnestly in favour of the nomination of President Arthur by the Republicans and of Cleveland by the Democrats. It was strongly opposed to Blaine because of the disclosures in the so-called Mulligan letters. When Blaine and Cleveland were placed in nomination by their respective parties the *Daily News* gave hearty support to Cleveland. That was a shock to Field.

Though accorded wide latitude in his column, he was not permitted to tear into the newspaper's presidential candidate or to sing the praises of the candidate whom the newspaper so determinedly fought on grounds of public morality. Thus was Field sorely handicapped during the campaign, being driven to amusing shifts in order that he might express his political views in ways fairly satisfactory to himself. Each evening was for him a time of crisis, for then his paragraphs passed under the critical eye of Editor Stone. In spite of Field's clever device of writing two or three particularly outrageous paragraphs in order that the editorial censor might not lack material so well fitted for slaughter that the rest would appear harmless by comparison, there were likely to be serious gaps in the column at the end of the winnowing process. It was on an evening when his pet paragraphs had fared exceedingly ill that Field retired to his room with fire in his eye and wrote "The Ahkoond of Swat" by way of expressing his disgust. With the defeat of Blaine, Field ceased to be a violent partisan.

III

A yarn which Field wrote about Chauncey M. Depew when the eminent New Yorker was supposed to be a presidential possibility seems worthy of being retold. It was ostensibly related by Samuel Kayser of Chicago, then director of the Chicago Conservatory, who was

represented to have travelled in Europe for some days
with Mr. Depew.   Field makes this report of Mr. Kayser's
impressions of his distinguished fellow traveler:

Mr. Kayser liked Mr. Depew very much, but found it hard work
travelling with him.   Mr. Depew felt bound to make an after-dinner
speech at all times and upon all occasions.   Stopping at Bologna for
refreshments, Mr. Depew delivered himself of a most graceful address to the restaurant garçon, which speech Mr. Kayser had to render
into Italian *ipsissimus verbis*, although, forsooth, the whole might
have been condensed into the simple, "Waiter, bring me a full order
of bologna sausages."   The born orator, however, is a creature of
sentiment—his tongue is, as it were, a tuneful harp upon which the fret-
ful fingers of his feelings (this is metaphor!) are forever striking responsive chords.   Mr. Depew is a born orator.   He talks all the time
and always well.   Mr. Kayser slept in an adjoining room for three
nights and he tells me that Mr. Depew talked all night in his sleep—
in fact, at the Hotel d'Europe in Verona about 4 A. M. Mr. Kayser
heard Mr. Depew formally accept the presidential nomination in his
sleep.   They parted at Turin.   Mr. Depew's last words were: "Kayser, I have had a delightful time.   The only thing I regret is that
there have been no shorthand reporters present."

One man whose early career Field watched with interest
and of whom he wrote occasionally, but in no spirit of
prophecy, was Theodore Roosevelt.   I sat by Field's side
in the Republican National Convention of 1884 when the
interesting young delegate from New York, whose reform
work in the General Assembly of his state had given him
an enviable reputation, voted with his fellow delegate,
George William Curtis, for Edmunds of Vermont until
Blaine won.   In the first session of the convention Curtis,
mounted precariously on a chair, made his fine speech
against the resolution that was intended to bind the
delegates to support the nominee no matter who he
might be.   "A free man I came into this convention,"
shouted the scholarly delegate into the teeth of the
ravening Blaine forces, "and by the grace of God a free
man will I go out of this convention."   That speech de-

feated the resolution. Field was thrilled, though he
commented then disparagingly on the dimple in Curtis's
chin, which he held to be a sign of effeminacy. Roosevelt sat at the side of Curtis and cheered the speech
enthusiastically—but he supported Blaine in the succeeding campaign, as Curtis did not.

Thereafter from time to time Field published paragraphs about Roosevelt, most of them in tenor somewhat
like the following, which appeared in January, 1891:

What has become of Theodore Roosevelt?   A short time ago he was
a Burning Issue; now he might parade up and down Christendom with
a bell and not find anybody who had ever heard of him.   Yet he
should be remembered at least as the great American firecracker.

In April, 1892, Field wrote:

Once in a very great while we discover obscure mention made
of one Theodore Roosevelt, and we are wondering whether he is the
same meteoric genius who sky-rocketed into conspicuousness eight
years ago.   What has become of all those promises of greatness he
was said to exhibit then?   Guess G. W. Curtis must have packed 'em
away in a cedar chest.

Three years later, however, Field discovered that Roosevelt after all was a force to be reckoned with in public
affairs.   He wrote:

Theodore Roosevelt would seem to be peculiarly qualified for the
head of the police commission in New York City.   He is, we believe,
several years this side of forty, but he has been in public life eleven
years, and his ability, sincerity, and conservatism have been pretty
clearly demonstrated.   Those people are sadly in error who, never
having seen him, imagine that Roosevelt is a prig or a dude.   He has
a distinct heartiness and vigour, a virile energy that is at once wholesome and pleasing.

These lines indicate clearly, I think, that Field had met
and conversed with Roosevelt and had taken a liking to

him.   Indeed, I am sure that Roosevelt and Field might readily have become famous friends.

IV

Field's determination to be original in everything led him to express himself about the Father of His Country in the following fashion when everybody else, in April, 1889, was eulogizing that great man while celebrating the one hundredth anniversary of the inauguration of the First President of the United States:

George Washington was a gentleman.
George had a red nose, a very red nose, and he was morbidly sensitive about it.   But George was a gentleman in spite of his bulbous and florescent nasal organ.

The next day he returned to the theme, thus:

It might be well to remember that although our first President was by no means a prohibitionist he neither got drunk nor approved of drunkenness.   If he had a red nose it was due to its having been frostbitten at Valley Forge.

By this explanation perhaps was the great shade of the First President placated, if not the indignant patriots who loudly protested against Field's original paragraph.

To illustrate Field's ability to produce laughter out of the most unpromising subjects I will set down examples of his delightful fooling at the time the interstate commerce law was about to go into effect.   First it is well to say, by way of explanation, that previous to April, 1887, when the new order was established by federal law, the average newspaper man thought he was disgraced if he ever found himself compelled to pay railroad fare.   Passes on railroads were about the most common things in the newspaper business.   It may be safely assumed, I think, that Field had never paid a dollar for railroad fare from the

day he became a newspaper reporter.   In this respect he
was, of course, no exception.   The railroads gave out
passes in abundance by way of making friends of all
dabblers in printers' ink.   So when the new law greatly
restricting the issuance of passes was nearly due to become
operative Field wrote this grim warning:

The colonels of the railroad business have but eight more days to
enjoy their titles.

Then on April Fool's Day, which came just before the
dread time for the revocation of passes, Field devoted his
entire column to paragraphs illustrating what he chose to
assume would be the sort of treatment the railroads would
receive regularly from an implacable army of passless
editors.   To some of the paragraphs were appended
certain cryptic letters— "d&wtf," "eodtf," and "1tpd,"
to mention a few of the meaningful combinations, intended
to make it appear that they were paid reading notices.
I quote two of these:

Colonel Marvin Hughett of the Chicago & Northwestern honoured
us with a pleasant call last evening.   The Colonel is looking as handsome as ever and he reports his road in superb condition. d&w.

Colonel O. W. Ruggles, general passenger agent of the old reliable
Michigan Central, has gone East for a day or two.   During his absence it is proper to state that his abilities are no less brilliant than
his personality is attractive.   Under his Napoleonic manipulation the
Michigan Central has been brought up to its preëminent standard of
excellence and Niagara Falls has been raised from the lowly condition
of a babbling cascade. d&w.

Field's column that day presented also samples of what
Field meant to imply was mere news, there being no
cabalistic symbols attached to them.   Here are two specimens:

The lightning express train on the Illinois and Iowa route came in
last night three weeks overdue.   The report that it had ivy and moss
growing on the driving wheels of the locomotive is not true.

It is stated on seemingly good authority that the president of the
Podunk Grand Trunk route was born in Connecticut and used to ped-
dle doorknobs as fresh eggs.

V

A curious practice in which Field took special delight
was that of attributing verses of his own to other people.
I have already mentioned his lullaby attributed to Henry
Ward Beecher, his poem about a seashell published over
the signature of Helena Modjeska and his improving
verses alleged to be by the good Dr. Isaac Watts.   In the
same way he assigned to Judge Cooley, then receiver of
the Wabash railroad and soon to become chairman of the
Interstate Commerce Commission, his "Divine Lullaby,"
his poem on the Holy Grail and minor verses.   His
method of carrying out this ludicrous plan was to publish
a long and extremely laudatory article, ostensibly a review
of many poems Judge Cooley was represented to have
written as a young man.   The reviewer favoured his
readers with copious extracts from these alleged poems,
most of them ridiculous enough.   Not long afterward the
serious-minded judge, having grown weary of his reputation for poetic genius which Field had thrust upon him,
formally denied that he had ever written poetry.   Thereupon Field wrote another long article, reproaching Judge
Cooley more in sorrow than in anger and accusing him
of trying to discourage other young men from following in
his footsteps and achieving poetic fame as he had done.
Field took occasion to publish still other alleged products
of the muse of the chairman of the Interstate Commerce
Commission.   One, I recall, was a purple lyric entitled,
"The Dimple in My Thisbe's Arm."
Of all the productions of Field's audacious pen that
were published by him as the works of others none is more
ingenious or more interesting than the material of his own
devising out of which he constructed his elaborate review

of a supposititious volume setting forth in detail the life
history of a mythical personage, one Florence Bardsley.
It seems to me that this carefully wrought piece of whimsicality has never received from the public the recognition
that it deserves.   Indeed, I know no other piece of humour
by Field that is quite so delightful.   It has been republished in various forms, having been originally rescued
from obscurity by Field's bibliophile friend, Washington
I. Way.

I have in my possession the author's proofs of the article
as it originally appeared in the *Daily News* late in 1892.
As published it gave no sign of its authorship other than
the unmistakable signs within the article itself.   It is
ostensibly a learned review of a newly published book
written in French by Whitelaw Reid, then American
minister to France.   I well remember the glee with which
Field worked away at odd hours for weeks on this elaborate hoax.   The review, being made up largely of extracts
from the precious biographical work which it celebrates,
contains long passages in French as well as a liberal sprinkling from end to end of French sentences and phrases,
together with solemn footnotes and parenthetical references to alleged authorities in German, Italian, and Spanish.   The article has also a flavouring of Portuguese, Latin,
and Greek.   He enlisted the services of his artist friend,
Frederick Richardson, in working up his French quotations, some of which would not pass muster in the
French Academy.   Finally, Field affects to point a moral
to his tale with a bogus extract from the edifying poems of
his old-time victim, Dr. Isaac Watts.

The notable work reviewed so felicitously by Field has,
one is told, the following on its title page: "Un Aperçu de
la Vie de Mme. la Comtesse de la Tour, par Whitelaw
Reid, Ministre plenipotentiare et Envoye extraordinaire
des États-Unis.   Bouchet et Fils, Paris."   Ostensibly it

tells how the daughter of Sir Robert Bardsley, an 18th century Englishman, was from childhood a persistent detractor of men. The reader learns that at the age of seventeen she published anonymously in a magazine a series of articles entitled "The Disadvantages of Being a Man," thus causing a mighty stir. Somewhat later she published a brochure entitled "The Horrors of Shaving Categorically Set Forth as Showing How Evil a Necessity It Is to Be a Man." Leigh Hunt is given credit for discovering and making public the name of Miss Bardsley as that of the author of the essay. "Immediately there was a great tempest," the women assailing the rash young author and violently "expostulating against the new and vicious doctrine." Even the learned Mrs. Piozzi denounced the "temerarious schismatic." Miss Bardsley, however, ably defended her position in a pamphlet entitled "The Pains and Cares of Masculinity." That work had "an enormous sale, passing into fourteen editions and being translated into half a dozen foreign tongues. Wolfgang Goethe used to say it was the most remarkable book he had ever read." All men, it seems, were delighted with the writings of the singular young woman, whereas all women cried out against her in horror. She bestowed her hand in marriage upon a certain Clarence Sidney Eastcourt, but her fond husband "soon died of quinsy contracted from exposure at tennis, a vice to which he was violently addicted (*absolument esclave*) and at which he exhibited marvellous agility."

Two years after her first husband's death the fascinating widow was wedded to the wealthy and cultured Comte de la Tour and thereafter she resided in Paris. One is assured that her titled husband "was in complete sympathy (*en pleine sympathie*) with his wife's extraordinary views." Thus was she enabled to put forth prodigies of effort in her special field of endeavour. In the twenty years following her second marriage she "wrote and published no fewer than sixty pamphlets in advocacy of her curious heresies." Among the sixty—the reader unfortunately is not enlightened as to the titles of the other fifty-nine—was "a thoughtful and charming treatise on the miseries of wearing suspenders ('Les Misères qui Rèsultent de ce que les Hommes Portent des Bretelles')." This imperishable treatise, one learns, was dedicated by its author to Schopenhauer.

Happily the review tells much concerning a famous public debate held in Brussels in the autumn of 1843 between the comtesse and a certain Frau Kathrina Winkelmann who for the good of the human race sought to refute the arguments of her opponent. The debate "lasted two days, vast crowds assembling from all over Europe. The women applauded Frau Winkelmann to the echo, while the men as rapturously indorsed the comtesse's utterances." At the end of the second day the great assemblage broke up in a riot after the fiery Kathrina had exclaimed: "If I could be a man for twenty-four hours the first thing I should do would be to go downtown and make a night of it with the boys." (*"Si je pouvais être homme pendant vingt-quatre heures, la première chose que je ferais ce serait de descendre en ville pour faire la noce avec mes joyeux camarades."*) Amid the tumult that followed might be heard the voice of the scandalized comtesse saying: "Nay, I should rather spend that time upon my knees imploring heaven's benignant offices to restore me once again and forever to womanhood, an estate free from the weaknesses, the temptations, the appetites, and the evils that beset all men."

At the end of a long life, one is told—and one is told it, according to Field, in Minister Reid's not very pellucid French—the comtesse, while on her death bed, confessed to the holy *père* who was at her side that from childhood to

old age she had unceasingly longed to be a man! **More;**
it was found after her demise that she had left a large sum
of money from which to provide an annual prize to be
awarded to the girl who should display the greatest skill
in riding a horse astride.   ("*La jeune fille, française ou
étrangère, qui, aborant courageusement le costume distinc-
tivement masculin, montrerait dans un manège de Paris le
plus d'habilité à enfourcher un cheval à la façon des hommes.*")

Field's final revision of the proofs of this article consisted
mainly of adding many sentences and phrases in French
and other foreign tongues.   These additions are written
at all angles and flow across and across the proof's broad
margins in Field's fine, yet exceedingly distinct, writing.

VIII

SATIRE AS A CONSTRUCTIVE FORCE

I

AN IMPORTANT and yet an imperfectly understood element of Field's work during his earlier
years in Chicago was his satirizing of crudities in
the city's somewhat ostentatious displays of its culture.
The innocent and easily satisfied pork barons, the com-
plaisant wholesale grocers and the other leaders in art
movements imported second-hand from New York were
extremely funny when they sought to be most impressive.
Field hated shams and fought them whenever he saw an
opportunity. "I'm not much physically, but morally
I'm not a coward," he once told Hamlin Garland, and he
added: "I like to illustrate the foolery of these society
folks by stories which I invent."

Back in the early '80's of the last century Chicago grate-
fully accepted the plausible Colonel Mapleson's frayed
opera companies and Chicago society revelled in the
golden voices of the gallant colonel's third-rate sopranos.
The superior East gave the Illinois city also glimpses of its
literary lions, who came to be admired and fêted, to read
from their writings or to lecture and then to write magazine articles of the most perfunctory sort about Chicago's
feats in slaughtering steers and its other industrial marvels. Field deemed it a necessary task to jolt the community out of the idea that anything imported from the
East was good enough to meet Chicago's cultural needs
and that a millionaire compounder of lard or a superla-

tively great pork butcher was by virtue of his money a competent leader in the finer things of community life. He wrote ludicrous conversations which he attributed to Chicago's first citizens, as if these expressed their feelings while taking punishment like heroes at Wagnerian opera or listening to and being submerged by the exquisite French of Sarah Bernhardt. It was all very wicked, but it was also very amusing and it caused a number of well-meaning rich men to become somewhat more modest in weighing their bank accounts against the culture of less dollarful individuals. And Field wielded a stinging lash against producers of musical or dramatic entertainments who tried to palm off obsolete singers upon the city or who surrounded theatrical stars with supporting companies of no merit on the comfortable theory that Chicago would unprotestingly accept anything.

Field found useful work to do also in taking down pretentious Easterners who visited the city to bear away its money in exchange for their shelf-worn products. Once James Russell Lowell came to lecture before a leading political club on the subject of American politics, but, taking alarm at the last moment lest the undeveloped intellects he was to address would not be able to assimilate or excuse his rarefied ideas, he changed without warning to a second-hand essay in which he inquired whether Shakespeare did or did not write the tragedy of "Richard III." Field whacked the eminent Massachusetts poet plentifully for this singular action and then he most irreverently poked fun at the next Eastern celebrity who came to irradiate Chicago with his presence, getting Charles Dudley Warner badly confused with a widely advertised maker of patent medicines. He expressed much doubt as to whether Warner would lecture on "Some Golden Remedies" or on "The Theory That Ben Jonson Did Not Write 'Rasselas'."

II

These satirical observations had an amusing sequel.
For Warner had come to Chicago primarily to write
articles about the city for an Eastern magazine. And in
Chicago he conferred with the city's leading publisher and
bookseller, General Alexander C. McClurg. Now General
McClurg felt that he had a grievance against Field. Not
long before he had offered to the trade a little volume of
which he was proud; it contained the surviving fragments
of the poems of Sappho. Field had made it an object of
mirth! He had contrasted the city's enthusiasm over a
circus parade with the far milder interest of the citizens
in Sappho's immortal lines. Field also professed to quote
the views of leading citizens on Sappho, all of these views
being painfully vague, except that there seemed to be a
feeling abroad that the lady, though gifted, was not all
she should have been. Altogether, the liberties taken
by Field with the poetess ground the iron into the soul of
General McClurg. One may even think that perhaps
Field's pleasantries about Mr. Warner's famous patent
medicines did not cause Chicago's distinguished visitor
any particular joy. In any event, Mr. Warner's extremely laudatory articles on the business enterprise and
the culture of Chicagoans incidentally lamented the short-
comings of Chicago's press. "It lacks tone, elevation of
purpose," wrote Mr. Warner. And he added:

It is curious also that the newspapers, or some of them, take pleasure
in mocking at the culture of the town. Outside papers catch this
spirit, and the "culture" of Chicago is the butt of the paragraphers.
It is a singular attitude for newspapers to take regarding their own
city. Not long ago Mr. McClurg published a very neat volume, in
vellum, of the fragments of Sappho, with translations. If the volume
had appeared in Boston it would have been welcomed and most respectfully received in Chicago. But instead of regarding it as an
evidence of the growing literary taste of the new town, the humorists

saw occasion in it for exquisite mockery in the juxtaposition of Sappho with the modern ability to kill seven pigs a minute and in the cleverest and most humorous manner set all the country in a roar over the incongruity.

Thus was Field transformed by the earnest Mr. Warner into a whole regiment of humorists and thus his trouncing was administered in a detached and casual manner.   So Field sarcastically joined in the hue and cry, thus:

Mr. Warner treats specifically of our culture.   We are particularly gratified by the attention which he pays to those baseborn scribblers, alleged humorists, and self-styled wits who eke out a miserable existence and entitle themselves to everlasting infamy by scoffing at the transcendent glories of our civilization.   The masterly manner in which Mr. Warner deals with and dissects this brood of buzzards, hyenas, and ghouls reminds us of the portrait Gustave Doré has left us of old Francis Rabelais, in which portraiture the most learned satirist is represented as stabbing his pen point through the very vitals of his enemies.

Field urged the people of Chicago to proceed at once to erect a monument to their fearless champion, Mr. Warner.   In short, the incorrigible Chicagoan was not at all cowed by the disapproval of the Eastern Olympian. He continued to make it clear that not everybody in the West was stricken speechless at the mention of revered names whose owners were accepted as great because they bore the stamp of approval of a particular section.   Here, for example, is a wicked paragraph written at this period which marked the height of Field's rebellion against New England's intellectual dictatorship:

Queen Kapiolani, the Hawaiian potentate, is charmed, positively charmed, with Boston.   "And, do you know," she said to Dr. Oliver Wendell Holmes the other day, "do you know, dock, that I never heard of Boston till a Washington gentleman told me about it last week?"   Dr. Holmes did not fancy this at all.   Subsequently he told his friend Aldrich that he knew by the queen's furtive glances at his

plump person that if she had him alone on her tropical isle she would
eat him.

III

This sort of treatment, liberally applied, soon had a
marked effect. It won for Chicago opinion deferential
regard from visiting notables, regard such as they had not
previously shown. Chicago was no longer looked upon as
a community to be patted on the head and fed with stale
intellectual nourishment. It was found to have standards
of opinion that were worthy of respect, and Field was its
prophet. For Field's condemnatory paragraphs were as
deadly as bullets. They were copied far and wide.
Particularly were they copied by the New York *Sun;* for
the discriminating and appreciative Charles A. Dana was
one of Field's earliest and warmest admirers. Field had a
standing offer of a position on the *Sun* at a salary larger
than that which he received in Chicago, but the offer never
tempted him. He liked Chicago; the people of Chicago
were fond of him. He had become the chief celebrity of
his town. Noted men from all over the country began
to make pilgrimages to his grimy little room in the *Daily
News* office. The New York *Sun* habitually called
Chicago "Colonel Eugene Field's town." Field liked that.
Other newspapers followed the *Sun's* example. Field
knew and frankly told his friends that he would be in a
measure submerged in New York; worse still, he would be
denied a free hand because of New York's tremendous
self-esteem. He wanted full freedom of expression and
Chicago accorded him that.

Did Field abuse this freedom? I do not think so. His
biting satire was a powerful agency in promoting true
culture, in substituting for the crude standards of wealth
standards of intellect, of gentle manners, and of artistic
achievement. To this day Field has not received the
credit due him for his pioneer work in breaking down the

old order. His many articles solemnly setting forth the teachings of a supposititious dictator of social forms, Professor Andrew J. Fishbladder—"that paragon, that pole star, that prototype of male and female etiquette"—most effectively satirized the fluttering anxiety of Chicago's society leaders whenever any Eastern or foreign celebrity was about to irradiate the city with the splendour of his presence. The hastily applied veneer of social elegance, the parading of local notables to do the honours, the general twitter of nervousness that prevented the good people of Chicago from being their own honest selves in the presence of company—these affectations Field always regarded as fair game.

IV

A typical piece of his satire aimed at the aridity of Chicago from a literary point of view begins with the announcement that a work of very special importance has just been given to the local public. "At this particular season of the year," Field unctuously asserts, "a literary revival is invariably expected in this centre of culture, for it is at this season that the straits of Mackinaw thaw out, opening up a highway between the copper and timber regions and our *cor cordis* of civilization for that commerce which no less a distinguished local poet than General McClurg has asserted to be the best of human employments." The new work, it appears, "is entitled 'Facts About Lard.'"

It comes to us under the indorsement, if not from the pen, of our wealthy and distinguished townsman, Mr. N. K. Fairbank. Whether it is an instinctive fondness for fine pastries or a tender regard for that substance which imparts to our fried victuals the most delicious flavour, or natural admiration of that product which is recognized as one of the bulwarks of our local culture—which of these considerations inclines us favourably to lard we know not, but we do know that for lard we have a rockrooted and ardent affection. And we maintain that the reading public has cause for self-gratulation in this valuable brochure which emanates from so eminent an authority as Mr. Fairbank.

Field proceeds:

In the treatment of his subject Mr. Fairbank employs that acuteness of perception, that fineness of discernment, that delicacy of taste and all those other rare analytical powers which have acquired for him preëminence as an art and literary critic in the midst of us.   Moreover, he brings to his discussion of lard a wealth of experience, a vast fund of research and a deliciously playful persuasiveness of style—a combination rarely met with in the chefs d'œuvres de belles lettres de Chicago.   A charming feature of the book is that it is written in the form of dialogues—not a new idea, truly, but always a good one.   It has been used with more or less effect by Sophocles, Lucian, Æschylus, Plato, Xenophon, Aristophanes, Izaak Walton, and Boswell; its adoption, therefore, invests this treatise with a certain atmosphere of classicality that gives the work an immediate and enduring charm. These dialogues purport to be conversations between Q and A before an inquisitorial body empowered to inquire into the qualities of different lards.

Field thereupon quotes a sample of the Socratic marvels of the dialogues and then adds:

A shroud, a vapour of mystery is thrown about the identity of the twain between whom this dialogue is sustained.   Who are Q and A? Ah, that does not appear; ages will roll on and posterity will be as much puzzled to identify Q and A as the present generation is in determining the authorship of the Junius letters and of the Shakespeare plays—unless, forsooth, there purls and percolates through these pages a cipher as yet undiscovered.   This mystery, however, constitutes another of those charms in which the masterpiece abounds.

At one time Field jestingly threatened to inflict upon the defenseless world his own translation of the epics of Homer.   "I follow the Homeric text pretty closely," he wrote, and then he added:

I transfer the scenes from Troy to Cook County, and for Hector, Ulysses, Priam, Ajax, and the rest I simply substitute the names of Pullman, McVicker, Gage, Ferd Peck, and other people now on earth.

I want to popularize Homer among the hustlers. Here, for example, is just a little bit which fairly illustrates the majestic swing and felicitous modernization of the noble poem:

> Ere from the east the many-tinted morn
> Peeped from the seas of lo! the poor Indian corn,
> The ox-eyed Armour from his perfumed halls
> Strode forth to boss things at the stockyards stalls.

*   *   *

> About his form a purple robe he wore
> And in his hand his shining weapon bore——
> The beef-producing spear! whose lightning blow
> Failed not to fell the corn-fed cattle low!
> The bull-eyed bull, likewise the steer-eyed steer,
> The cow-eyed cow, stood not before that spear;
> Last but not least, full many a calf-eyed veal
> Had felt the fatal force of Armour's steel.

*   *   *

> Three cubits long in length from end to end,
> And these two ends adjusted were so true
> That the same distance lay between the two.
> Big two-pound diamonds in the hilt made light
> Of nature's darkness—even day of night!
> 'Twas not yet morn (as I remarked before),
> Yet as he issued from his palace door
> The blaze-compelling spear changed nature so
> The neighbours' cocks straightway began to crow,
> And Pullman, waking up, was queered to see
> 'Twas half-past five at only half-past three!

v

Certain of Field's favorite methods of promoting the gayety of existence not infrequently proved extremely embarrassing to friends of his. The emotions aroused in them were expressed with great mildness by the Rev. Newell Dwight Hillis when he said pensively not long after Field's death: "'Sharps and Flats' was a terror to some of us, who often wished that its writer did not have

so much humour." A not extreme example of the immo-
lation to which Field subjected persons whom he particularly liked is afforded by the following paragraph:

Mr. H. H. Kohlsaat, editor of the *Inter Ocean*, goes to Minneapolis
next week to urge the Republican Convention to give the second place
on the national ticket to a coloured man. The elevation of the Negro
race has long been one of his fads. He is ready to take a delegation
of coloured citizens to Minneapolis with him, paying all the expenses of
the trip, if a sufficient number can be got together to present an
effective appearance.

Any unsuspecting man of colour who chanced to read
this ingeniously worded announcement may well have
thought that he would bestow a favour upon the earnest
Mr. Kohlsaat by consenting to accept a free trip to the
convention while at the same time helping to obtain a high
honour for a member of his own race. The implied
anxiety of the alleged promoter of the expedition lest there
should not be a sufficient number of applicants was, of
course, a particularly effective bit of detail. Needless to
say, the number of applicants who rallied to the cause was
a source of infinite worry to the innocent victim of the
joke.

Mr. Edward W. Bok in his autobiography has related
some of his embarrassments resulting from grotesque
yarns invented by Field and widely circulated by the
newspapers of the country. Curiously, Mr. Bok thought
that Field had caused these reports to be disseminated
by the Associated Press. Field's first story of a love
romance involving his friend Bok represented him as soon
to marry the granddaughter of Mrs. Lydia Pinkham, renowned because of countless patent-medicine advertisements. Mr. Bok says:

Field was wise enough to put the paragraph not in his own column
in the Chicago *Daily News* lest it be considered in the light of one of

his practical jokes, but on the news page of the paper, and he had it put on the Associated Press wire.

Yet here is the original item as it appeared in Field's column June 1, 1892:

The talk in Eastern literary circles is that Mr. Edward W. Bok, the handsome young bachelor editor of the *Ladies' Home Journal*, is to wed with Miss Lavinia Pinkham, the favourite granddaughter of Lydia Pinkham, the famous philanthropist. The young lady has been a contributor of verse to Mr. Bok's paper. She lives in East Braintree, Mass., is tall and slender, with a wondrously sweet face, and aside from her distinct intellectual charms might be considered interesting in the possession of a fortune estimated at nearly half a million dollars.

Field's sole, but sufficient, method of putting this item "on the Associated Press wire" was to write it in such a way that it would deceive the news-hungry representative of the Associated Press. Field would have regarded it as quite unsportsmanlike to use personal blandishments upon any news agency to get his jokes into general circulation. It was an astonishing circumstance that Field's notoriously unreliable column, so commonly the repository of the most extraordinary inventions, continued to the end to furnish the newspaper press with "news" which was glaringly bogus if intelligently analyzed but which nevertheless was solemnly accepted and published far and wide as authentic. The particularity of the description given of the engaging Miss Pinkham—who of course existed only in Field's imagination—convinced the press and the public that the tale was as true as gospel. Who could doubt that the beauteous damsel, "tall and slender and with a wondrously sweet face," actually existed and actually had captivated the romantic Mr. Bok?

But a worse experience for Mr. Bok was still to come. On June 27, 1893, Field published in his column—and from there it went everywhere—the following sentimental tale:

There is now a rumour to the effect that Mr. Edward W. Bok, the talented editor of the *Ladies' Home Journal,* is about to link his destiny with that of Mrs. Frank Leslie. Although the lady in question is Mr. Bok's senior by several years, it is easy to understand how one of his impressionable nature would reverence a woman so long and so conspicuously identified with those reforms in which Mr. Bok himself is interested and of which he writes so sweetly and forcefully in his excellent journal. It is also easy to understand that the tempest-tossed heart of this superior lady should only too willingly commit itself at last to the tender keeping of this valorous young man whose career so far has been a constant and discreet battle in behalf of womankind.

While we have not always indorsed Mr. Bok's views upon the subjects of corset-covers and toilet soaps, although we have not infrequently criticized his recipes for lemon pie, chapped lips, and angel-food, and although the system advocated by him of pulling out basting threads with forceps instead of with the fingers does not meet with our approval—in spite of this we cordially approve of that prospective event which promises to bring two sympathetic hearts into permanent union.

"It so happened," says Mr. Bok, "that Field put this new paragraph on the wire"—Mr. Bok had an unduly exalted opinion of Field's ability to command the resources of the Associated Press when he wished to perpetrate a joke—"just about the time that Bok's actual engagement was announced." And in fact only three days after Field published the preposterous Leslie canard he reported in his column the engagement of Miss Mary Louise Curtis to the gifted young editor of her father's celebrated journal for women.

It is pleasant to record that in the last months of Field's life Bok engaged Field as a contributor to the *Ladies' Home Journal* and published in that periodical at least three notable contributions by his poet friend.

IX

Artistry in Writing

I

THAT Field was an exceedingly efficient worker is the testimony of all who were familiar with his methods and with the effective service of his pen. His brother Roswell has told how Eugene, when nearly thirty years old, deliberately changed his handwriting from the ordinary size to that clear and regular but singularly minute script which was the wonder of his correspondents. "I had to clap a virtuoso glass to my eye to read this damnably exquisite writing," declared Stedman when he first encountered it. The employment of that kind of penmanship was a labour-saving device on the part of Field, but it doubtless appealed also to his esthetic taste. Writing much in little, each pen stroke being reduced to the smallest possible dimensions, was a practical method of avoiding needless effort. But before the day's serious work began, Field with great care and no little skill frequently elaborately ornamented the first letter of the first word which he was to write. Manuscripts thus adorned with old English capitals done in inks of various colours were always returned to Field from the composing room, and these he bestowed on friends or retained to form a part of his legacy to his family.

A cluster of little bottles of coloured inks was a permanent feature of Field's writing table. Gold and yellow, green and blue, red and purple and any other colour that might chance to strike his fancy, provided such ink was obtainable, were there and were used along with black in preparing manuscripts for the printers or letters to friends. There were likely to be on his table, also, various books in which he was especially interested at the time.   Field had little use for standard authors.   An old book was to him far preferable to a new one, though he delighted in such new volumes as Alice Morse Earle's studies of life in old New England and Henry T. Frinck's "Unhappy Loves of Men of Genius."   Field especially loved fairy tales of all sorts and what he commonly called "fool books"—that is to say, books on quaint and whimsical subjects.   I remember that at one time he was greatly fascinated by a curious old volume on odours.   The New England Primer he not only read with delight but bestowed as a gift upon friends.   My own copy bears on its fly leaf Field's autograph and the inscription, "Christmas, 1887."   The rhymes in this little book were frequently on Field's lips. He was particularly fond of repeating in his deepest chest tones:

> "Young Obadias,
> David, Josias,
> All were pious."

When, in his usual flow of spirits, he descanted, as was his custom, upon his own immense moral superiority over any friend or friends then present, he would sometimes clinch his grotesque arguments by saying: "And surely you recall the testimony of that godly volume, the New England Primer:

> "Old Field, Josias
> And Obadias,
> ALL were pious!"

This odd little volume, because of the pleasure Field gained from it, richly deserves the conspicuous place he gave it in his "Love Affairs of a Bibliomaniac."

Of "fool books," according to his classification, the old book stores supplied him with as many as he could contrive to purchase. Through daily conversations with him and otherwise I shared his pleasure in many of the volumes that particularly appealed to him. In presenting me with Alice Morse Earle's "China Collecting in America" he wrote in it: "To the mild chinaphile, Charles H. Dennis, from the rabid crockeromaniac, Eugene Field, June 11, 1892." A distinctively "fool book" among the others which he gave me is "Adventures of Master Tyll Owlglass." The great and desolating theft of a Field souvenir from which I have suffered is that of a first edition of Longfellow's "The Golden Legend." It was indeed a prize to tempt a hardened book collector. The passages that were omitted from the later editions of this poem Field had marked in gold ink and inside the cover he had pasted the most beautiful manuscript of his that I have ever seen. It was a copy of his "Lollaby," all in gold lettering, with a toy house, a tin soldier, and a toy dog—strongly reminiscent of "Little Boy Blue"—drawn at the top of the poem by Field in inks of various colours, while at the bottom a lively company of small gold fairies in the capacity of bell ringers drew music from a flower on its slender stalk with the aid of a rope of spider web. The date of this gift, March, 1888, follows rather closely the date of the composition of "Little Boy Blue." The theft which I here lament taught me—too tardily, alas—to keep my Field souvenirs under lock and key.

Among the books read by Field in the years of his earlier creative work I recall some that particularly impressed him. I name them as they come to my mind: Keightly's "Fairy Mythology," Wright's "Provincial Dictionary," "The Golden Ass," Suetonius' "Lives of the Cæsars," McNish's "Anatomy of Drunkenness," Burton's "Anatomy of Melancholy," Hilderic Friend's "Flowers

and Flower Lore," Rees's "Pleasures of a Bookworm,"
Wagner's "Epics and Romances of the Middle Ages,"
Baldwin's "Book Lover," "The Greek Anthology," "The
Compleat Angler," "A Lyttel Geste of Robin Hood," King
James's "Counterblaste to Tobacco," Blades's "The En-
emies of Books," "The Reliques of Father Prout," "Noctes
Ambrosianæ," Thorpe's "Northern Mythology," "Shake-
sperian Jest-Books," "The Ingoldsby Legends," "The
Travels of Sir John Mandeville." For many months
Field carried in his pocket a copy of Horace, the Latin
text being accompanied by a literal translation in English. This was while he was engaged in turning out paraphrases of those poems of Horace that particularly struck
his fancy.

Always having possessed a hunger for quaint books,
Field was inspired with a still greater passion for them
through his companionship with such confirmed book
collectors as Francis Wilson and a number of Chicagoans,
who possessed extensive and carefully selected libraries.
One of his fellow workers on the *Daily News*, Dr. Frank
W. Reilly, was an ardent admirer of "Kit North," of
"Father Prout," and of Horace. Field read them on Doctor Reilly's recommendation and fell in love with them.
From that time forward they were particular favourites
of his. At Doctor Reilly's suggestion he began to write
rhymed paraphrases of Horace. On various occasions
Field acknowledged his indebtedness to his older friend,
who outlived him many years. Doctor Reilly was the
Doctor O'Rell of Field's "The Love Affairs of a Bibliomaniac."

II

Thoroughly to understand Field, one had to take into
account his haunting sense of loneliness which caused him
to seek companionship on every possible occasion and to

revel in sympathetic friendships. His imagination was
so active that it peopled the sunlight no less than the
dark with objects of his fancy. He was medieval in his
acceptance of the grotesque as an element of the unseen
world about him. His thoughts dwelt upon elves and
pixies, upon werewolves and all manner of low-comedy
bogies because his imagination demanded that he think of
them. They were present in the books he read by preference. And they were not cheerful companions. He did
not like to be alone unless his mind was sunk deep in a
book or unless he was thinking out a poem At other
times he needed to bask in any ray of friendship that came
to illuminate his corner of the world. He was at all times
a lovable acquaintance and a helpful friend. He was
generous in notable ways. Indeed, he poured out the
riches of his mind and heart lavishly in exchange for a
little appreciative comradeship. Such comradeship he
commonly treasured quite beyond its worth.

His walks and talks of evenings with any friend were
made memorable to his companion by his stream of
reminiscences, particularly of his boyhood in New England, by his discussion of plans for poems or stories and by
his recounting of strange lore that he had picked up from
some book that he had recently read.

One night I walked with Field from his Fullerton
Avenue home to the studio of an artist on North State
Street who was working on an etching of Field. When we
reached the studio we found that Ballantyne and another
friend had arrived ahead of us. The portrait was nearly
completed. Ballantyne, after studying it gravely for a
while, blurted out: "Gene, it makes you look half-witted."

Then arose the artist, his whole frame one frenzied
gesture. There were cries of indignation. There were
shouts of protest. The rest of us, having recovered from
our temporary state of stupefaction, began to bestow un-

measured praise upon the portrait.   It was declared to be perfection and worthy of Whistler or any other master of the needle.   Ballantyne, we assured the outraged artist, knew rather less about real art than did his own setter pup.   So peace was gradually restored.   On our walk home Field frequently broke into chuckles as he thought of "the bad break of my Scotch brother-in-law."   The portrait in question is reproduced in Melville E. Stone's "Fifty Years a Journalist."

Much has been written by Thompson, Wilson, Stone, and others of Field's humorous methods of extracting advance payments of salary from Collins Shackelford— invariably called "Sheckelsford" by Field—the cashier of the *Daily News* during Field's first years on that news-paper.   Later, when Shackelford was succeeded by Miss Harriet Dewey, that experienced, kindly, and competent business woman, who still holds her position on merit, arranged, with Field's approval, that Mrs. Field should always draw his salary with the exception of a certain margin fully agreed upon.   Thus Field's passion for buy-ing books and curios was reasonably well subordinated to the needs of the Field household, and his affectionate admiration for his wife was still further heightened by the skillful way she parcelled out the family income.   Miss Dewey's boundless good nature, firmness, and tact were always equal to any emergency that arose by reason of Field's marvellous ability to spend more money than he possessed.   Field always called her "Cousin Hattie," and he showed his appreciation of her practical friendship by dedicating to her one of his most beautiful poems.

III

One of the amusing battles fought by Field with the cashier's department under Miss Dewey is worthy of being recorded here.   It began when Field to his horror discovered that the weekly pay-day was soon to be changed from Monday to Tuesday. His verbal protests having failed to alter the decree that had gone forth, he proceeded to prepare the following argument against the impending revolutionary procedure:

Shakespeare hath said that use doth breed a habit in a man, and Montaigne tells us that habit is second nature. But we do not require the authority of the ancients to fortify us in a conviction that mankind is truly a creature of habit, and not mankind alone but every other thing into which animal life has been breathed. The writers upon natural history have gathered together a vast quantity of material illustrative of the theory that habit exercises the most potent of influences upon brute animals, and there is no one of us that does not know of his own experience how important, not to say how essential, a part the item of habit plays in the daily life of each. Of so great consequence is this item considered that there is among mankind a sort of tacit understanding that one shall not do that which is liable to embarrass or conflict with the habits of others—in short, society, as it exists in this refined and enlightened age, is little more than a condition of thoughtful, if not cheerful, acquiescence to habit.

As this acquiescence is most properly respected and lauded as contributing to universal peace and comfort, so do men as properly deprecate and condemn everything that operates to the confusion of habit or to the neglect thereof. The evils with which a jeopardy of habit is fraught are so vital that to be hated they need but to be seen, nor will any continued contemplation of them so accustom us to their hideousness as to reconcile us first into pity and then to an embrace of them.

In illustration of the misery which is precipitated by a revolution in habit we would fain point out the manifold embarrassments and evils certain to arise from the proposition to make Tuesday a pay-day instead of Monday, if that proposition is carried into effect.

It has always seemed to us (and we doubt not that other people see and think, as they should, as we do) that of all the days in the week Monday is the fittest for the acquirement of one's salary or wages There was a time when this noble day was commonly called blue Monday—the opprobrious epithet having originated in the mediæval practice of paying wage workers the sum of their hire upon Saturday. In that barbarous time men devoted their wages to a conscientious and zealous disregard of the Fourth Commandment; their wages coming to them on the eve of a holiday enabled them to evade lawful creditors and to spend in Godless rioting the moneys which should have been applied to honest purposes. Therefore, when Monday dawned it was indeed a blue day; blue to the wage worker who returned to his toil with a jag upon him, blue to the employer who demanded honest work but could not get it on account of that jag, and blue—oh, so very blue!—to the creditors whose honest dues had been diverted to foolish purposes.

But Monday ceased to be regarded and designated blue when civilization, eager to correct the evils that had come down from mediæval ages, demanded that the time for paying off hands should be changed from Saturday to Monday. This change not only invested Monday with a proper amount of dignity but restored to the Sabbath that peace, that calm, that restful piety, which so become it. All men are very human, and when a human being winds up the week without a sou markee in his pocket it is the nature of the creature to spend Sunday in the dual condition of physical repose and of spiritual rapture—the physical repose necessitated by the circumstances over which he has no control and the spiritual rapture induced by the apprehension that the next day is Monday, which is to say pay-day. It has been said none the more wittily than truly that gratitude is the lively anticipation of favours to come. Is it not a fact, O men and brethren, that the prospective joys of pay-day have invested our Sabbath devotions with peculiar earnestness and enthusiasm? Have not the thoughts of the certain worldly rewards of the morrow thrilled us more keenly than the pious expositions of the preacher, and inspired us to combine our pulmonary functions with those of the choir in rendering with marked fervour such vocal devotion as only "Mears," "China," and "Brattle Street" abound in?

This Sabbath quiet and these pleasing anticipations put the human being into admirable condition for renewing his labours upon a Monday. He begins the week cheerfully—ay, with enthusiasm. When he returns home of a Monday night (and return he does regularly and promptly) he is contented and happy; no trace of a Sunday jag lingers in his system; mayhap his wife has been at the washtub all day, but when he doles out her share of his weekly stipend all sense of fatigue is lost in the pleasing delirium which the chink of gold impels. So, all in all, Monday is a dear, never-to-be-forgotten day.

The poets held Monday in high dignity. The name itself is one that compels respect. Originally it was Money-day, that is to say the day upon which men got their money. In time the word naturally became contracted into Monday. Chaucer tells us that—

"Ye carle did says hys prayers on Sondaye
But drew hys paye upon a Monnaie-daye;
Ye which ben called by that name yet,
For that men then their monnaie gette."

If, then, the proposition to make Tuesday the common pay-day is carried into effect, we shall not only lose Sunday as a day of zealous devotion, but violate every poetic and beautiful tradition that has come to us from the ancients. Nor should we underestimate that widespread embarrassment which this proposed change will involve. The debtor will no longer be able to look avaricious trade in the face and say, "I'll fix this Monday"; he will no longer be in a position to negotiate trifling loans from his wife upon the solemnly reiterated promise to make them good on Monday; he will be no longer provided with the means wherewith he may redeem his shirts and collars from the laundry nor hath he the wherewithal to purchase a reserved seat for a first performance of a new comedy. His lot is altogether miserable. The habit that has constituted him a cheerful, confident, and solvent human agent is now so truculently and so wholly reversed that, as it were by one fell swoop, he loses the respect of his neighbours, of his family, and of himself. The watch which he has been in the habit of carrying four days of the week he now carries but three. His whole business economy is metamorphosed, his entire system of credit is disordered, and his social, domestic, physical, moral, intellectual, and spiritual machinery, as by the fantastic operation of a diabolical automatic lever, is thrown irreparably and hopelessly out of gear. Then anarchy succeeds, and following it a train of horrors too hideous for contemplation.

It is painful to record that this learned and eloquent disquisition did not prevent Tuesday from being made payday in the *Daily News* office.

IV

A few years after Field came to the *Daily News* two of his early comrades retired from the staff of that newspaper. Ballantyne was succeeded as managing editor by Doctor Reilly, and Thompson resigned to assume the editorship of *America*, a new literary journal. Previously, however, a still greater change had come in the editorial department of the newspaper. Mr. Stone sold his interest in the business to his partner Victor F. Lawson. Thereupon Mr. Lawson took over the editorship of the *Daily News* and also continued to discharge the functions of publisher.

The members of the editorial staff were informed of the change at a dinner given to them by Mr. Stone.

We all received the news with the greatest possible astonishment.   As Mr. Lawson did not relieve himself of any part of his heavy duties as publisher we could not understand how he could take on, also, the work of editor. However, we soon discovered that the quiet, courteous young man who was now the sole owner of the *Daily News* was capable of doing anything well that he undertook. He knew precisely what he wanted done and how to get it done.   There was a steady forcefulness about him that completely won the staff's confidence and admiration. Field had offered his resignation at the time of the change, so that Mr. Lawson might suffer no embarrassment in case he did not approve of "Sharps and Flats," but the new editor's cordial assurances quickly made it apparent that Field was as highly valued by him as by his predecessor.   Indeed, Field was at all times an editorial adviser whose suggestions were esteemed by the *Daily News* management.   His practical knowledge of newsgetting and of methods of arousing public interest by special features was a real asset, and his unique column had become famous.

v

Field loved journalism and he not only sought constantly to improve his work but he urged self-improvement on all other writers.   He believed in close application to the job on hand at any given time and he had no patience with those who awaited special inspiration or who looked upon their environment as an aid or a detriment to composition.   On one occasion he wrote:

A current paragraph is to the effect that Mr. W. D. Howells finds that the noise and hurry of New York are fatal to literary inspiration and that he has therefore returned to Boston.   There comes in the old, old idea of "atmosphere"; it would seem as if literary greatness could not be achieved nowadays without "atmosphere." Bah! . . .

The rot about atmosphere discourages many young writers, who are led to believe that they can never get on in the world unless they can move into one of those alleged localities where this so-called atmosphere is said to abound. This is very sad; but the saddest thing about this atmosphere heresy is that it induces and encourages writing on the part of a great number of peaceful idiots who have no qualification whatever for writing except that atmosphere which another has made and which they, fool-like, have invaded. We think that the atmosphere heresy is largely responsible for the vast amount of wretched stuff that is annually spawned in this country in the name of literature. So on general principles we despise, we fear, and we cry out against that monstrous evil commonly called "atmosphere." There is but one atmosphere which we believe in and reverence; that is the atmosphere which every strong intellect surely creates. But that is an atmosphere of individual personality, and its glory cannot be shared except as toads wallow in a congenial pool, or as lizards scuttle forth to warm themselves in the sun, or as silly flies and moths caper gleefully about a street lamp.

To young writers everywhere: Attend diligently and patiently to your work and atmosphere will come to you. You can no more subsist upon the "atmosphere" of another than you can do your breathing with another man's lungs.

Several years later Field wrote:

Down East they have a great regard for what they call "atmosphere," and to a Western man that word, as the Eastern man uses it, is peculiarly exasperating. A Western man does not depend upon "atmosphere," and therefore he is not likely to believe in it. His loathing of "atmosphere" is intensified when he visits the East and breathes and smells what manner of thing this so-called "atmosphere" is—a sticky incense burned continually before narrow, vainglorious intellectual pigmies by busy little parasites. . . .

What makes the moon a particularly beautiful orb, in our thinking, is the pleasing fancy that it is wholly without atmosphere and that, consequently, the man in the moon must be a Western man.

Field gave much good advice to young writers. At one time he wrote:

A young writer cannot be too careful in his choice of words; eternal vigilance is the price of a correct English style. Colloquialisms are

not to be fought out of existence—they can't be.   They are exceedingly useful and at times they are exceedingly effective, for the same
reason that the introduction by adroit public speakers of homely
phrases or popular proverbs into their speeches invariably catches
the ear and wins the heart of the audience.   But a writer must know
his weapons before he can use them with effect.   It is brutal of him to
employ a bludgeon when the services of a rapier are demanded, and he
exhibits unpardonable senselessness who fritters away time at fencing
when only a club can achieve his purpose.

There are now, we think, 120,000 words in the English language;
the possibilities in the use of synonyms are remarkable, and we should
say that to the study of synonyms the young writer should apply himself diligently.   To the newspaper writers we are looking with solici-
tude and hope, for the reason that outside of the columns of the press
our literature does not seem to be making any progress at all.   Our
literature of the press is, on the other hand, constantly improving, and
in the last ten years that improvement has been marked.

Then Field gave a long list of words commonly used out
of their correct meanings.   He added:

It was not our intention to enter upon any elaborate essay upon the
choice of words, for, however earnest and enthusiastic may be our
desire to see correct expression of vigorous thought, we are sensible of
our disqualification for the honorable task of instructing young writers.
We would, however, renew our warning to young writers not to take
the English language as they find it in commen and vulgar usage.   It
is their duty to study, test, and prove words, to retain that which is
good and cast away that which is bad in speech.   In the performance
of that duty they shall find delight and profit and therefore shall duly
accrue permanent benefits to mankind.

In reply to a young man who wrote asking him how one
might become a newspaper reporter, Field gave these
instructions:

To be a good reporter these qualifications are necessary: Health, the
news instinct, a sense of humour, the ability to write a simple style in a
legible hand, eternal vigilance, temperance, amiability, patience,
determination, and ambition.   Then, furthermore, it behooves the
reporter to be a constant student and reader, informing himself fully
upon every variety of subject that interests mankind.   For the profession of newspaper reporting we have the highest regard, and we find

pleasure in this opportunity of saying that from the companionship of newspaper reporters we have derived incalculable profit; for of all classes and conditions of men (excepting, perhaps, the printer) the newspaper reporter seems to abound most liberally in wit, humour, invention, generosity, good nature, patience, pluck, fortitude, and those other qualities and accomplishments which do so much toward brightening and bettering human life.

Field's constant harping on precision in the use of words is amusingly illustrated by the following:

"Pedagogue" writes: "Poets should conserve the purity and elegance of the language.   Mr. Kipling commits a grave error in representing the monkeys as 'holding each other's tails,' when presumably he means 'holding one another's tails.'   Do you not regard this as a serious blow at our language?"

That depends.   Maybe there were but two monkeys; in that case the poet is correct.   If there were more than two the poet should have said, "Holding one another's tails," unless in sooth, the poet, recognizing the demands of rhythm, chose to avail himself of that license which is accorded to poets in the construction of their wares.   In prosaic life, monkeys, if outnumbering two, cannot carry each other's tails, but must carry one another's tails.   In the realm of poesy, however, monkeys—no matter how many there may be of them—are privileged to carry "each other's tails" in full of all demand of rhyme and rhythm, without recourse to reason or benefit of clergy.

X

GIRDING AT THE REALISTS

I

FIELD wrote a good deal of dialect prose and verse. He felt that he knew the New England speech, because of the associations of his youth, and also the Missouri dialect, which was much like that in parts of the South. He was less proficient in the authentic dialect of the Western mining camps, yet I think his experiments with it are distinctly more successful than are Bret Harte's. The provincial speech of the Middle West, which James Whitcomb Riley knew so well, was for a long time a puzzle to Field. He worked at it faithfully, however, and finally mastered it well enough. The careful workmanship that he put upon "Our Two Opinions" furnishes a good example of the methods that enabled him to give a satisfactory account of himself in whatever he undertook. I have the manuscript of this poem as Field first wrote it. At that time there was on the staff of the *Daily News* a reporter who had an exceptional knowledge of the speech of rural Illinois. Paul Hull had grown up in the Spoon River country and his interminable stories of the people he used to know there might lead one to conclude that he had been intimately acquainted with the life histories of those immortals who were later embalmed by Masters in "The Spoon River Anthology." Indeed, he knew the Middle Western backwoods dialect, Western country village life, and Western river steamboat life as did few persons. Like Field, he was a capital mimic. One of his favourite bits of mimicry had to do with the words and actions of a deckhand on an Ohio river boat as he made soundings in shallow water. These ranged from the startling singsong cry:

> Look out on the larboard si–ide,
> For she's three—feet—SCANT!

To the satisfying shout:

> No—o—o BOT—tom!

To Hull, then, Field submitted "Our Two Opinions" for revision of the dialect. The verses originally bore the title, "Me and Jim." The manuscript shows that Field renamed it "Jim's Opinion and Mine." Therefore its permanent title was the third Field chose for it.

Hull's suggested first line—"Us two wuz boys when we fell out"—was accepted by Field as better than his own "We wuz boys when us two fell out." Hull's "wunct" for "oncet" was not accepted. His "Abe Linkern," his "sergeant" for "gin'ril" and his "shuck" for "shook" were accepted. Hull's "a-havin'" was rejected, but his "a-hatin'" was approved. Hull suggested "thar" for "there"; the word became "ther." At the top of the second page of the manuscript Hull wrote these lines, which he suggested for the first two of the last stanza:

> I never seen Jim alive ag'in,
> But I'll not fergit that last dark night.

Field, however, gave the preference to his own lines:

> Jim never come back from the war ag'in,
> But I'll not fergit that last, last night.

Hull's "knowed" for "knew" was rejected, presumably because Field preferred euphony to faithful reproduction of dialect.

The original heading of the manuscript, in accordance with Field's custom, is done in old English letters, and there are elaborate initial letters to mark the beginning of the various stanzas.   The first of the series is executed in red ink, the second in green, the third in yellow, the fourth in blue, and the fifth in red—a sufficient indication that there were just four kinds of coloured inks on Field's desk the day he wrote that copy of the poem.

Other verses done by Field in Middle Western dialect include "Deep Rock," which he wrote long before he published it.   To the copy of these verses in my collection Field attached the name of James Whitcomb Riley, but when he put them into print he attributed them to Howells.   They were inserted in a long and solemn criticism by Field of some of Howells's early poems.   Field asserted that "Deep Rock" had first appeared in the *Ohio Farmer* when Howells was a young man.   In making Howells the father of the lines instead of Riley, as he had first intended, Field merely changed the line "Clear as the Wabash River" to "Clear as the Miamy River."   Soon after the appearance of the article on Howells, Field wrote in his column:

Not very long ago Mr. B. H. Ticknor, the eminent Boston publisher, wrote us a letter saying that he had read with profound interest our review of the early poetical work of William Dean Howells.   Mr. Ticknor said that about a week after that review was printed in the *Daily News* Mr. Howells happened to come into the Ticknor publishing house and was shown the paper containing our critique upon his early poetry.   Mr. Ticknor says that Howells read the paper eagerly and rolled over on the floor with it; that when he left the office he took the paper with him for the ostensible purpose of showing the review to his wife, but, Mr. Ticknor continues, "he has never brought the paper back and I want you to send me another copy."

We do not know why Mr. Howells rolled over on the floor when he read our review, but we can guess Mr. Howells was transported with joy; in no other way than by rolling on the floor could he express adequately his delight that the early fruits of his versatile genius should be revived in so ostentatious a manner for the edification and delectation of the thousands upon thousands of admirers of his maturer work.

II

In thus disclosing his appreciation of an elaborate joke played upon him, Howells showed better sportsmanship than did Thomas Bailey Aldrich, who at one time expressed considerable irritation because Field wrote a ridiculous article ostensibly quoting criticisms of Aldrich's "The Last Cæsar" by "Professor W. Thackeray Wilkerson, the well-known litterateur and dentist of the West Side." Field announced on the authority of this eminent man that "Colonel Aldrich belongs to the same literary clique with Colonel J. Russell Lowell, emeritus professor of Shakespearian politics, and Dr. O. Wendell Holmes, author of numerous T. B. Peterson novels and composer of the famous Greek poem entitled 'The Iliad'!" Being ostensibly much impressed by this information, Field charitably wrote:

So it is to be taken for granted that Colonel Aldrich is a very cultured and very affable gentleman; although, so far as we can learn, he has never done anything for Chicago.

Aldrich's manifestation of annoyance at this harmless fooling astonished Field, who wrote to his friend Ticknor that he could scarcely believe that "a man of Mr. Aldrich's intelligence and humour" would take exception to "so slight a thing." However, to display resentment at one of Field's jokes was a reasonably certain way of becoming a victim of a still more memorable joke. In Aldrich's case Field went to the trouble of composing a set of verses, written amusingly in the Aldrich manner, and attributed the production to Aldrich, intimating that

it was a highly admired bit from a volume of his poems.
Here are the verses:

That day at Villa Ste. Marie—
    Oh, how the memory glows!
A day of calm and murmuring sea,
    Of asphodel and rose;
Pomegranate bloom and fragrant vine
    Spiced the cool breath of day,
The sunset sky flamed red as wine—
    And then I heard you say,
Rolling your nutbrown eyes to mine,
    "Caro, sto macha che."

Fruits hung inviting all around—
    Fig, orange, olive, lime
And other glories that abound
    In that impassioned clime:
But when I caught your pleading tone
    I thrust them all away—
You see, though I am older grown,
    I've not forgot the day
When with a gasp, half sigh, half moan,
    You breathed: "Sto macha che."

The sea below, the sky o'erhead,
    The flowers that decked the scene—
These were a deep portentous red,
    But you and I were green;
And green perhaps—quite likely so—
    The fruit you plucked that day—
I don't remember; this I know,
    A tempest of dismay
O'ercame me when you murmured low:
    "Caro, sto macha che."

Oh, perfume of the faded rose!
    Oh, swashing of the sea!
Oh, paragon of *quelque chose*—
    Oh, Villa Ste. Marie!

> And, oh, the dear, fantastic art
>   Wherewith doth memory play
> Upon the tendrils of my heart
>   To mind me of the day
> When you and I were torn apart
>   By one "Sto macha che!"

The simple process of resolving the bogus Italian phrase into plain stomach ache suffices to disclose that here we have once more the theme on which, years earlier, Field had hung the tragic story of Johnny Jones and his sister Sue. But how in the intervening years had Field's Missouri Valley muse bedizened herself! Here we have melody and art and atmosphere—anything you please— to cast a glamour of romance about the indiscreet maiden who ate green fruit and suffered the consequences. Indeed, I cannot help thinking that Field deliberately set about the experiment of demonstrating how elaborately he could ornament the theme of "The Little Peach," which previously he had handled with the engaging frankness of a man in overalls hammering rivets in a boilershop.

The original manuscript of these verses, which is in my possession, shows that Field laboured over them not a little while polishing them to his satisfaction.

III

Before leaving the subject of Field's experiments with Middle Western dialect I wish to present what seems to me a very beautiful as well as an extremely amusing tribute paid by Field to his friend Riley. An Indianian tells the story:

Do I know Jim Riley? Well, I should smile to murmur. Me and Jim has been pardners (as one might say) ever since we was boys; for Jim was never too proud to train around with us 'at knowed him when he was a child of genius before he got to be, as the Terry Hut *Gazette* says, the pampered darlin' of fame. I have knowed Jim Riley for thirty years, more or less, and there never was a time when I hain't been ready to go my last cent on him, like every other sensible, patriotic Indiana man.   Riley has got true genius; can't call it anything else.   When he was born God give him the tongues of men and of angels, and threw in charity for good measure.   There hain't no Shakespeare business about him, nor no Byron.   Jim is a straightaway poet, and his pieces are as full of honey and dew as the flower the hummin' bird plays tag with in the cool sunlight of an early summer morning!   You don't have to have anybody tell you what Jim means in them pieces; there hain't no need o' footnotes and there hain't no disputed passages.   It is all plain music from the word go, and that's the kind of music a feller's heart loves to dance to.

But when God give Jim them gifts when he was a-bornin' He didn't mean that Jim should be what folks call a practical business man.   Jim hasn't got no more business about him than a child—why, anybody can do Jim in business, for Jim don't know anything about that sorter thing, and he don't keer, and it would be the last thing on earth for him to suspicion that anybody was tryin' to do him.   He always had difficulty findin' his way around; city always kinder confused him; never came to Terry Hut but what he'd make 'Gene Debs or Bill Ball or some other feller stick to him all the time so't he shouldn't miss his bearin's and lose his way.   Jim was peculiar in this respec' and, jes' to show what might come of it, I'll tell you a dream I dreamt a spell ago a-illustratin' this p'int.

I dreamt that the end of the world had come and that all us kind o' people had arrived in heaven.   We found there that the specially reserved seats was for the eleck (which was the Indiana folks), and these seats was up front and was separated from the rest by a gold rail called the Indiana state line.   It was a beautiful sight to see all them Hoosiers gathered to their reward—Democrats and Republicans alike, with here and there a Farmers' Alliance representative lookin' like a bean in a button bag or a dandelion in a clover patch.   But all to oncet somebody asks, "Where's Riley?   Sakes alive, where's Jim Riley?"

Sure enough, Jim wasn't there!   And jes' as we was huntin' him and callin' him and worritin' ourselves almost to death about him, in come John C. New—he slipped in jes' as the pearly gates was closin', and his pores was all open and his eyes was wild and his beard was blowin' four ways for Sunday.

First thing he sez was: "Hev any of you seen Jim Riley—has Jim Riley showed up here yet?"

"Of course he hain't," sez 'Gene Debs.   "We left Jim with you, and you promised to show him the way.   You know jest as well as we do that that pure, poetic sperrit o' his'n don't know nothin' about streets an' crossroads an' turnpikes an' sich, specially when there's a crowd, as there happens to be jest now. If you hain't brought Jim along, why, he's done lost!"

Then there *was* a lively time, sure. The children cried and the womenfolks sobbed, and the men stormed round, and there was worritin' and trouble. Some of us come near lickin' Colonel New for bein' so careless about neglectin' his duty; reckon we *would* have licked him if he hadn't come to the front with a suggestion.

"We was comin' along up here," sez he, "when Jim kinder dropped behind to talk to a little kid what had curvature o' the spine. First thing I knowed, when I looked around, them two had disappeared, an' though I went back an' called an' called an' hunted, I couldn't find hide nor hair of 'em. But suppose we telephone—maybe we'll be able in that way to find out somepin'."

Well, sir! Of all the time we had a-telephonin' for Jim! Saint Peter allowed that in all his experience he'd never had such a time.

"What's the matter with you people?" sez he, addressin' the central office.

"There's nothin' the matter with *us*," sez the central. "The trouble is with them folks we're tryin' to call up."

"Wires crossed?" asks Saint Peter.

"No, that can't be possible," sez the central; "the only connection we have out of here is with that other place."

"Well, maybe they're busy and you'll have to call us later," sez Saint Peter.

"No doubt about they're bein' busy," sez the central; "they're always busy, but never too busy to answer the telephone when there's a prospect of *more* business."

"Then shake 'em up again," sez Saint Peter, givin' the bell a terrible turning. . . .

"Jiminy Christmas! we've raised 'em at last," sez the central office.

Then Saint Peter sez, holdin' the tube up to his venerable ear, "Hullo," sez he, "hullo!"

"Hullo yourself," answers somebody in a subdued, sorroful, snivelin' tone that had a teeny weeny odour of brimstone about it.

"Who be you?" asks Saint Peter.

"I'm Bilzybub," sez the person at the other end.

"Oh, you be, eh? Well, what's the matter with you folks to-day? Asleep?" asks Saint Peter.

"Worse'n that," sez Bilzybub. "We've been havin' an awful time down here the last hour or two."

"Glad to hear it," sez Saint Peter; "serves you right."

"Yes, we're all broke up," sez Bilzybub, "all on account o' one o' them Hoosier fellers what strayed in here a while ago."

"Why, that's the man we're lookin' for," sez Saint Peter; "slender, pale feller, ain't he?   Got blue eyes and wears specs?"

"Yes, that's him," sez Bilzybub. "About one-thirty o'clock this afternoon he come a-ganglin' in here. Said he'd missed his way and would like to stop here till he got his bearin's. We told him that he didn't b'long here, but that didn't make any difference, he said; he had so many friends here it almost made him want to stay, and he declared he'd be eternally hornswoggled 'fore he'd go back to Indianapolis!"

"He done right," sez Saint Peter.

"Well," sez Bilzybub, "we humoured him—cussed fools that we wuz!   Told him he could come in an' get warm an' rest himself till we could let you folks know where to come to get him."

"Thank ye," sez Saint Peter.

"Well, now you've got to get him right out o' here, or we'll have to give up business," sez Bilzybub, whimperin' like, an' sure enough he'd been cryin'. "He's been recitin' his poetry for the last half hour, an' he has got us all to snivelin' an' weepin', so that operations here have practically suspended. The tears has been flowin' so freely as to put out the fires an' the water is four foot deep on the dead level all over the shop. I'm tellin' you this now a-standin' on a keg o' bichloride o' sulphur, an' my feet is so wet that I reckon I've caught my death o' cold."

Field saw much of Riley from time to time, as Riley not infrequently visited Chicago and Field was an occasional visitor in Indianapolis, which was a favourite meeting place for Western authors. The two poets were fond of each other and after Field's death Riley wrote a sonnet in his memory. However, Field once confided to me with a humorous air of dolour that the appearance in his office doorway of the famous Hoosier poet was not always an unalloyed delight. "Riley," he complained, "insists on my going with him to all the dime museums"— those places of weird horror furnished entertainment for the many in that day when motion pictures were unknown—"and there he likes to stand around making jokes at the expense of the bearded lady and the other freaks. He thinks it funny to present the bearded lady with the business card of some barber shop, and he gives advice to the fat lady on healthful forms of exercise to reduce her avoirdupois. That sort of thing gives me a pain." I have tried in vain to picture to myself Field standing speechless and bored during such conversations between poet and museum freak. I suspect that on such occasions two poets actively participated in the fun.

IV

Field's Red Horse Mountain poems were his most ambitious attempts at versification in dialect. In view of those productions and of his other poetic ventures of a similar nature the following remarks on dialect verse, written by Field about the time "Our Two Opinions" and "Our Lady of the Mine" appeared in print, are of special interest:

Dialect verse is a precious fraud. It is a wretched vehicle utilized by wretched poets to carry stale thought and bad mechanics. It involves a certain prostitution with which a strong mind will have little to do; even the most virile of men will occasionally condescend to dalliance. It is a foe to rhythm; it debauches taste, and it engenders a false and maudlin sentiment; worse yet, it corrupts and weakens our language, which, in its natural purity, is direct and strong enough for the expression of every natural sentiment.

Upon general principles it can be assumed, we think, that the writer of dialect verse is either a lazy poet—for dialect appears to be the natural refuge of the lazy, the doddering, and the inefficient—and its practice is either the first flicker of crude ambition or the last flicker of a decaying intellect. Take it as we may, it is a sneaking but no less dangerous foe to our literature.

Of course some pinheaded person will now bob up with a conventional remark about Robert Burns. We shall anticipate this unseemly reference by saying that the so-called Scotch dialect is not only a language but also a poetic language, essentially.

Field took a more tolerant view of dialect when used in prose fiction, as is indicated by him in the following:

During her recent visit to Chicago Mrs. McEnery Stuart made the acquaintance of a certain book reviewer who is pronounced in his antipathy to dialect.   Mrs. Stuart took occasion to refer to this anti-pathy for which her newly made acquaintance is noted, and she added: "I fancy I dislike dialect just as much as you do, and that is why I am emboldened to ask your advice.   Now, what am I to do?   I detest dialect and yet the people I write about talk just that way."

The critic was compelled to admit that Mrs. Stuart's case was hope-less.   Her candid confession gave him a view of the matter he had never before taken.

V

Field was always a convinced adherent of the romantic school of writers and an outspoken opponent of the realists of his day.   He was particularly fond of exchang-ing cudgel strokes with his friend Hamlin Garland.   They engaged in a hot controversy during the summer of the World's Fair in Chicago, a controversy that developed many points of humour.   Field began it by declaring that he stood with Mrs. Mary Hartwell Catherwood for the fanciful in fiction and against bald realism.   "She believes with us in fairy godmothers," wrote Field, "and valorous knights and beautiful princesses who have fallen victims to wicked old witches.   Mr. Garland's heroes sweat and do not wear socks; his heroines eat cold huckle-berry pie and are so unfeminine as not to call a cow 'he'." Field then mourned over Garland as a young and im-pressionable author who had fallen "under the baleful influence of William D. Howells."

The next day Field published in his column a rejoinder from Garland, who wrote:

I had my share in the general hearty laugh over your most excellent fooling yesterday, for I realized (as no doubt others did) that a layer of serious meaning ran under it all.   It certainly is a curious thing to see the lords and ladies who partake of ambrosia and sip nectar mak-ing a last desperate stand in the West—the home of Milwaukee beer and Chicago pork.   There they strive to maintain the aristocratic party in literature.   .   .   .   .

The baleful influence of Mr. Howells seeks them out even there and

makes life miserable for them.   There is no pause now in their story
from start to finish; they appeal to their reader's sensibility in a pite-
ously direct fashion; they can't languish any more, nor stride in
stately pride through lordly halls; they rush and gasp and talk in husky
whispers; their ancient dignity is almost a memory.

Realism or veritism or sincerity or Americanism (at bottom these
words mean practically the same thing) is on the increase.   We are in
the minority, we admit, but we're fighters and we've got truth on
our side.   We're a minority that grows; we're likely to be a majority
soon.

Because (and this is the most terrible fact of all) realism or Americanism *pays*.   People buy the poems of James Whitcomb Riley in un-
heard-of quantities—the plain people buy him: they buy Miss
Alice French's novels and Mr. Cable's and Mr. Harris's, and even Mr.
Howells contrives to live on $10,000 or $15,000 a year.   And it is
this sorrowful revelation which casts a gloom over Chicago romanticism—judging from the tone of your plaintive pipe.   I admit I have so
few acquaintances among people who really believe in the lance and
morion and nectar and tapestry that only at rare intervals do I get a
glimpse into the sad court where you romanticists sit upon the ground
and wail the death of kings.

A day or two later Mrs. Catherwood entered the fray.
She wrote:

I, too, had my laugh at your droll impalement of Mr. Hamlin Garland and myself, and did not intend to lift either lance or embroidery
needle in defense.   I think you have that honest love of a fight which
Thomas Hughes says is in Anglo-Saxon blood.   But Mr. Garland
brings me up in spite of myeslf, as he brought me up before.   Mr.
Garland is a man one would admire and disagree with every day in
the year.   His big, sympathetic, manly heart is so burdened with the
human struggle of to-day that he will not let himself look away
from it.

But what does he mean by "the morion and nectar and tapestry"
and the "aristocratic party in literature"?   Is it aristocratic to remember those who have by great effort and sacrifice opened ways for
you?   Then, since the foundation of the world, most men have been
instinctively aristocratic.   We keep aristocratically covering our
soldiers' graves with flowers every 30th of May.

Where was "the lily-white hand" of La Salle?   "He belonged,"
says Francis Parkman, "not to the age of the knight-errant and the
saint, but to the modern world of study and practical action."   He
was "pitiless to himself, bearing the brunt of every hardship and every

danger." If Mr. Garland would look at these great men of the past he would see the same human soul struggling with human problems that he sees to-day.

Shall all the prosperous families of this country say to the shades of their grandfathers: "Old gentlemen, we repudiate you; don't pose for effect before us; there is nothing pathetic in your life. A spade is a spade. *We* are realistic and of the present day. Your revolutionary cocked hat and rusty gun are back numbers. We are sincerely and modernly taken up with corn planters and riding plows."

There was a young physician who years ago met his death on these winter prairies; but his grave is yet a garden; and every birthday of his, every Christmas and every Memorial day, it blooms with new wreaths. Should I say to the sleeper in that grave: "Father, you are behind the times. We don't think any more as you used to think. You lived a heroic life, but you are dead and gone, and I can find interest only in the people I see around me"?

Is looking at the beautiful side of life insincerity? What is sincerer or more truthful than love and gratitude?

I knew a little girl who in her miserable orphanhood was made to grope to bed in the dark, to a lonesome wing of the house. But she painted the dark with pictures of heroic people who encountered and overcame everything. We live in our thoughts. Readers seize on Mr. Riley's and Mr. Howells's work for what is beautiful and uplifting in their presentation of life. There is nothing common or unclean. But pulling down, trampling and denying Yesterday and setting up an apotheosis of To-day was what the French revolution vainly tried to do.

To Mrs. Catherwood's outburst Field appended this comment:

We approve everything this lady says—everything except that passage in the beginning of her letter in which she speaks of what she is so indiscreet as to term Mr. Garland's "big, sympathetic, manly heart." That is an admission which we shall not make. In dealing with Garland and his piratical crew we propose to concede nothing, for we know full well that if those ravening heretics can get close enough to us they are going to disembowel us and all our kind. They are worse than iconoclasts; they are but one remove this side of anarchists. In his lucid moments Garland himself has confessed that one of his purposes is to subvert the grand old Republican Party—in fact, that shameful confession was the first thing that opened our eyes to the wickedness of the whole realistic brood. Then, too, he would burn up all fairy tales and ghost stories—just think of that! Do you suppose that any person bent upon such a purpose could, by any possible freak of nature, be possessed of a "big, sympathetic, manly heart"?

Some weeks later Field issued this warning:

When Hamlin Garland made his appearance upon the scene early last summer we began to scent trouble. Garland tried to make us believe that he came simply as one crying in the wilderness; that he was merely the forerunner of one the latchet of whose shoes he was not worthy to loose. He alluded, of course, to William Dean Howells, the Mahommed of the realistic religion, skilled in all those wiles which proselyte, but prepared to exterminate where his sugared sophistries fail. Garland opened out headquarters in Dearborn Street, a locality long sacred to the uses of insurance agents, epic poets, mortgage brokers, and idealistic novelists. This was what he termed "carrying the war into Africa," and he had not been here ten days before he ran afoul of the queen of Western romanticism, Mrs. Mary Hartwell Catherwood. The scrimmage was short but earnest. For a time the circumambient air was full of hayrakes and pitchforks and excelsior shovels and other weapons with which the aggressive Garland is so handy; but, laying about her with her enchanted sword Bon-Temps and pressing to her lips the magic ring containing a relic of the ever-to-be-revered Saint La Salle, Mrs. Catherwood soon dispersed her audacious assailant and for several weeks he was laid up for repairs at that quiet asylum for realistic invalids, Tie Siding, Indiana.

In his dire emergency, Garland sent a piteous message to his lord and master Howells, the pole star—nay, the great central sun of the realistic system—and lo and behold! Mr. Howells has answered the call with his presence. Yes, the prophet of veritism is in the midst of us, his face illuminated by a smile that disarms suspicion, but his bosom heaving with emotions that prognosticate war.

We have had several serious talks with Mr. Howells, so we have a pretty intelligent idea of the situation, and we advise the romanticists to "watch out." Mr. Howells loves Garland; he confesses that he is responsible for Garland, as Garland exists to-day. When he took Garland up, Garland was a mere boy hustling around the streets of Boston with his trousers fringed with burdocks and his hair thick with hayseed. Howells said, "Let there be light," and there was light— we'll leave it to Garland if there wasn't. Yes, Howells molded and shaped that plastic Wisconsin survival as a potter pottereth his clay, or, to use a contemporary realistic phrase, as the buxom country wench spanketh the golden butter into short-weight pound gobs.

Having created Garland, it is Mr. Howells's duty to protect him. Mr. Howells admits all this. Nobody can—metaphorically speaking

—dispossess Garland of an ear or an eye or a tooth without receiving from Mr. Howells an intimation at least of his disapproval. This also has been given to us in confidence by Mr. Howells, and we should not divulge it but for the stress of threatening times. So again we bid the romanticists to "watch out." Particularly does it behoove the queen of Western romanticism to be on her guard, to fortify herself in her stanch castle at Hoopeston, and to have that enchanted sword Bon-Temps always at hand and that magic ring of Saint La Salle always within reach.

Mrs. Catherwood having escaped the rage of the veritists, Field was able to publish the following some months later:

At the risk of striking terror to the hearts of Colonel Hamlin Garland and his followers we will vouchsafe the information that Mary Hartwell Catherwood is writing a romance upon scenes of two hundred years ago, involving a hero who did not know a hayrake from a scoop-shovel and a heroine who possessed lily-white hands and read chansons in the original.

But Field's earlier report of the outcome of the veritist invasion of the Middle West should not be overlooked.

Hamlin Garland has gone up into Wisconsin for a fortnight's rest and William D. Howells has returned to New York. The latest raid upon Western romanticism was by no means successful, and it is understood that further proceedings will be delayed until that season when, as the poet informed gentle Annie, "the springtime comes and the wild flowers are budding on the plain." The talk is that the failure to prosecute the war upon the romanticists was due to a disagreement between Garland and Howells as to the tactics which would better be adopted. Garland was for the utter annihilation of the audacious brood that stood in the path of realism, but Howells insisted that the poor creatures should be conciliated and proselyted rather than exterminated. The result of this wide divergence of opinion was a postponement of the campaign, and Howells has gone back East with a copy of "Old Kaskaskia" in his possession, while Garland is immured in a Wisconsin farmhouse reading through Lew Wallace's latest quarto exploit in 32-mo romanticism.

VI

Field's final assault on the realists, written less than three months before his death, began with a pen picture of a railway train in Russia. Then he proceeded with his story in the following fashion:

One day not long ago two men sat near each other in one of the compartments in a first class car in one of these railway trains. It was easy to see that they were intellectual forces. Both had high brows and soulful eyes; both wore beards and slouch hats; both suffered. These are the trademarks of genius. One of these two men was older than the other. It was he who spoke first. "We have travelled three hours and eight minutes together," said he, "and we are in sympathy. Yet we do not know each other's names. We are in sympathy, I am sure, for when we saw the officers at the last station knouting the peasants into line we groaned simultaneously."

"Yes," said the other, "and when a moment ago we saw the guard creeping along the outside rail in the bitter morning air we groaned again."

"The contemplation of all this misery tears our hearts agape," said the older man of genius.

"Life is hard; fate is pitiless," said the younger.

The conversation proceeds. Presently the younger man remarks:

"From bad humanity goes to worse. Its condition becomes harder and harder all the time. This barren country about us will eventually be cultivated, these trees felled, these mountains quarried, these plains plowed and irrigated."

"And all involves more labour, more suffering, more sorrow!"

"That will be the harvest of realism," continued the younger genius. "There will be more sweat, more sore feet, more lame backs, more callous hands, more evil smells, a greater destitution of socks, and a vaster plenitude of patched pants than the philosophy of veritism even dreams of in these days."

"And we shall not be here to enjoy these miseries and the telling of them! It is this thought that makes our lot even more wretched! Alas!" sighed the older man. And then the two groaned again simultaneously.

"It is now noon," said the younger man after a moment of melancholy reflection. "I suppose we should sustain miserable life by partaking of a wretched morsel or two. Will you share these *pâtés de fois gras* sandwiches with me?"

"With melancholy pleasure," said the older genius, "provided, however, you will upon your part gratify me by sharing this quart of Chambertin with me."

"I have so often drunk the potion of misery," answered the younger genius, "that I cannot now decline the humble but honest draught you proffer. But first let us know each other's names, since we are so heartily in sympathy upon all that demonstrates the horror of human life."

"By all means," said the older genius with a profound sigh. "I am Leo Tolstoy."

"And I," said the younger genius with a half-suppressed groan, "I am Hamlin Garland."

XI

A Few Drolleries

I

FIELD'S acrobatic attitude while writing—his feet on his desk and his tablet and paper either at his side or, more often, on his lap—has already been described. Thus established to his liking, he wrote steadily and rapidly, chuckling every now and then as some quaint fancy developed under his pen. When it had been transferred to paper he would read it aloud in order to hear my comment, but especially to enable his own fastidious ear to apply its test. It might be some brief paragraph or an article of considerable length. The following I recall especially because of the cumulative enjoyment Field got out of it as he built up the imposing structure of absurdities:

Our Senator Farwell is not getting much from the national administration, but he has the finest collection of old Bibles in the West. He is now getting together a collection of prayer books and psalmodies. His latest acquisition is an original Bay Psalm Book, for which he paid $1700. He sings from this precious volume every Sabbath evening, his distinguished relative, Reginald de Koven, playing the accompaniment upon the family melodeon. Mr. Farwell has a barytone voice of more then ordinary quality and power and Mr. de Koven hopes to make much of it by the course of instruction which he is now giving the Senator. We asked Mr. de Koven the other day what tune Mr. Farwell sung best, and Mr. de Koven said that was a hard question to answer. "I like his rendition of Wesley's hymn,

'God moves in a mysterious way
His wonders to perform.'

But that is merely a matter of taste. He probably throws more feeling into 'The Heart Bowed Down with Weight of Woe' than any other

137

piece he has learned, but I am teaching him a 'jubilate' which I hope he will be able to execute with credit from the front steps of the post office presently."

"But why a 'jubilate' and not that famous basso solo, 'The Old Sexton'?" we asked.

"He hasn't enough whiskers to sing 'The Old Sexton,'" said Mr. de Koven. "To sing that song properly a man should have long and fierce whiskers and a smooth upper lip—one of the typical Ohio beards. I have discovered that only persons of certain physiques can sing certain songs intelligently. It takes a fat man to sing 'Old Shady' with proper feeling, and no one but a bald-headed man in checkered trousers can give 'The Sword of Bunker Hill' as it ought to be given.

"There are certain omens, too," continued Mr. de Koven, "that are infallible when it comes to piano playing. When a young lady exclaims reproachfully, 'Maw, why do you insist upon my playing when you know I haven't practised any for three months?' you can set it down for certain that she is about to perform 'The Maiden's Prayer' or 'Silvery Waves.' Girls who are troubled with insomnia dote on 'Tam o' Shanter' and those who are addicted to bangles and showy bracelets always evince a predilection for 'Monastery Bells.' These 'Monastery Bells' fiends invariably take off their bracelets and bangles with a great splurge and lay them solemnly on the piano case (where they'll jingle) before they begin to play."

Mr. de Koven said that whistling had done a great deal toward driving cheap music out of favour with women.

"A whistling boy is unconsciously a great boon in a family. You never hear his sister playing 'The Mocking Bird' or things of that kind—oh, no; she's too smart for that! She plunges as fast as she can into sonatas and symphonies and things that can't be whistled."

Field's regulation three sheets of paper having been filled with his extremely fine writing, his feet came down promptly from the top of his desk, he squared his elbows to place the sheets in order and then, for my benefit, he would emit a loud, provocative "Oh, well!" That was his daily declaration of release from labour, his signal that he was ready for any kind of mischief. As Field was a phenomenally fast worker and I was decidedly nothing of the sort, my day's tasks were never done when he was ready to depart. Consequently, after a little verbal sparring, Field would give me his copy to turn in along with

my own and would amble out of the office, headed for some
old book shop.   Frequently he would return later in the
afternoon with his pockets full of newly acquired volumes
and with other volumes under his arm.   These would be
stowed away in his desk until he could find favourable
opportunities for smuggling them home without attracting
the attention of his wife to their number and their probable cost.   Because he was continually buying more
books than he could afford the problem of getting his
purchases home without having to confess his fault
frequently taxed his ingenuity.   Books were his tools
and he profited greatly by his love for them, but it was
unfortunate that they were so serious a drain on the family
resources.

I have estimated the length of Field's normal working
day in the *Daily News* office at about two hours.   He was
able to accomplish so much in so short a time, however,
because of his many and diverse activities elsewhere
throughout most of the day and also most of the night.
He was gathering material for his column when he prowled
in old book shops, when he met his actor friends at or
after the theatre, and when he read or wrote late at night.
He even had the faculty of turning to account the visits of
bores, who took up a good deal of his time when he could
not escape them.   He had, also, not a few extremely
profitable callers—brilliant men with ideas in abundance,
from whom Field gathered many delightful stories.

II

I recall, for example, one afternoon visit of William J.
Florence, an old and warm friend of Field's.   When he
and Field put their heads together two of the greatest
practical jokers of their day went into conference.   Field,
however, was rather in the metaphorical position of sitting
at the feet of Florence, since with all his imagination and

daring Field lacked the Napoleonic strategy essential in carrying on such elaborate, such cosmic jests as made Florence the greatest living exponent of that highly specialized form of weird artistry, the hoax.   I have often regretted that I did not preserve in writing as best I could the conversation of that afternoon; for Florence and Field conferred at length on the fine points of historic hoaxes, both ancient and modern.   From the wealth of his own experience Florence related stories that proved him an adept at making game of vast crowds of representatives of the singularly credulous human race.   Florence ordinarily found fooling one person or a handful of persons entirely too tame.   He went at the business wholesale, with the mental illumination gained from his impish study of mass psychology.

A typical hoax by Florence was one he had perpetrated in St. Paul some years before while he was appearing in a theatre in that city.   As I recall its details, which he related to Field and me, he advertised in one or more St. Paul newspapers, ostensibly as a foreign worker of wonders and under a fantastic name, that at a certain hour on the succeeding day he would descend beneath the waters of the Mississippi and would walk upon its bottom the entire length of the city's river front without once coming to the surface for air.   Come one, come all!   This stupendous, this unprecedented exhibition would be given in the interest of science and therefore would be absolutely free.

The next day at the appointed hour the St. Paul river front from end to end was black with people.   They waited and watched until dark, but they waited and watched in vain.   Finally they went home.

On the succeeding morning the St. Paul newspapers contained in their advertising columns a heartbroken apology from the foreign wonder worker with the fantastic name.

He had kept his word! At the appointed hour he had descended to the bottom of the river and, moist but triumphant, had walked under water the entire distance through the city. Unhappily he had forgotten to provide himself with a suitable contrivance to make his presence known to the watching throngs as he made his way past them. For this grievous oversight he humbly begged everybody's pardon. More; he would make amends. That afternoon at the same hour he would descend again to the bottom of the Mississippi. Once more he would walk under water past the entire river front. This time there should be no mistake; at every step he would make his presence known in a most striking and novel way.

That afternoon greater throngs assembled to view the promised spectacle than had assembled the day before. They waited and they watched. There was no sign of any marvel above or below the surface of the river. Finally the throngs dispersed in deep perplexity. The newspapers next day had no explanation to offer of the second failure of the wonder worker to make good his promise, and indeed no explanation was ever vouchsafed.

At another time Florence perpetrated a similar hoax on the people of Buffalo.

III

A story illustrating the passion of the elder Sothern for practical joking was told by Florence during that afternoon visit to Field. One time when he and Sothern were in New York they played so many pranks at each other's expense that finally, in parting from Sothern late one night, Florence proposed a truce. "Now, Ned," he remarked, "we've had enough of fooling. Let's drop it." Sothern agreed

About 8 o'clock the next morning a messenger boy

knocked at Florence's door in the Fifth Avenue Hotel. He bore a parcel which Florence took and immediately opened. It contained a handkerchief which Florence recognized as one of his own. Inside the folds of the handkerchief he found a note in a feminine hand. It was worded about as follows:

Glenham Hotel,
Thursday morning.

DEAR WILL:

After you left me yesterday I found this handkerchief on the floor. Knowing that my husband would become suspicious if he saw it, I hasten to return it to you.

Yours devotedly,

EMILY.

Florence knew no person of the name of Emily. He at once suspected a plot. A little reflection convinced him that Sothern had broken his promise and that the handkerchief had been stolen by his waggish friend the day before to furnish material for the joke. Accordingly he wrote this note to Sothern:

SIR:

Your jokes are as bad as your acting and both are highly distasteful to me. Until you are prepared to keep the promise you recently made me you need not seek any further communication with me.

W. J. FLORENCE.

When this note was delivered to Sothern he was quick to observe that there was no one's name upon it except that of the sender. Immediately seeing possibilities of further mischief, he put the note into a fresh envelope and sent it off addressed to Dion Boucicault.

IV

During his conversation that afternoon Florence confided to Field and me that he was doing very well with his latest hoax and he described in some detail how he operated it. A few weeks later Field wrote an article which effectually destroyed Florence's fun just when he was preparing for an especially elaborate demonstration of his ability to make game of an entire city. Here is what Field wrote:

Our valued friend, Mr. William J. Florence, the comedian, is a gentleman whose humour is of a peculiar kind. He loves a practical joke and he enjoys it most when its authorship remains a dark, impenetrable mystery. It is always a pleasure to betray a friend who takes so much delight in selling his fellow mortals. We take immense satisfaction, therefore, in exposing the practical joke which Mr. Florence has played with more or less success upon several communities within the last five years.

Mr. Florence's scheme has been to advertise "The ascension of a human rocket" and to attract together at a given time at a stated place an enormous crowd of people anxious to see a man who, tied to an enormous rocket, blazes away from earth to a preposterous height and subsequently descends safely by means of a parachute. Our ingenious friend told us all about this hoax when he was last in Chicago, and he gave a graphic description of the crowds that waited patiently for the "human rocket" that never came. This was Mr. Florence's idea of an ideal joke. While he was in the northwest last winter the Minneapolis *Tribune* (January 13th) printed a long and harrowing description of the human rocket and gave several woodcuts of the alleged machine in operation. The description and illustrations purported to have come directly from the inventor of the rocket, Professor D. Edselle, at that time said to be a sojourner in Minneapolis. On the 18th of January, Mr. Florence, who is always around when the "human rocket" is being agitated, addressed the *Daily News* the following autograph letter:

St. Paul, Minn.,
January 18.

To THE EDITOR:
    Do you think that the police authorities would permit my giving an exhibition of my ascension in some of the public parks during the coming spring? I will give the ascension free in the interest of science. Can you aid me?

Yours truly,
"D. EDSELLE, the Human Rocket."

Mr. Florence has now reached northern New York, and, of course, his hoax is with him. Yesterday morning the daily papers all over the country printed telegrams from Buffalo giving information about the remarkable invention of Professor D. Edselle, which was to be exhibited at the International Exposition. This wonder was said to be a human rocket. "The apparatus consists," says the dispatch, "of a combination of rockets of immense power with a parachute attachment which folds over the apex. Four tubes form the framework and contain the explosive. The nature of the explosive is a secret and it is called dynoascenimite. Its peculiar property is that it is detonating. A small quantity of the solid makes an immense volume of vapour and lifts the machine with lightning rapidity into the clouds. The test took place under Peruvian government patronage near Callao in December. The charge, touched by electricity, sent the machine over 15,545 feet, and the descent by parachute was perfect. The dauntless aëronaut landed five miles from the starting point, no worse for the trip. Fifteen thousand people were present and watched with telescopes the rise and fall of the machine. Mr. Edselle will start for Buffalo within a few days."

Well, of course thousands of people will believe this yarn and will pour into Buffalo for the purpose of seeing D. Edselle and his preposterous machine. And Mr. William J. Florence will meanwhile laugh, laugh, laugh and grow fat. It seems strange that so few folk should have recognized the "dead sell" in that peculiar name, D. Edselle.

V

This seems to be an appropriate place to tell of one of Field's innumerable office jokes. "Monty" Bennett, a member of the staff whom Field had chosen to nickname "Birdie," went to Wisconsin for his vacation. On the morning of his return he telegraphed the office: "I will arrive to-day at 3:15 P. M." The wording of this message filled Field with glee. He saw in his mind's eye a heroic general rushing up reinforcements in a desperate battle. Accordingly he prepared and hung up placards conspicuously about the office bearing such words of cheer as these:

HOLD THE FORT!
Once more unto the breach, dear friends!
BIRDIE WILL POSITIVELY ARRIVE
at 3:15 P.M.

Field also laboriously chalked footprints of enormous size on the stairs and marked them "Birdie's." They indicated that Birdie had taken the three long flights three steps at a time in his eagerness to enter the fray. When Birdie finally arrived there was in the local room a band of merry villagers, recruited from the "deckhands," drawn up to give him an appropriate welcome, and there was Field to greet him with a grandiloquent speech.

A year or two later Field transferred the nickname "Birdie" to another member of the staff, a small, soft-spoken, gentle-mannered artist. On one occasion the two were sent to Kansas together to get a news story that Field desired to write up. While they were away Field sent numerous telegrams, all written in his favourite rôle of martyr, describing his sufferings at the hands of his comrade. Here is the wording of the one message that I recall: "Birdie has been, oh! so rude."

All such performances serve to illustrate the truth of George W. Cable's comment:

Only to total strangers was his name Field, and no man worthy to be anyone's friend could call him by any name but his first after three days' acquaintanceship. In all the word's best meaning he was a boy, and all men and women were his boy and girl friends and play-mates.

As Field grew in reputation he received an extraordinary number of requests for assistance in literary composition or in getting marvellous products of genius brought to the attention of publishers. One curious instance of Field's unfailing kindness and helpfulness came to my attention. A young man terribly crippled for life by the explosion of a cannon at a country Fourth of July celebration wished to obtain a set of verses that he might have printed and sell on street corners by way of earning a livelihood. A friend of the cripple's, possessed of far more good will than poetic ability, wrote some rhymes and sent them to

Field for his judgment. Field wrote a kindly letter in reply, saying the verses would do very well, so they went into circulation through the efforts of the maimed man, who, as well as the writer of the verses, was grateful to Field for the interest he showed in the humble enterprise. I recall certain of the lines which might almost lead one to suspect that Field had added a touch of pathos and whimsicality to them:

> Beside the booming cannon
> I boldly took my stand,
> And I was blown to pieces
> To the music of the band.

VI

In the early months of 1887 Field had begun to find himself intellectually. His prose stories—and his best work at that time and in previous years was mainly prose, his verses being almost invariably light and ephemeral productions—were carefully wrought, when they were not broad farce, and displayed much understanding of the human heart. Field, in his boyish manner, would still roll under his tongue delightedly for days such a phrase of his own as "I opine that some gentleman has drawed a boot"—a protesting remark of one of his characters who found conditions not wholly to his liking in an unventilated day coach on a Western railroad late at night—but he was studying and practising the art of true expression, of accurate interpretation of human emotion, and he was carefully gauging the effect of his experimental appeals to the sympathies of his readers.

"The Little Yaller Baby," one of the stories that has always been a favourite with readers of Field's works, belongs to this period, though it was written some months later than the time I have mentioned. A curious thing about this story is that it has caused a charge of plagiarism to be brought against Field—the only charge of the sort that I ever heard associated with his work. George A. Vinton, a teacher of elocution in Chicago, who as a young man had worked under Field on the Denver *Tribune*, wrote me many years after Field's death a letter in which he said:

The "Yaller Baby" story was written by me. My title was "The Motherless One." I gave the story to Ballantyne to give to Field, expecting to be given credit for it. Field changed it a little, putting in the coloured porter, which spoiled the story for me. The rest was all mine. But I did not mention that the woman who gave the baby her breast was the wife of the lieutenant-governor of Texas. The time was 1877 or 1878. I told the story in Texas Southern dialect. It was a true incident. There were two children with the lady in my story, one about three, the other one year old.

Accepting Mr. Vinton's story as true, I find it easy to believe that Field thought the manuscript a gift from an old friend and proceeded to dress it up very much to the story's advantage. Knowing Field's honesty of purpose, I am convinced that he regarded "The Little Yaller Baby' as wholly his own after he had carefully recast it.

XII

THE STORY OF "CULTURE'S GARLAND"

I

FIELD thought well of his serious stories and of those in which humour and pathos were mingled, but in the early months of 1887 he realized that as a rule his work was a bit too boisterous and that not much of it was up to the standards he had set for himself. Then, most unexpectedly, he received a shock. An Eastern publisher wrote to him asking material for a book. On a morning of early spring in 1887 Field found among his letters at the *Daily News* office one from B. H. Ticknor, the Boston publisher. He read it standing by my desk. Then he handed it to me and said: "On this"—naming the day; I think it was the 26th of March—"in the year of our Lord 1887, I have received my first letter from a publisher who asks me to furnish him material for a book." He made no effort to conceal his pleasure.

I read the letter. In it Ticknor said that his attention had been called to Field's writings by E. C. Stedman and that he would like to take up with Field the question of issuing a volume of his selected humorous articles and poems.

"But I have nothing of that sort that I want to put in a book," said Field when I had finished reading the letter and had tendered my congratulations.

"Nonsense," I replied. "Make a collection of your best work, reshaping as much of it as may be necessary, and take this opportunity to get a start in productive authorship."

"No," he said, "I will not rewrite any of my humorous stuff. It is too ephemeral, too local in its application, to be effective in book form."

Field thought the matter over for a week, meantime taking an inventory of what he conceived to be his available literary product. Then he wrote a reply to Ticknor. The publisher's daughter, Miss Caroline Ticknor, has made public Field's letter in her "Glimpses of Authors." Field wrote: "I made up my mind a long time ago that my verse never did and never would amount to a ———." He went on to say that he had written about forty stories or sketches, that he had a good opinion of them and that on their newspaper publication they had been received with favour. He expressed the desire to see them in book form and gave it as his belief that such a book would sell. "If you were to indicate a desire to publish them," added Field, "I should want to rewrite them." He went on to describe their character, saying, "They are stories for young and old; perhaps I should say that they are (most of them) children's stories so written as to interest the old folk. I have made them as simple as I could and in many of them the fairy element predominates. In two of them there are a number of lyrics, humorous and serious."

Field sent with this letter a list of his forty stories and sketches. It was so made out that his passion for coloured inks was gratified. The titles were in blue ink, the estimated number of words in each story was set down in red, the subtitles followed in green, and the character of the stories—"humorous," "pathetic," "satirical," and the like—was written in blue.

Ticknor forwarded the letter and the list to Stedman and asked his advice. In his reply Stedman wrote:

I did and do strongly advise you to take a book from this gentleman. My notion is that some publisher will seize upon him and develop his selling potentiality and make the "paying" author of him that your

firm so much needs.   He is just the sort of man, methinks, that
Carleton used to pick up and rush—e.g., Josh Billings, Artemus Ward,
etc.

But I never dreamed of your asking him for a *novel*.   .   .   .

My suggestion is that you either send for the whole lot, or ask him
to pick out 75,000 words of the best of them—making the selection as
varied as possible.   Then read them yourself or hire one of your slaves
to do so and see what they amount to.

Stedman wrote further that he had seen "scores of
short sketches, skits, humorous poems, satires, etc.," by
Field, all of which were original and "taking."   "I do not
know," added Stedman, "whether he is the author of the
famous 'Lakeside Musings'—if so, so much the better."
Stedman thought that, all things considered, Ticknor
should get out a book of Field's humorous material, with
only a seasoning of the more serious stories in the Westerner's list.   "At the same time," he conceded, "pathos
is an attribute of every true humorist, and very likely you
could make just as good a first book of a selection (say one
half) from the rather staggering list which he sends you."

II

Ticknor chose to make the book humorous throughout.
When he communicated to Field his wish for humour and
nothing else Field lost interest in the project.   However,
he finally concluded to comply with Ticknor's request that
he send on a quantity of material and let the publisher
look it over.   Accordingly Field fished out of a drawer in
his desk a mass of newspaper clippings, made a parcel of
them and sent it to Ticknor.   I recall how he jestingly
crowded the clippings together and wrapped them up.
In his biography of Field, Slason Thompson quotes Field
as saying: "I simply sent on a lot of stuff and the folks at
the other end picked out what they wanted and ran it as
they pleased."   Denying the accuracy of Field's words,
Thompson says:

Field himself, to my knowledge, selected the matter for "Culture's Garland" and arranged it in the general form in which it appeared. He then delegated to Mr. Ticknor authority to reject any and all paragraphs in which the bite of satire or the broadness of the humour transgressed too far the bounds of a reasonable discretion.

In the face of these positive assertions I merely say that my memory tends to confirm the truth of Field's statement. Indeed I can see no reason why Field should have wished to misrepresent the matter. In my opinion Thompson had in mind the carefully compiled list of stories that Field sent to Ticknor, only a few of which found their way into the book. I recall that when the proofs of the material selected by Ticknor came to Field from Boston the articles were devoid of headings, so that Field and I went over the proofs and supplied the lack. For example, there was a bit of verse beginning:

> The world is drear and the sedges sere,
>   And gray is the autumn sky,
> And sorrows roll through my riven soul
>   As lonely I sit and sigh
>   "Good-by,"
>   To the goose-birds as they fly.

When we came to this soulful effusion Field said, "What shall we call the foolish thing?" "Call it 'A Lament,'" I suggested, and thereupon Field wrote down the words. The title so appears in the book published by Ticknor. In Field's collected works, published after his death, the verses bear the title "November." The beautiful little poem entitled "November," beginning:

> The night is dark and the night is cold
> And the wind blows fierce and strong,

which appears in the Ticknor volume, I do not find in Field's collected works.

Stedman's amusing confusion of mind which left him in doubt as to whether Field did or did not write "the

famous 'Lakeside Musings'" discloses that his knowledge
of Chicago writers was extremely rudimentary.   Indeed,
Stedman knew of them only through their articles that
were copied on the editorial pages of the discriminating
New York *Sun* and certain other Eastern newspapers.
"Lakeside Musings" were written in a wholly different
style from Field's.   Their author, Henry Ten Eyck
White, was an enthusiast on trotting horses.   His "Musings," originally published in the Chicago *Tribune*, either
gave the opinions of "The Horse Reporter" on all manner
of topics, somewhat as Mr. Dooley's opinions are expressed,
or else presented in a style of high romance conversations
which had ridiculous endings.   These sketches were widely
copied by the press and later were issued in book form.
At the time Stedman wrote of them, however, White was a
member of the staff of the *Daily News*, occupying the
position of managing editor of the evening editions.   He is
entitled to be remembered not only as the author of
"Lakeside Musings" and "Life with the Trotters"—
which he attributed to John Splan—but also as a dis-
coverer of young geniuses.   White picked up promising
unknowns in all sorts of ways, set them to work as reporters on microscopic salaries, and inspired them to their
best efforts by a discriminating blend of sententious praise
and scathing criticism.   Among his discoveries may be
mentioned Finley Peter Dunne, Will Payne, Charles D.
Stewart, and Eugene Wood.   Stewart once wrote of him:

My favourite editor was "Butch" White of the *Daily News*. He was
decisive and peremptory, but he was a good fellow at bottom and you
always felt on good terms with him.

It is an odd coincidence that Ticknor selected for
Field's book an imitation of White's style of humour
written by Field while White was still a member of the
Tribune staff.   It was entitled "A Novelette" and it was

supposed to be a conversation between the two principal
stockholders in the *Tribune,* one a free trader and the
other a protectionist.   It began in White's characteristic
manner:

"Sing me the old song!"
The words rang out clear and bell-like upon the mellow September
air and coquetted with the autumnal zephyrs that ruffled the cerulean
bosom of the mighty lake.   It was night.   The moon rolled proudly
through the azure heavens, bathing the landscape in a shimmer of
silvery sheen and tipping the dark waters of the Chicago River with
a wavy, tremulous light.

This was the sort of thing that Ticknor preferred to
Field's "children's stories so written as to interest the old
folk"!

III

What, then, were those rejected stories?   Among them
were quite two-thirds of the beautifully imaginative writings that two years later appeared in an appropriately attractive dress as "A Little Book of Profitable Tales."   So
it is not surprising that Field took only a casual interest
in Ticknor's volume.   He used to say to me laughingly
when I mentioned it to him: "Remember, I take no
responsibility for this atrocity.   You and Ticknor are the
criminals."   He linked me with Ticknor because I had
urged him to go ahead with the venture.

While Ticknor was tempting Field with offers to publish the material that Ticknor had selected, Field asked
whether Stedman would agree to write an introduction
to the volume.   When approached by Ticknor on the subject Stedman somewhat brusquely declined.   The legend
that Field thereafter bore a grudge against Stedman and
so lampooned him on every occasion is quite without
foundation.   The fact is that Field and Stedman soon
became excellent friends and remained friends until
Field's death.   The introduction to Field's first volume

was actually written by Julian Hawthorne, one of Field's very few literary acquaintances at that time. When Hawthorne consented to perform this service Field withdrew his objections to the book and Ticknor proceeded at once with its manufacture.

Straightway Field began to bombard Ticknor by mail with grotesque suggestions about the book, suggestions made in mere horse-play. The title, "Culture's Garland: Being Memoranda of the Gradual Rise of Literature, Art, Music, and Society in Chicago and Other Western Ganglia;" the wreath of sausages following the title-page; the atrocious sketch of the author, drawn by himself, which appears as the frontispiece; the gallows which serves as a colophon, and the page of alleged advertisements at the back of the volume—these were so many bits of sarcasm leveled by Field at the book and its publisher. Somewhat to Field's dismay, I think, Ticknor serenely incorporated Field's jokes in the book, by way of embellishing the satirical articles describing Chicago's heroic struggles to achieve culture through Italian and German opera, through listening to the French plays of Sarah Bernhardt, and through study of the legs of the various tragedians who essayed the rôle of Hamlet. Field's extended review of the alleged poems of Judge Cooley was there. The book contained also "The Story of Xanthippe," "Isaac Watts, Tutor," and a number of other worthy pieces of humour, including the review of Sappho's poems which had so horrified Charles Dudley Warner. There, too, was much sorry stuff, which I am sure Field himself never would have selected to put between covers.

IV

One of the best things in the book was Julian Hawthorne's introduction. It showed that Hawthorne in his contact with Field had gained a clear understanding of his character and his intellectual powers. Hawthorne wrote:

He has a gentle yet intrepid heart, a penetrating but broad intellect, a pen that is at once trenchant and kindly, sensible and imaginative. He is the author of some of the purest and most charming fairy tales that have been written since Hans Christian Andersen's time. He has produced poems whose effortless art and tender pathos have brought them to the knowledge of perhaps half the newspaper readers of America; and withal he has poured out genuine and spontaneous fun enough to restore that gayety of nations which the death of a certain renowned comedian was said to have eclipsed. Yet, in all his jesting, he has never jested heedlessly or cruelly. If he has laughed at what is foolish, he has honoured what is good; if he has unsparingly satirized what is absurd or unworthy in our civilization, he has always reverenced what is sacred and holy in our nature. His is no common mind, and we have as yet seen but a small arc of its complete circle.

Stedman in a letter to Ticknor had called Field "the great apostle of culture in the Porkopolis by the lake." In view of the New Yorker's reluctance to take Field seriously and his belief that Field should cut funny capers for Ticknor instead of appearing as the author of "some of the purest and most charming fairy tales," to use Hawthorne's words, it is hardly surprising that Field wrote a year later:

The fear that the West will not be fairly dealt with in the "History of American Poetry," now being written by two eminent New York litterateurs, causes us a good deal of anxiety. The litterateurs engaged in this stupendous work are Mr. Edmund Clarence Stedman and Miss Nellie Hutchinson; we know that both have honest intentions, but how can it be possible for them to treat with becoming dignity and intelligence of a locality which they have never visited—a locality as generous in its intellectual as in its physical products, whose culture is as ineffable as its territory is boundless? Mr. Stedman is a learned man and a charming man, but he has never been farther West than 104th street in New York City, and as for Miss Hutchinson—we admire her greatly—her idea of the West is that it begins just on the other side of Syracuse, a town she visited some years ago.

In due time "Culture's Garland," a compact little volume inexpensively printed and bound in a grayish paper cover, made its appearance. My copy, bearing the inscription, "With the affectionate regards of Eugene Field," has also in Field's writing the date, August 22, 1887. The book, which attracted some attention at first, had only a relatively small sale. Still, I have always believed that if Field had taken the trouble to "dress up for company" his humorous and satirical material and had made his own selection of the contents of the book he would have produced a volume that would have had a fairly broad appeal, a volume that would have possessed a permanent value as a basically truthful, though exaggerated, picture of wealth recently acquired undertaking to put on culture along with its evening clothes. Field's refusal to improve in any way the material chosen by Ticknor made of the venture a sort of literary outcast. However, for a year or so it brought in substantial royalties. After that it was practically forgotten and then it went out of print. One day in 1891 Field took another friend and myself to luncheon at Kinsley's. We had a very modest luncheon—perhaps it was Kinsley's famous corned beef hash with tartar sauce, which in that day was known throughout the country. When he was handed the check by the waiter Field looked at it and laughed. "What an absurd coincidence!" he said. "To-day I received from Ticknor my percentage on last year's sales of 'Culture's Garland,' and, to a cent, the amount was the same as the figures on this check."

v

The volume published by Ticknor was the third of Field's to appear. The others also had paper covers. The first was his uncouth but famous "Tribune Primer"— Field wrote primer lessons similar to those written in

Denver for a time after he began work on the *Daily News*, but they were more sophisticated and made no special hit. The second little book constituted Field's initial experiment in producing a privately printed work of real beauty, though it was modest enough.   His imaginative tale, "The Symbol and the Saint," published in the *Daily News* at Christmas, 1886, was immediately reproduced in a booklet of ten pages made up of photographed sheets of Field's beautiful script.   Eight of the pages were embellished with appropriate illustrations by **J. L. Sclanders**, a capable artist then employed by the *Daily News*. Upon the paper cover was a holly wreath, inside which appeared, in Field's writing, the title of the Christmas tale and the names of the author and the illustrator.   The whole was printed in brown ink and the sheets were held together by a double loop of narrow red ribbon strung through holes in their margins.   This unique little book Field distributed among his friends as a holiday gift.   A year or two before he died Field told me with much satisfaction that book collectors had bid up the price of this rare publication to $35.

When a third paper-covered book bearing his name as its author appeared from Ticknor's press Field vowed that it should be the last.   From that time forward, he declared, his name should be associated only with beautiful books.   Indeed, he expressed the desire—and that desire was fulfilled—to become a positive force for the general improvement of the physical quality of books published in the United States.   In the last years of his life he frequently voiced his abhorrence of cheaply printed books—and these were the rule rather than the exception in that day of pirate publishers.   Finally, in 1893, he published in his column this significant notice:

The writer of "Sharps and Flats" requests that publishers and authors send him no more paper-covered books.   He simply throws away all books of this kind, it being his notion that a book that is worth reading is surely worth keeping, and is therefore entitled to a durable dress.

A day or two later a writer in another Chicago newspaper commented upon Field's scornful attitude toward paper-covered books and remarked that he possessed a certain humble volume of that description. Field promptly replied:

A writer for the *Times* announces that he has a paper-covered book, published in Boston in 1887, and entitled "Culture's Garland." As this work is now out of print and, curiously enough, somewhat in demand, we are prepared to pay the *Times* correspondent double the original price of the book for his copy.

VI

Not many weeks after "Culture's Garland" came off the press Field began his first long vacation since he had come to Chicago four years earlier. He visited New York, Boston, and various other Eastern cities and towns, including Amherst and Newfane, places dear to him because of childhood memories. In Newfane the old home on the village square, built by Field's grandfather, General Martin Field, was still standing and there it remained a landmark until it was destroyed by fire August 6, 1917. Field's vacation extended over six months and during that time "Sharps and Flats" was suspended.

Ticknor showed Field many attentions in Boston, and in New York Stedman and Hawthorne introduced him in literary circles. In Amherst he visited his beloved cousin and second mother, Miss Mary Field French. He saw much of Richard Henry Stoddard and Mrs. Stoddard, and of those two clever and kindly old people he grew very fond. He took delight in Hawthorne's household, which was overflowing with children, whose romps he shared. Everywhere he was received most cordially by writer folk and he discovered that they expected much of him. He determined that he would fulfil their expectations. This play spell was for him a time of inspiration and orientation. It brought him to the threshold of a new intellectual period in his life. Of his experiences he told me much, but I now remember little of what he told me. On one occasion he was taken to a dining club of New York authors and journalists. When his identity was made known the roomful of diners rose and applauded him and immediately demanded that he give some of his famous recitations and impersonations. He answered, in some embarrassment: "Look here, I don't know many of you fellows and I don't know what you want me to give you, but I'll try to do a few little things for you." His efforts to entertain them proved so successful that he had some difficulty in getting the company's permission to discard his rôle of entertainer and sit down to dinner.

Field also told me with amusement of an extemporaneous bit of sentimentality invented by Stedman for his edification. The two were riding on an elevated train near the lower end of Manhattan Island when Stedman suddenly directed Field's attention to a certain grimy window in an upper story of an ancient tenement. "There," said Stedman in a voice charged with emotion, "is the window of a room in which I lived many years ago when I was very poor. See, it has the same cracked pane and there across the pane is the very strip of paper that I pasted over the crack to keep out the winter cold."

XIII

A POET FINDS HIMSELF

I

NOT a little has been written about the supposed hardship to Field of having to supply daily a long column of original material for the *Daily News*. The fact is, however, that Field was free at any time to abandon his work for a day, a week, a month, or even six months if he had a good reason for so doing, his salary being paid him regularly in the meantime. There were frequent gaps in his service, though no other was so long as that extending through the fall of 1887 and the succeeding winter. A few years after Field's death Julian Ralph wrote:

> He once said to me that his contract with his employer was almost as hard as the sale of his soul would have been. "I must do it to live," said he, "and yet if I do it I cannot produce the better and greater work that I long to be at. I can do nothing but trifling work in literature so long as I am forced to go down to that office every day and grind out my column." He spoke seriously, and if he felt bitterly he only did as hundreds of other bright newspaper attachés have done and are doing to-day under similar circumstances.

Yet when Ralph knew Field the latter never went near the office of the *Daily News* to do his work. During the last four years of his life he did his writing at home and his son Fred (Daisy) drew a small weekly wage from the newspaper, his task being to carry his father's manuscript to the office. However, up to the autumn of 1889 Field did regularly go to the office, as he did also for a time in 1891, after his sojourn of about fourteen months in

Europe. Doubtless it is true that his newspaper work irked him at times; yet his considerate employer gave him every possible freedom.

After Field got back into the harness in the spring of 1888, following his long vacation in the East, his work went on much as before, except that he had begun to do a great deal of planning. He felt that the time had come for him to begin to harvest his dreams, but he was still in doubt how to begin. He wrote many anecdotes that he had picked up during his Eastern trip. He wrote some amusing articles on fishing. He wrote two Christmas stories and three of his best pieces of mingled humour and pathos—"Bill, the Lokil Editor," "Dock Stebbins," and "The Little Yaller Baby." He composed the well-known verses, "Little Mack." More significant still, he began to write much on books and book collecting. His first bibliographic note appeared in March of that year. Here it is:

The Rev. Frank Bristol is in trouble. An evening paper announced the other day that at a meeting of Methodist clergymen he had avowed that he didn't believe in the doctrine of everlasting punishment. Of course Mr. Bristol made no such avowal. Those who know Mr. Bristol at all know that if he has one deep-rooted conviction it is that there is a hell and that to the torments thereof will all unrepentant sinners be condemned for eternity. Mr. Bristol so earnestly believes in this that he takes a seeming pleasure in collecting books and pictures treating of the everlasting miseries of the damned. He has perhaps the finest "hell" library in the country, and many of the illustrations of this subject (such as woodcuts, copper plates, and steel engravings of the old masters) are so vivid that they would seem calculated to throw even the vilest scoffer and the most callous reprobate into a tremor of penitence.

The year 1888, however, will be regarded by lovers of Field's verses as most noteworthy because it saw the birth of "Little Boy Blue." This poem unquestionably is the greatest favourite of all the poems that Field wrote. He wrote it in bed one April night and read it to me as soon as he reached the office next morning. He recognized at once that it was a remarkable production. I was enthusiastic about it, and his smiling satisfaction with the lines told plainly that he saw no way to improve them. However, as was his custom, he put the poem into his desk for further consideration at some other time. He had written it because he had promised Slason Thompson to furnish a poem for the first number of *America*, a weekly periodical. "Little Boy Blue" duly appeared in that number. Its powerful appeal to human hearts caused it speedily to become known the world around. Here it is:

LITTLE BOY BLUE

The little toy dog is covered with dust,
But sturdy and stanch it stands;
And the little toy soldier is red with rust,
And his musket molds in his hands.
Time was when the little toy dog was new
And the soldier was passing fair,
And that was the time when our Little Boy Blue
Kissed them and put them there.

"Now, don't you go till I come," he said,
"And don't you make any noise!"
So toddling off to his trundle-bed
He dreamed of the pretty toys.
And as he was dreaming, an angel song
Awakened our Little Boy Blue—
Oh, the years are many, the years are long,
But the little toy friends are true.

Ay, faithful to Little Boy Blue they stand,
Each in the same old place,
Awaiting the touch of a little hand,
And the smile of a little face.
And they wonder, as waiting these long years through,
In the dust of that little chair,
What has become of our Little Boy Blue
Since he kissed them and put them there.

One other poem appeared in that first number of
America—"St. Michael the Weigher," by James Russell
Lowell. There speedily developed a curious race for
popularity between Lowell's poem and "Little Boy Blue,"
a race that was watched with very great interest by Field
and myself. Here was the product of a poet of long-
established reputation pitted against that of a mere
aspirant to the title of poet. Which would receive the
greater degree of recognition from the newspapers of
the country? We kept a close lookout, searching daily the
columns of the hundreds of newspapers that came to the
office. Both poems were widely copied. Wherever found,
we clipped them and matched the two sets of clippings
numerically against each other. To Field's immense
satisfaction "Little Boy Blue" soon began to outrun its
more pretentious rival. Its lead grew longer day by day,
until there was no doubt that the younger poet's verses
had scored a notable success over Lowell's in point of
newspaper popularity.

At this advanced stage of the contest I undertook to
perpetrate a feeble joke. I had the composing room
strike off a number of proofs of the title, "St. Michael the
Weigher." Then I clipped from the exchanges many
pieces of verse of about the length of Lowell's poem and
having the same kind of verse formation and pasted the
bogus title at the top of each. Thus I prepared a sheaf
of doctored clippings that at first glance might pass for
what they were not. These I laid on Field's desk over
against two or three fresh clippings of Field's own poem.
When he reached the office that day the clippings immediately attracted Field's attention. He caught them up
and there was silence for the space of half a minute. Then
his sudden shout of laughter showed that he had dis-

covered the fraud. "Oh, no," he said to me. "That won't go down. Mike needs your help badly, but the Little Boy will beat you both."

The widespread affection for Field and his verses that developed in succeeding years was due in large measure to this poem. It was speedily set to music. It was read in the schools. Of many instances tending to show its universal popularity I recall one. When a young woman novelist of my acquaintance visited the Shetland Islands some years ago she found the Scotch schoolmaster of the parish school in Mid Yell teaching his pupils to recite "Little Boy Blue." Those fisher children, penned up in their rocky islet by the racing waters—children "whose only toys were sea shells and who sucked dried fish for sweeties"—thus profited spiritually by the most famous poem of the tenderest of children's poets.

Many have supposed that the poem was written in memory of Field's son Melvin. But Melvin died a year and a half after "Little Boy Blue" was written, and his father wrote other beautiful and tender verses in his memory. Twelve years before he wrote the poem he had lost an infant son, when the family was living in St. Joseph. That may be the reason why Melville E. Stone, in his "Fifty Years a Journalist," makes the curious error of asserting that Field wrote "Little Boy Blue" while residing in that Missouri city. Another story which has gained some circulation is that Field wrote the poem on being told of the death of a little boy whose parents thereafter never moved the child's toys from the bay window where he left them, even leaving the window unchanged when making extensive alterations in the rest of the house. However, Field never intimated to me at the time the poem was written or at any other time that it was anything more than the product of his imagination.

There is still a strong tendency to build up legends

about this well-loved poem. And recently it has been a
subject of dispute between learned gentlemen, one of
whom challenged the authenticity of the accepted text.
He wrote an article in a book collectors' magazine to prove
that the lines:

> And they wonder as, waiting the long years through
> In the dust of that little chair,

should be so changed as to make the second line read,
"In the bust of that little chair." He explained that he
had examined the original manuscript of the poem and had
found that the word was "bust," not "dust." Then he
made this argument:

> If Mr. Field had written the line "In the dust of that little chair"
> it would have been false to his purpose. "Dust" in this particular
> sense means nothing, and during all these years the world has printed
> and read this poem erroneously and meaninglessly. But "bust of
> that little chair" is more to the purpose and to the meaning. "Bust"
> in the old English usage was applied to the trunk of the body, the
> main or solid part, hence was used in speaking of the trunk or sub-
> stantial part of anything. In the making of chairs for children an
> enclosure or box was fastened under the seat, the latter forming the
> lid, and in the box (the trunk) the child was supposed to keep his toys
> or playthings.

This earnest person wrote in conclusion:

> It is to be desired that in the future editions of Mr. Field's poem this
> long-standing error, this mistake of forty years, shall be corrected and
> that "bust" supplant "dust" in the popular mind whenever this
> favourite poem is read or quoted.

The article drew a reply from the pen of James Shields,
of Philadelphia, a writer on Field's life and works and a
collector of Fieldiana. Mr. Shields also had studied the
manuscript of "Little Boy Blue"—the same manuscript
that was bought in Chicago a few years ago at a war
bazaar for $2400 by John McCormack, the tenor—and

had found that in writing it Field had made fourteen
"d's" precisely as he had made the letter which the other
investigator pronounced a "b."

All of this is, of course, trivial enough, but it is interesting as illustrating how busy commentators can torture
new and amazing meanings out of the simplest lines of
dead and therefore unprotesting poets.

III

Doubtless, after all, the most important work performed by Field in 1888 consisted of his preparations for
the remarkable tasks which marked the earlier months of
1889.   At first he was eager to produce many pieces of
"Alaskan balladry."   Later he hit upon the idea of writing lullabies for children of all lands, and he read widely
to collect material for the fascinating series.   His success
in working out this plan is known to all who have read his
poems.   He was also making notes at this time of his
memories of his Western mountain experiences for a
series of poems dealing with life in a Colorado mining
camp.   Then came to him the plan of writing paraphrases
of Horace.

Here indeed was a wealth of material for poetic treatment.   He studied it, made trial flights, hummed sample
lines, and generally saturated himself with the subjects
that so appealed to him.   By the end of the year he was
ready to enter upon an extremely fruitful period of composition.

Field has told how he came to take an interest in the
poems of Horace.

It was in the autumn of 1888 that, at the suggestion of an editorial
associate, I began to make paraphrases of the odes of Horace.   I soon
became much interested in the work, or perhaps I should rather call it
play, for seldom has my dealing with the rare old Venusian cost me
labour and never fatigue.

The editorial associate who turned Field's attention to Horace was Dr. F. W. Reilly, then managing editor of the *Daily News*. Field's method of dealing with the Latin poet has been adopted by many imitators, but not more than one or two of them has approached him in felicitous treatment of the verses. In all seriousness Field defended his method to me. "In paraphrasing the lighter verses of Horace," he said, "I begin by asking myself how Horace would write them if he were alive to-day amid surroundings similar to mine. His was a joyous spirit and certainly he would express himself rhythmically and with mirthful lightness if he were now on earth. So I try to interpret Horace in a way to bring his pagan poetry up to date. At least I give him the best I have in the shop."

His bold rendering of Horatian verse created a sensation. Some solemn critics denounced his "insolence" in turning famous classic poems into modern slang, but as a rule lovers of Horace acknowledged the force of Field's argument that his paraphrases merely modernized the poems while retaining their spirit. Field wrote in 1891 in defense of his method:

The genius of Quintus Horatius Flaccus appears not only in the poetic work of that preëminent master but also in the increasing popularity which that work enjoys in spite of the translations, paraphrases, and imitations to which it has been subjected. For hundreds of years scholars, theologians, poets, pedants, soldiers, barristers, pedagogues—the representatives of every class and condition of society—have had their fling at the grand old pagan; they have threshed and rethreshed the straw with unflagging enthusiasm, producing results at once diverse, amusing, shocking, and humorous. But neither solemn pedantry nor ribald tomfoolery has served to abate posterity's love for the Sabine poet's songs; the voice which answered to the call of the muse in parched Apulia nineteen hundred years ago sings to-day as sweetly as of old, and the lyre which the hand of the freedman's son swept in praise of love and wine still awakens with its rapturous music the liveliest responses of which the human heart is capable.

The fatal error which most of the translators of Horace have made

is a failure to detect this thing which seems so very certain and clear
to us—that Horace wrote for all times and for all time.   That charming and crafty old *ingenue*, Voltaire, has said: "None argues the
possibility of changing the nature of beasts, and pray how then shall
it be possible to change the nature of mankind, who are simply beasts
in the higher scale of animal life?"   Humanity has been the same
from the beginning, and Horace, as a very human being, wrote for
humanity as it was and is and ever shall be.   Yet our ancestors
(peace be to their husky old bones, their musty ashes, and their
solemn shades!) seemed ill content to regard the genius as a genius
for all time and for all conditions; they insisted upon dragging themselves back through the dreary centuries into what they fondly
fancied was a classic atmosphere and then, environed by a pedantry
and a pomp which Horace himself always lampooned, they laboriously and solemnly delivered themselves of the awful waste of dullness
which was calculated to serve as a stimulus to the study of the most
remarkable lyrist the world has ever known.

Four years later Field returned to the subject of
Horatian translations, as follows:

We must despair of having any satisfactory rendering of the Venusian's work until the old-school college professor has passed away and
until the poets-in-embryo are made to understand, as youths, that
Horace was not a demigod or a bugaboo, but simply a mortal man
imbued with the weaknesses, the appetites, and the passions as well as
the stronger, nobler qualities of humanity.   If he were on earth
to-day how Horace would scout at the solemn asses who, with no sympathy for those kindly, genial qualities which make his verses immortal, plane and saw and hammer at his genius like so many job-lot
carpenters!

IV

On New Year's day, 1889, Field published in his column
"Casey's Table d'Hôte"—an auspicious beginning for the
golden year of his literary life.   Having started so well
the task to which he had set his hand, he wrote and
published other poems in rapid succession.   Those appearing in January included "A Paraphrase of Seneca"—
"Happy the man that, when his day is done"; Horace
I, 11—"Seek not, Leuconöe, to know"; Horace I, 13—
"When, Lydia, you (once fond and true)"; "A Para-

phrase of Heine"—"There fell a star from realms above";
"The Bibliomaniac's Prayer," and Horace I, 23—"Chloe,
you shun me like a hind," with its various paraphrases.
On the last day of January appeared "The Cyclopeedy,"
a story written from the heart, for Field himself through
weary years had been purchasing, volume by volume, an
encyclopedia, much as did his harassed but hopeful hero,
Leander Hobart.

In February there were more Horatian verses, including
Horace I, 19—"Incendiary passions fill," and the celebrated paraphrase of Horace III, 9—"When you were mine
in Auld Lang Syne." There appeared in this month also
the following verses:

A Lamentation

Oh, if I were a poet
The world should surely know it—
Ye gods! how I would go it
   From morning until night!
I'd write no rhymes jackassic,
But carmina as classic
And as redolent of Massic
   As old Horace used to write.

I'd quaff Falernian yellow
Till my muse got good and mellow—
Then I'd flatter some old fellow
   Who had sordid gold to strew;
Let him give it—let him lend it—
Did I only comprehend it
I'd devise a way to spend it
   To advantage p. d. q.

I'd forswear McClurg and Morris—
Hic difficilis laboris!
And I'd do as did old Horace
   When he'd touched his wealthy friend;
I'd refresh my muse with bumming
And I'd keep creating humming
In a fashion most becoming
   To a bard with cash to spend.
     *   *   *

Alas! I am no poet—
These maundering verses show it,
And I can never go it
  As old Horace used to go;
But through his numbers lyrical
And in his lines satirical
I'll learn, as 'twere empirical,
  What wise men ought to know.

In February appeared also "Lollyby, Lolly, Lollyby,"
"De Amicitiis" and "The Twenty-Third Psalm," all on
one day, the three nearly filling Field's column.   March
brought more Horace, "Our Lady of the Mine," and a
splendid succession of lullabies.   The "Japanese Lullaby"
appeared on March 8th, the "Norse Lullaby" on March
9th, the "Dutch Lullaby" ("Wynken, Blynken and Nod")
on March 11th, the "Orkney Lullaby" on March 18th
and the "Cornish Lullaby" on March 22d.   This month
saw also the publication of "Good-by—God Bless You"
and "Mother and Child."

v

Field's desire now was to dazzle his readers with the
number as well as the beauty of his verses.   So on April
4th he published poems that occupied a column and a
quarter of newspaper space.   They were: "Our Two
Opinions"; Horace I, 4—"'Tis spring! The boats bound
to the sea"; "Love Song," by Heine; Horace, I, 20—
"Than you, O valued friend of mine"; Hugo's "Pool in
the Forest"; Horace I, 5—"What perfumed, posie-
dizened sirrah"; Beranger's "Broken Fiddle"; Horace I,
38—"Boy, I detest the Persian pomp"; "Chloe";
Uhland's "Three Cavaliers"; Horace VI, 11—"Come,
Phyllis, I've a cask of wine."

This notable demonstration did not satisfy Field's love
for the spectacular.   Though he brought to the office and

read to me many poems in the later weeks of April, in May and June, he published none. Meantime the reserve supply of verses in his desk grew to formidable proportions. "I'm going to accumulate a lot of them and then astonish the natives," he said. Finally he was ready. In the week beginning July 15th he filled his column every day with nothing but poems of his own. Here is the list of them:

Monday: "Professor Vere de Blanc" (It is "Vere de Blaw" in his collected poems).

Tuesday: "Horace to His Patron" ("Mæcenas, you're of noble line"); "Poet and King," Alaskan Balladry, I—"The Wooing of the Southland"; "Lizzie"; Horace I, 30 —"Venus, dear Cnidian-Paphian queen."

Wednesday: "The Conversazzyony."

Thursday: "Egyptian Folk Song," Beranger's "To My Old Coat," Horace's "Sailor and Shade," Uhland's "Chapel," "Guess," Alaskan Balladry, III—"Skans in Love."

Friday: "Marthy's Younkit," "Fairy and Child," "A Heine Love Song," "Jennie," Horace I, 27—"In maudlin spite let Thracians fight," Heine's "Widow or Daughter?"

Saturday: "The Happy Isles" of Horace, Beranger's "Ma Vocacion," "Child and Mother," "The Bibliomaniac's Bride," Alaskan Balladry, II—"Krinken," "Mediæval Eventide Song."

Having prepared to fire this astonishing broadside, Field went to a summer resort in Wisconsin. From there he wrote letters to Mr. Gray and other friends expressing his happiness at having performed so notable a feat. Ten days elapsed after the week of poetry before "Sharps and Flats" again appeared. On July 31st "In Flanders" was published and "Rare Roast Beef" followed on August 22d. Then on September 2d "Forty-Nine" saw the light.

VI

Thus in barest outline I have set forth his achievements of a few months by which Field forced the American public to recognize his fine ability as a poet. The newspapers of the country copied his verses with the greatest avidity. How his poetic feats impressed newspaper writers is indicated in the following verses which appeared in the Philadelphia *Times* at the height of Field's extraordinary burst of song:

An Editorial Lullaby

Wynken, Blynken and Nod one night
   Sat in a room sky-high,
Sat in a blaze of electric light
   Rubbing each weary eye.
"Where shall I put them and what do you choose?"
   The office boy asked the three.
"Pick us out the Chicago News
   If that it has come, perdie!
   Tired of other exchanges are we,"
     Said Wynken,
     Blynken
     And Nod.
*   *   *   *   *   *   *
All night long the News they read
   And drank the Pierian cup—
Then down from the sky dropped the foreman and said
   That the paper was not yet up.
*   *   *   *   *   *   *
Wynken and Blynken their Horace knew well
   And Nod was college-bred;
Not always on grosser food below
   Have these three editors fed.
And they shut their eyes while the poet sings,
   And forget their cares, maybe,
And recollect other and pleasanter things
   Than turning out of copee.
And, poet, you rock the editors three,
     Wynken,
     Blynken
     And Nod.

Critical Eastern editors commented on Field's versatility and on the faultless rhythm that characterized all his poems. The New York *Evening Post*, conceding that he was "quite a dabster" at preserving the flavour of Horace in his extremely modern lines, quoted some of Field's verses as models of their kind. In short, Field had succeeded in his purpose. He had "astonished the natives."

XIV

Manuscripts and Memories

I

FIELD'S feverish production of poems during the first eight months of the year 1889 had a special purpose. He was eager to carry out a cherished plan of publishing two volumes, one containing the tales that Ticknor had not found comical enough for his use, together with stories written after the appearance of "Culture's Garland," and one containing poems. When this plan was conceived, most of the material for the book of verses had still to be written. So Field set about providing the necessary contents of the book that was to be. The poems were mainly composed in bed late at night. During those months of furious composition one of my common experiences was to be interrupted in my morning's work by the joyous entrance of Field with a new poem to read to me. The reading would begin as soon as he was seated at his desk. "I finished this thing at 2 o'clock"—or some other unearthly hour—"this morning," he would say.

Thus one morning in the preceding year he had read to me "Little Boy Blue." But of all the poems produced in that remarkable creative period I remember with the greatest pleasure the first reading of "Wynken, Blynken and Nod," or "Dutch Lullaby," as its author preferred to call it. I hailed it with particular delight, assuring Field that it was the most charming of all his poems, and Field smilingly agreed with me. In thus reading aloud the first drafts of his verses it is probable that Field did not so much seek my verdict upon them as he did the verdict of his own fastidious ear. Lines written in bed long after midnight naturally were weighed by him with some anxiety when they confronted him in the cold light of day. Field would ask me which of two words or which of two phrases I preferred in some line or lines when a reading was over, and he freely invited suggestions and criticisms. I tried to be frank, saying exactly what I thought, but I am not so conceited as to think that I exercised more than the remotest influence in the final shaping of the poems of that period. Field had so much the finer ear for melody and so much the nicer discrimination in the choice of words that he never was really in doubt as to the best way to produce the effect he desired.

Two pages of manuscript, written in lead pencil, lie before me. They constitute the original draft of Field's "Child and Mother," beginning, "O Mother-My-Love, if you'll give me your hand." The paper is ruled, and down the left margin the lines are numbered from 1 to 8 for each stanza. Field had written above it the title, "Child's Lullaby," and then had stricken out the first word. The title, "Child and Mother," appears first on the printer's copy of the poem, which is also in my possession. At the bottom of the second page of the original draft appears the penciled line, "June 4, 1889, 2 A.M." June 3d was the date first written there, but then Field had marked the "4" over the "3," doubtless when he discovered that midnight had struck two hours before.

Only two changes were made when Field came to revise the original draft of this poem. In the third line "the beautiful land" became "a beautiful land," and the line next to the last was changed from "Away hand in hand to the beautiful land" to "Away through the mists to the beautiful land." This is a fair example of the degree of perfection commonly achieved by Field in the first drafts of his most admired poems.

II

Other first drafts of poems written in bed by Field about this time and now in my possession are "Apple Pie and Cheese," "The Happy Isles," "Contentment," "The Death of Robin Hood" and these lines from Horace (I, 19) which do not appear in Field's collected works:

> Fierce passions do my breast to-fill—
>   Invincible whene'er they choose to be,
> They mould me to their hideous will
>   And make me human, as I used to be!
>
> And Parian splendours pale before
>   The fairer comeliness of Glycera—
> She hath of every charm such store
>   As to inflame my very viscera.
>
> I fain would write of Sythian deeds,
>   Of Parthian cunning all embattled,
> But Venus frowns upon these screeds—
>   And as for me, I'm badly rattled.
>
> Fetch me, O slaves, a fresh sod hence—
>   I hope to find Dame Venus milder
> When with vervain and frankincense
>   And young red wine I've reconciled her.

This manuscript is dated January 31, 1889. On its margin Field wrote: *Herrick. Old English ballad. Sir John Suckling. Thos. Moore. John Skelton.*

Field at that time was studying English verse forms with the purpose of bringing back into use some of the admirable old vehicles of poetic expression. It was not only a worthy quest but well directed, if one may judge by the scribbled list here presented.

In "Echoes from the Sabine Farm," by Eugene and

Roswell Field, the latter's paraphrase of Horace's lines celebrating the charms of Glycera stands alone, his brother having contributed no version of that poem, though to my thinking Roswell's are inferior to the verses I have here quoted which Eugene's good judgment and fastidious ear rejected after he had written them. Compare Eugene's fine last stanza with these commonplace lines by Roswell:

> Here boys, bring turf and vervain too,
>   Have bowls of wine adjacent;
> And ere our sacrifice is through
>   She may be more complaisant.

On the back of the sheet containing Field's version of Horace's "The Happy Isles" the poet had carefully laid out working plans preparatory to writing a very different set of verses, presumably "Professor Vere de Blaw," which, like "The Happy Isles," appeared during the famous "Golden Week," as Field called it, of July, 1889. Numerals written on the left-hand margin of the sheet prepared the way for a series of stanzas of eight lines each. At the top appear a couplet and a broken line, manifestly constituting a false start on the verses he had in mind. Here is what he wrote and then rejected:

> When Casey run his restaurant in Red Hoss Mountain days
> His enterprise wuz manifest in many pleasant ways.
> Besides—

One may suppose that, finding himself not then in the mood to write of the doings of Casey, Field turned the sheet over and went to work on Horace. But this latter task did not go any too smoothly, or else Field wrote the poem at breakneck speed, as was sometimes his custom, pausing not if a word failed to come to him on the instant. In this first draft of the poem there is a broken line in the

third stanza and a gap where a missing word should be in
the fourth, while the fifth appears in this wise:

> There no vandal foot has trod
>   And none of the————that wander
> Shall ever profane the————sod
>   Of those beautiful isles off yonder.

In the completed poem the stanza runs:

> There no vandal foot has trod,
>   And the pirate hosts that wander
> Shall never profane the sacred sod
>   Of those beautiful isles out yonder.

Another poem the first draft of which indicates that it
was written at high speed is "The Death of Robin Hood."
In its final form this poem differs materially from the first
draft, which does not have the last two beautiful stanzas.
The penciled lines with which the first draft begins are
these:

> "Give me my bow," quoth R. H.
>   "An arrow give to me—
> And where 'tis shot marke thou that spot,
>   For there my grave shall be."

> Then Lyttel John shed not a tere
>   And not a word he spake,
> But he smiled altho' with mickle woe
>   His herte ben like to break.

> He raised his master in hys armes,
>   And set him on hys knee,
> And R.'s eyes beheld ye skies,
>   Ye shawes—ye greenwode tree.

III

I have the original draft of Field's well-known poem
recounting the delights of reading in bed. "De Amicitiis," he named it, but the title was a later inspiration, as
in its first form it is titleless. It shows many erasures and

many recast lines.   Curiously enough, it is evident that
this poem was one of the relatively few written by Field
in that fruitful period that were not written in bed.   Not
only is it set down in ink, which is proof that it was
produced while Field was sitting at his desk, but I well
remember how its author toiled over it from time to time
during a period of some days.   While he was whipping it
into its final shape he read to me with special delight this
stanza:

> And when I'm done,
>   I'd have no son
> Pounce on these treasures like a vulture;
>   Nay, give them half
>   My epitaph
> And let them share in my sepulture.

That Field particularly valued this poem from the time
of its birth is indicated by his carefully written signature
at the bottom.   It bears the date February 14, 1889.

Among Horace manuscripts of Field's in my collection
is the one containing the poem that later received the title
"Horace and Lydia Reconciled."   At the top of the sheet
it bears the words in Field's handwriting, "Original draft."
When Field read it to me before its publication he expressed particular satisfaction with the poetic bull:

> I'd gladly die if only I
> Might live forever to enjoy her.

The first line of this poem was originally written "When
you were mine, O nymph divine."   It later became,
"When you were mine in Auld Lang Syne"—a sufficiently
free rendering of the original.

Though Field's birthday fell on September 3d, in pub-
lishing his poem "Thirty-Nine" he affixed to it the date
September 2, 1889.   The first draft of this poem, which
I have, shows Field still more emphatic in his use of

the wrong date, for he put it into the title, thus: "Thirty-Nine; September 2, 1889." At the end of the manuscript Field placed his name and the date August 1, 1889, the day on which the poem was completed. It was not until several years later that Field learned from family records the true date of his birth.

Another interesting manuscript of Field's that is in my possession is the original draft of "A Proper Trewe Idyll of Camelot." There are numerous indications in the manuscript of the special enjoyment that Field got out of writing it. There is a jest in nearly every line. He wrote it from time to time at his office desk and he laughed a great deal while he wrote, composing at high speed. That he undertook to set down the story as rapidly as possible is shown by the manuscript itself. For, whenever a problem of rhyme or rhythm arose, he simply left a broken line hanging in the air and proceeded on his merry way. For example, the description of King Arthur's hospitable table runs in this wise:

> Oh, 'twas a goodly spectacle to ken that noblesse liege
> Dispensing hospitality from his————siege;
> Ye pheasant and ye meate of boare, ye haunch of velvet doe,
> Ye canvas ham————

When, however, Field began to deal with the king's list of drinkables his imagination so ran riot that he concluded later to shorten materially the tale of those strong waters which played such havoc with the monarch and his knights, according to the veracious chronicle. Here are the lines that Field eliminated from his revised verses:

> To-wit: there ben Falernian in amphoræ or skins,
> Madeira, Malmsey, Tinto and divers forreine vins;
> Lafitte, Châlons, Latour, du Pape and others hight châteaus,
> Chinon, Lamont and Haut Brion, Neuf, Thierry and Margaux;
> With every kind and size and age of sparkling Spanish vino,
> The which I wolde be pleased to name, but, wit ye well, damfino;

Hochheimer, Sauterne, Burgundy, port, Muscatel and sherry,
Johannisberger, Bodenheimer, claret, elderberry,
Catawba, currant, Rhenish, sack, Malvoisie, Osey, Massic,
And divers other stimulants, ye moderne and ye classic.

One gets a glimpse of the tenor of the Chicago board of trade man's conversation which appealed so strongly to Queen Guinevere and the ladies of her court, for on the margin of the manuscript Field penned these rudimentary lines:

Ye tables in the west ben round,
And in the middest of eche one there ben a slit
Into ye whiche ye custom ben to slip a chip
As truage for ye——

Having an intimate knowledge of round tables, every seat at which is a "siege perilous," naturally the stranger from Chicago was in nowise awed by King Arthur's table round.   Field did not develop this idea, which manifestly was in his mind, presumably because his verses had grown to a very considerable length.   He wrote his "Idyll" in the same year that Mark Twain published "A Connecticut Yankee at King Arthur's Court," but it is my impression that Field's verses were the first to appear.

Owing to my daily close associations with Field I made it a point never to ask for manuscripts of his.   All that I possess were voluntarily given to me by him from time to time, for he knew that I valued them.   He saved most of his finished manuscripts for his family, but he gave away many.   Some of the latter in my possession—"Krinken," "Our Two Opinions" and "The Brook and the Boy"— bear lines written by Field presenting them to me.

IV

When, early in 1889, Field decided that he was ready to put between the covers of books his best work in both prose and verse, he determined that the volumes should be beautiful examples of the printer's art. He enlisted the friendly assistance of Slason Thompson, who sent out in Field's name to a selected list of Field's acquaintances and to a few others a prospectus announcing the early production by the University Press at Cambridge of a volume of Field's poems and a volume of Field's stories. Subscriptions to these limited editions were invited, each subscriber to receive for $10 two sets of the volumes. One hundred subscriptions were asked and they were readily obtained. Then additional subscriptions were accepted, so that two hundred and fifty copies of each book were required. They were printed upon the best hand-made paper with beautiful type and the pages had broad margins. In all respects they were admirable specimens of book-making.

Field found immense enjoyment in his long-distance relations with the Cambridge printing house of John Wilson & Son while it was producing the volumes. The arrival of each batch of proofs threw him into a joyous flutter. For what he was pleased to call my assistance in going over the proofs with him Field insisted on giving me his extra set of author's proofs as they came to him from the printing house. Unfortunately for me, there were some omissions in forwarding duplicate proofs, so that my set is not complete. Field conceived a particular liking for the conscientious and competent proofreader whose queries and suggestions he found freely scattered over the margins of his proofs. He laughed whenever he thought of the shocks that excellent person manifestly suffered on coming in contact with wild Western expressions employed in some of the stories and also in some of the poems.

The tribulations of that Puritan proofreader as he strove to discover substitute words and phrases that might pass muster under the shadow of the walls of Harvard never failed to stir Field's risibilities when he reviewed the gentleman's noble efforts recorded on the margins of the proofs.   After the first three or four parcels of proofs had reached him Field wrote to the printing firm to express his admiration of its proofreader's erudition.   He added that the quality of the worthy individual's work led him to believe, first, that the proofreader was a native of Massachusetts; second, that he was a graduate of Harvard; third, that he was a Unitarian minister.   Field received in reply a letter from John Wilson & Son expressing the thanks of the firm for Field's complimentary remarks and reporting that on inquiry it had learned that the proofreader who had dealt with Field's proofs was indeed a native of Massachusetts, a graduate of Harvard, and a Unitarian who had studied for the ministry.   Field was much pleased by his success in reading the past of his proofreader friend through his study of the latter's mental processes as disclosed in penciled comments on words and phrases.

It has long been my belief that the proofreader who thus aroused Field's amused interest was the Rev. James Henry Wiggin, who for a time was literary adviser to Mrs. Mary Baker Eddy.   Mr. Wiggin, a somewhat noted character, was long in the employ of John Wilson & Son. He is described as "a man of enormous bulk and immense geniality," a great lover of Shakespeare and of the theatre and fond of telling humorous anecdotes.   Such a man quite naturally would have won Field's delighted approval if he had read the proofs of Field's volumes and had set down comments and suggestions on the margins.

v

The list of subscribers to the limited edition of "A Little Book of Western Verse" and "A Little Book of

Profitable Tales," as Field had felicitously named his volumes, is interesting as showing who were Field's personal friends of that day.   Seventy-three of the one hundred and fourteen subscribers—a few took more than one subscription each—were residents of Chicago. Though there were few book collectors in the list, these were honourably represented by three ministerial friends of Field's, F. W. Gunsaulus, M. Woolsey Stryker, and Frank M. Bristol.   There was a sprinkling of St. Louis, Kansas City, and Denver acquaintances and friends, including Joseph B. McCullagh, Colonel William R. Nelson, and Frederick J. V. Skiff, who was publisher of the Denver *Tribune* when Field was its managing editor.

Subscribers from among Field's stage friends included Emma Abbott, Kate Field, William H. Crane, Francis Wilson, Sol Smith Russell, and Stuart Robson.   New York City furnished a few well-known names for the list— Edmund Clarence Stedman, Charles A. Dana, Brander Matthews, Whitelaw Reid, Daniel Frohman.   Nor should one omit to mention the name of Miss Mary Field French of Amherst, Mass., to whom Field dedicated "A Little Book of Western Verse" in lines beginning:

> A dying mother gave to you
>   Her child a many years ago;
> How in your gracious love he grew
>   You know, dear patient heart, you know.
>
> The mother's child you fostered then
>   Salutes you now and bids you take
> These little children of his pen
>   And love them for the author's sake.

Field continued to send on to the Cambridge printing house new poems to be added to the book until, late in the summer, he forwarded "Thirty-Nine," practically closing the list.   By September he was making preparations to sail with his family for Europe with the intention of taking a long rest amid new surroundings, as he was suffering intense pain from nervous dyspepsia.   Before the end of September he was on the Atlantic.   His friend Thompson was left to see the new volumes through the press and to distribute them to the subscribers.

The volumes duly appeared and were received with great favour by those who were so fortunate as to obtain them.   Some weeks later, George M. Millard, manager of the department of old and rare books at McClurg's, called me on the telephone to ask for Field's European address, saying that a leading New York publisher wished to communicate with him on a matter of importance to Field. I gave Millard the desired information and immediately dispatched a letter to Field telling him to be on the watch for an offer from a publisher.   It is probable that Millard also wrote him at once.   I received this line in reply: "Thanks for your kind letter.   I will answer it anon."

Not very long afterward Field wrote me that Charles Scribner's Sons had arranged with him to publish a popular edition of his two books from the plates of the privately printed edition.   He asked me to forward to that publishing house a recently published poem of his to round out "A Little Book of Western Verse."   It was needed to fill the space that had been occupied by the names of the subscribers to the other edition.   The new poem was "Yvytot."   Field had laboured upon it for years and had finished it only after he had gone abroad. Knowing how highly he thought of it, I did not wish to run the risk of overlooking typographical errors in the printed poem as it had appeared in the *Daily News*, so I copied it from the original manuscript, which I held with others of his to be delivered to him on his return from Europe.

In due time the popular edition of Field's books appeared and sold at a highly satisfactory rate.   Speaking of them a few years later Mr. Millard said:

I happen to know that he received a check for a few cents less than $2000 as his royalties for six months on two volumes of his works. And that was exceptionally good—very large, as royalties go.   There were more of his books sold that year than of any other publication of that house.

VI

Before leaving the subject of Field's first successful book of verse I will mention briefly two or three more of the poems contained in it.

"At the Door" was one of Field's earlier poems, having been written in 1884 and first published in the Chicago *Current*, a weekly publication, of which Miss Rose Elizabeth Cleveland, President Cleveland's sister, later became a contributing editor.

"Soldier, Maiden and Flower," when published in the *Daily News* in 1887, bore this note below its title: "A piece for little Miss Trotty to speak at school on Decoration Day."   "Little Miss Trotty" was Field's daughter, Mary.

"In Flanders," verses that were lucky to get into such good company as that of the other contents of the volume, was written by Field at my suggestion, though his treatment of Uncle Toby's remark that "the army swore terribly in Flanders" was wholly original with him.   In suggesting the subject I had said that it would be amusing to have Mrs. Shandy or some other woman express curiosity as to what oaths the army used, mentioning some ladylike expletives of the time, such as "Lawks!" and "Odd's bodikin!"   Field chose to leave the oaths to the readers' imagination and merely to express his own virtuous horror at such improper language.   The verses were written very rapidly at his office desk, certainly in half an hour. Field was particularly pleased with the lines affirming that the army's embroidered speech

> Would never go down in this circumspect town
> However it might in Flanders.

XV

TABLE DELIGHTS OF A DYSPEPTIC

I

SOMEWHERE in the files of *Puck* of the middle '80's—*Puck* was the best-known American humorous publication of that day—is to be found an article by Field on "The Soul-Destroying Pie Habit," or bearing some similar title. The article itself, as I recall it, was a travesty on the stock arguments of the prohibition orators of the time, the unfortunate wretch whose downward career was traced by Field being the victim of an insatiable appetite for pie.

Field might have written seriously from his own experience on the perils of pie unwisely eaten. His "Apple Pie and Cheese" was a poem from the heart. Irregular meals, including many midnight suppers, also played their part in reducing him to a serious condition of ill health through nervous dyspepsia. Along with too much pie and coffee at unseemly hours he had to answer physically for the smoking of too many cigars and particularly for habitual reading and writing in bed late at night at the cost of needed rest.

His unfailingly sunny disposition made it difficult for even his closest associates to realize that he suffered severe discomfort and often great pain. He was merry in the midst of his distress. But his strength dwindled and his suffering increased with the passing months of 1889. The pangs of indigestion which caused him to describe Nesselrode pudding as a cross between ice cream and the Spanish

Inquisition caused him also to name the southwest corner of LaSalle and Washington streets "The Place of Groaning," because that was where he regularly alighted from a street car to go to the office.   There daily he stood writhing until his rebellious stomach ceased to protest at the jar caused by its owner's descent from the car to the street level.

In this distressful physical condition he worked on, hoping to see his two volumes issue from the press before he started on his long-contemplated European trip. However, at the solicitation of his friends, he gave up finally and sailed without having seen the eagerly awaited books.   It was in London that he first had the satisfaction of seeing and handling them.   Their beautiful type and their heavy, hand-made paper delighted him and his letters at that time contained many expressions of satisfaction at the outcome of his undertaking.

II

Marked as was Field's New England predilection for pie, it might still be thought but a phase of the poet's amused interest in anything weird in the form of eatables. Strange and perilous articles of diet had a fascination for him.   The German dishes in a well-conducted restaurant that flourished under the shadow of the *Daily News* building were for him the subject of many jests.   But pie and coffee were his particular reliance at luncheon except when he occasionally succumbed to the enticements of some such comestible as *kalter aufschnitt* or boiled tongue with raisin sauce.   He professed to regard the consumption of pie as a very special proof of good citizenship and intellectual power.   He even made a classification of womankind according to the nature and quality of the pies constructed by its fair representatives.   Thus to have reduced the characteristics of the sex to a formula for the convenience of pie eaters must be regarded as a notable feat:

Among the savants with whom we associate there obtains a well defined theory that the age and the disposition of the donor of a pie may be accurately determined by the nature of the pie itself.   We do not violate any confidence in submitting the following rules as a guide to this determination:

If the pie be a custard pie, right joyously bestowed and happily composed, the sender thereof is surely not more that twenty-one nor less than nineteen years of age, and the likelihood is that she was born north of the James River and south of Lake Champlain.

If the custard pie be gummy, oleaginous or fluidistical as to the nether crust (by which is meant the sediment occurring between the custard and the baking pan), the maker is a sentimentalist and is addicted to Browning and marshmallows.

If the pie be a lemon pie and hath lather over it, the donor shall surely be less than nineteen years of age and it may truly be reckoned that she hath loved and lost.

Without the lather the lemon pie betokeneth a lack of delicacy of sentiment and an absence of those finer qualities so admirable in femininity.

If the pie be a cherry pie and containeth the pits of the cherries, it argueth either that the donor is callow to a degree or that she was born at the conjunction of Saturn and Sirius, with Venus in apogee, which bodeth full great evil and is a thing as grievously to be lamented as is the pie itself.

The same rule shall be applied unto the giver of those pies in which occur unpitted prunes, peaches, and such other fruits as are at certain seasons woven with sugar, shortening, and baking powder into practical poems that fall like benedictions upon the stomach and thrill the whole being with unspeakable rapture.

If the pie be a pumpkin pie of ample circumference, of goodly diameter, of generous depth and of proper complexion (*id est dicere*, of a hue happily between an old gold and a Roman purple), wit ye well that the sender thereof is a woman of bounteous nature, of comely aspect and of noble practices, and that she was born under a lucky star, and that she shall wed a prince—or if she be already wedded to one that is not a prince, so much the more reason have all princes of every principality to be regretful.

An apple pie wherein the apple hath been grated to the consistency of mucilage betokeneth an exacting and a jealous nature; dried apples in a pie argue a mean and sordid economy which all praise in women but dislike in pies.

Cocoanut pie bodeth evil dreams and a sorry morrow; the best way to eat cocoanut pie is to let thy neighbour eat it, and if he smite thee turn over to him thy lemon pie also, for thus shalt thou heap coals of fire into his system.

A pie, if it be a mince pie of justly magnificent latitude and longitude and of proper deep soundings, betokeneth that the sender hath in exceeding fullness all beauties of body, of mind, and of soul.   And by as much as there is abundance of plums and sweetmeats and savoury juices and pleasant liquors in the pie, by so much shall you presently know, do all sweet, savoury, pleasant, and gracious qualities abound in the woman that hath possessed you of that pie!

III

Field's most noteworthy rhapsodizing on this subject was confined to his beloved concoction, mince pie. One who reads it will have no cause to wonder that the rhapsodist was a victim of dyspepsia:

A pleasant and profitable pie which we would fain commend to all that desire long and active life is one that we shall now describe:

It is called mince pie.   There be pies and pies, but there is but one mince pie, and you shall know it by these measurements and signs. First, concerning the measurements: It shall possess a diameter of half a cubit, and therefore a circumference or perimeter of a cubit and a half, or, in secular parlance, a diameter of nine inches and a periphery of thrice that number; the depth of the pie shall be, from the inferior aspect of the superincumbent layer to the superior surface of its lowest stratum, one-sixth of a cubit, which is to say eight and twelve hundredths centimeters, or, in other words, three inches. And, unless the pie conform strictly to these measurements, you shall know that it is not a righteous pie and that there is no good in it.

Now, to the signs of the pie, showing it to be a worthy instrument for your apprehension and comprehension. The surface exposed to the visual organs shall have all the hues and shadings of the prism, the darker colours obtaining near the edge of the pie and the inferior or softer colours abounding in the middest of the pie, wherein philosophers agree the centre of gravity doth lie.   If the pie be a righteous pie it shall please the eye, and none but the blind shall eat the pie that offends the sight.   That pie shall be accounted of special noble quality wherefrom, in the baking of it, certain precious juices have escaped, inundating certain tracts of the superincumbent stratum, and, through natural infrigidation, congealing into a gum or balsam more pleasing to the palate than the honey of Hybla or of Hymettus.

The contents and component parts of the pie shall be spiced meats, pungent juices, gustful liquors, savoury fluids, delectable saps, aromatic gums, piquant herbs, and ambrosial fruits; the covering thereof (by which we mean the superior crust) shall be made and cemented with such nice discretion that in the baking of the pie none of the odours, vapours, gases, and essences engendered in the bowels of the pie shall by any chance escape therefrom.

This pie, whose composition and measurements we have defined, shall be eaten hot, and it shall be heated in this wise: Cut the pie with a silver knife (for a silver blade alone becometh the carving of this noble pie), and in your cutting have a care to cut from the edge of the pie to the very centre, axis, or hub of the disk, for elsewise the substances in the pie are like to be crowded outward toward the periphery, inducing ruptures and confusion alike displeasing to the eye and prejudicial to the pie. The cut of pie (which must be an even quarter of the whole) shall be placed in a deep plate and upon the surface of the upper crust shall be spread cheese to the thickness of a barleycorn. Of the cheeses suited to this delectable purpose you shall prefer Herkimer, since that learned and ingenious scientist, M. Jean-Marie Coulomb, has demonstrated that the potential energy in one hundred grammes of Herkimer cheese is equal to 7.2394 foot-pounds, and Professor Grove, collaborateur with the eminent Michael Faraday, has shown that, if this could be converted into motive power, one kilo of Herkimer would do the work of nine kilos of the best Newcastle coals.

The pie thus placed upon the plate and the cheese thus spread upon the pie, a second plate, inverted, shall be placed upon the whole, and these two plates, with the interjacent viands, shall be put into an oven and kept therein for the space of nine minutes and fifteen seconds (Greenwich time) in a heat not lower than 750 degrees (Fahr.).

Then presently, O fortunate man! you shall see this pie, so devised, so constructed, and so garnished, come steaming from the furnace. What a pleasing delirium will its savoury smells induce, and when its melting glories are unfolded to your ravished vision the joys of the *dii immortales*, feasting upon high Olympus, will be yours!

Should you think this glorified disk sufficiently deadly for all practical purposes perhaps you will not care for certain viands which Field discovered on his dyspepsia-haunted tour of Europe. However, they seem worthy to be added to the collection of culinary wonders to which

Field gave his allegiance.   He wrote in 1890, during his stay in Germany:

I came upon a viand in Hanover which is quite new to me, and I have had to do with pretty nearly every edible from the meek and lowly 'possum that blooms in midwinter in Cole County, Missouri, to the orthodox pumpkin pie that graces the festal board in puritanical New England—from the infinitesimal and indigestible cove oyster that abounds in Colorado to the prize-rebus and sphinx-riddle conserves compounded in Oxford Street, London.   This new viand is sausage served in a beer broth.   The sausages are first fried and then the fat juices that have escaped therefrom are thoroughly mixed with lager beer, the whole liberally sprinkled with pepper.   Served upon a warm plate that has been rubbed over with a little garlic, this edible is most pleasing.

My friend Cowan, who recently made his escape to America, told me that in Vienna it was the fashion to serve beef gravy on sponge cake for dessert and to eat roasted meats with a sauce composed of whipped cream and melted sugar flavoured with vanilla.

Carthusian puddings make a very satisfactory dessert. They are so called because they are a favourite viand with the Carthusian monks during the Lenten season.   They are made in this wise: Take stale rolls or stale bread and cut into squares, which soak until thoroughly saturated in a sop composed of milk, eggs, and sugar, and then either bake in a quick oven or fry, as you would a doughnut, in hot lard. Over these puddings sprinkle a mixture of cinnamon and sugar. There may be eaten on or with the puddings apple sauce or whipped cream or any kind of sweet jam with whipped cream.   In Germany apple sauce alone is most commonly served with the puddings, but there are many folk of most discriminating judgment who hold (quite properly, I think) that cream improves every eatable.

IV

Field took a special interest in foods and he well realized that folk commonly gave joyous response to the calls of appetite and liked to get new suggestions appertaining to the pleasant business of dining.   He once conceived the idea of presenting to the readers of his column—for the solace of their imaginations—the most exquisite meal that could be devised.   Accordingly he enlisted the aid of his friend William J. Florence, the comedian, a famous *bon vivant.* Florence and Field put their heads together one afternoon in the little room at the *Daily News* office that Field and I occupied. They seriously discussed many viands that tempt the pampered appetites of good livers. Florence put at Field's disposal all the lore of cookery and of dining that he had accumulated in a lifetime of choicest eating and drinking. By way of making a beginning, Florence told how to make a salad, first having pronounced a lettuce salad the best of all. He said:

The lettuce should be fresh and crisp and should have that greenish-white tinge which betokens succulence and tenderness. It should never be touched with metal of any kind, nor should it be bruised by any instrument except the teeth. I do not care for mayonnaise or any dressing but that compounded of salt, pepper, and vinegar, which should be first well mixed apart from the lettuce. Never put eggs into a salad. If oil is to be used, the best I know is the Lucca oil, which comes from Leghorn (I think), and is imported in small tin cans. A tablespoonful of Tarasçon vinegar imparts a delicious bouquet to a salad—a tablespoonful to every four portions.

Field's method of setting down the results of his and Florence's long consultation on ways and means to construct the best of all possible dinners condensed their rambling and fascinating discussion—interlarded with delightful anecdotes of dining—into the following:

"A friend was asking me only a day or two ago," resumed Mr. Florence, "what I would suggest as a bill of fare for a charming little dinner party—and we all understand that a dinner can hardly be charming unless the party be small and congenial. My answer was that I should first of all set down before each guest half a dozen cherrystone or Lynn Haven oysters, with one small glass of Chablis. Mark you, I said *one small* glass. I should follow this beginning with terrapin——"

"A soup?"

"There is but one terrapin, and that is terrapin. When Father Tom went to see the Pope he undertook to give His Holiness a recipe for the making of punch. 'First,' says he, as nearly as I remember the words, 'first you pour in the whisky; thin you add the sugar and

the limmon, and ivery dhrap iv wather afther that spiles the punch!'
It's the same way with terrapin. Terrapin—why, men can tell you
how an apple tastes or how a peach tastes; there is scarcely any
flavour that can't be defined until you come to terrapin! Terrapin
has a taste, a flavour, a bouquet, an essence, that can't be described.
When a soul has once tasted it the next best thing is sitting around
thinking about it.

"Stew the terrapin," said Mr. Florence, earnestly, "putting in no in-
gredients except butter, salt, and pepper (black pepper). I should say
no sauce at all for me; but of the sauces I prefer Madeira rather than
sherry. Still, in order to please the tastes of my guests, I should have
both sherry and Madeira at hand. The wine to be drunk with terrapin is Burgundy, and my favourite brand is Clos de Vougeot; second
best, Chambertin. I should be particular to serve but one glass of
wine with each course; this is a pretty safe rule to follow, for it insures
a complete enjoyment of the viands.

"Next in order," continued Mr. Florence, "would come ducks—
canvasbacks, of course—and to each guest a whole duck! This
should always be insisted upon. The ducks should be baked seventeen or eighteen minutes, basted meanwhile with pepper, salt, and
butter. Inasmuch as they should be eaten hot, I should serve
these birds upon chafing dishes; with them I should give boiled hominy grilled (by which I mean boiled hominy browned over coals) and
cold, white, brittle celery. With the canvasbacks Pommery should
be drunk."

"What next?"

"A cigar—a Santiago Rosa perfecto," said Mr. Florence, "and
maybe a black coffee."

"Then a pousse-café?"

"Never a thing after coffee. Some may prefer a small brandy with
the coffee, but no epicure will take liqueurs into his mouth after a
dinner such as I have specified. The chances are that when he gets
that perfecto lighted the guest will be so completely satisfied that anything further would be distasteful."

It was mainly a very different kind of dining that occupied Field's attention during his trip to Europe in search
of health. He recorded the rules laid down for him by the
English doctors whom he consulted about his diet:

1. Do not eat beef; it is too hearty for the average dyspeptic.
Eat the lean of mutton (boiled preferred).
2. Bacon in small quantities may be eaten; also thin slices of

aërated bread fried in bacon fat; also boiled pigs' feet and tripe, and the fish not known as oily fish.

3.   Eat no fruit.   Of vegetables partake sparingly of baked potato, rice, and boiled peas.

4.   Bread may be eaten (aërated bread preferred) in thin slices toasted till they are brittle.

5.   The brown meat of fowl may be eaten.   Avoid all gravies and sauces.

6.   Abstain from all liquors, and drink no tea unless it be fresh made.

7.   Eat no eggs, except fresh raw, well whipped.   Sugars should be avoided.

8.   Drink no iced water; partake freely of hot water and of hot milk (not boiled).

9.   Lie down for twenty minutes after each meal.

V

In his search for original anecdotes of his beloved Father Prout, Field came upon one during his sojourn abroad that was destined to play a considerable part in his later social activities.   Here it is:

It was a custom with Father Prout to invite a company of jolly good fellows from Cork to dine with him at his home at Watergrass Hill.   He would seat this company at a table upon which there was no cloth and which was bare of plates, knives, and forks.   When the guests were seated upon rude forms two lusty servants would bustle in, bearing a pot of boiled potatoes and these steaming hot vegetables they would shoot along the table between the guests.   Then was there a great rushing and ostentatious haste in fetching a wooden vessel filled with cold milk for every two guests.   Then Prout would say gravely, "Your dinner is before you, gentlemen; let us say grace." Eminent jurists, poets, journalists, and ecclesiastics would vie with one another in the delicate task of peeling hot potatoes with their fingers, and when the joke seemed to have gone far enough the host would rise and announce dinner in the next room.

After Field returned to the United States he imitated the Father Prout joke on various occasions.   The best-known of these occasions was his celebrated luncheon at the Union League Club in Chicago in honour of the Rev. Dr. Edward Everett Hale.   Preparations for that luncheon gave him great delight.   For days he was bubbling over with anticipatory mirth as he planned the menu.   I recall that he was particularly entranced with the idea of serving boiled potatoes "with their jackets on"—precisely the special viand provided at Father Prout's dinner.   He added corn bread, corned beef, and other substantial fare, with apple pie and cheese for the final course.   To partake of this repast and to meet Doctor Hale he invited a large number of friends, both men and women.   I remember to have observed there the handsome ruddy-gray countenance of Marshall Field, the great merchant. Thomas Nelson Page was there.   And as Henry B. Fuller and I were introduced to Doctor Hale at about the same moment, I recall with what warmth the young author of "The Chevalier of Pensieri-Vani" was greeted by the Boston veteran.

The guests disposed themselves about the great room and an army of waiters served them with eatables on plates poised precariously on their knees.   There was an abundance of drink for the thirsty.   Waiters poured it out expertly into fragile glasses from lordly champagne bottles swathed in faultless napery.   When so served, however, it proved to be a good quality of water.   Beaming hospitably, Field circulated among his guests.   Into the ear of each man whom he approached he breathed softly, but with impressive solemnity, this helpful warning: "Be careful; don't drink too much—remember your failing."

When the repast was over Field introduced Doctor Hale, who made a felicitous little speech, in which he did not fail to compliment his host upon the luncheon.   I recall no other intellectual feature of the occasion except the recital of "Casey at the Bat," by De Wolf Hopper.

At another time a similar feast was served in honour of the Rev. Robert Collyer.   James Whitcomb Riley was

among the guests on that occasion.   Mr. Riley afterward
recalled that the luncheon, which was served with "punc-
tilious ceremony," was "of the old settlers' character,
consisting of beans, corn bread, buttermilk, and similar
dainties."   On that occasion, everybody present was
called upon to say something.   "Field came forward,"
said Riley, "and gave an imitation of the admirable good
nature of his special model, Sol Smith Russell."   Then
Russell gave an imitation of Field reciting "Little Boy
Blue."   Both imitations were extremely funny.

Edward W. Bok's story of a dinner party given by
Field at his home in the absence of Mrs. Field, where the
guests, after long waiting, were informed by their host in
shocked tones that through some error nothing to eat had
been provided, records another variation of the Father
Prout joke.   Bok and Riley volunteered to go out and get
provisions, but they found the doors locked and the
windows nailed shut.   However, they finally made their
escape through a basement window.   Having loaded
themselves down with eatables purchased at the nearest
delicatessen shop, they returned and crawled back through
the basement window only to find Field and the rest of his
guests dining merrily on viands that had been in con-
cealment until Field chose to produce them.

Field's freakish hospitality furnished a number of other
good stories.   Madame Modjeska told this one in her
amusing reminiscences of Field:

I remember a dinner *en forme*, which he called a "reversed one,"
beginning with black coffee and ice cream and ending with soup
and oysters.   After the first course he delivered a most amusing
toast.   We were laughing so much that tears stood in our eyes.   He
looked compassionately around the table and, saying, "I see that you
are sad and depressed; let us have some fun," he went to the mechanical piano and gave us a few bars of a funeral march.   After
each dish he returned to the instrument and treated us to some doleful tune.

On one occasion Field, when entertaining guests, talked a good deal about the deftness of the family maid, Marie. After all were seated at the table, however, Marie failed to appear. The bell was rung for her in vain. Field bustled out impatiently to discover what was wrong. Soon Marie entered the dining room in cap and apron, with a mincing gait, her countenance wearing an expression of conscious rectitude. But Marie was Field himself, and he proceeded to serve the dinner, ignoring, as a proper maid should, the laughter and comments of those at table.

XVI

THE PLEASURES OF READING IN BED

I

FIELD'S passion for indigestible dishes probably had less to do with the acute stomachic disorder that caused his doctor to banish him to Europe than did his habit of reading and writing in bed until far into the early hours of the morning. Even after he was brought finally to a realization of the physical harm he suffered from this practice he was an unrepentant sinner. While abroad trying to get back his health he wrote:

If reading in bed is a vice, what shall you say of writing in bed? But for those hours which I stole away from the other end of my life I should not now be an exile. Still, like the churl who peeped at Godiva, I find much consolation in the thought that I had a very pleasant time inducing my calamity. It was only a day or two ago that I happened upon a bit of versification done in that period of damnable, delightful indiscretion.

Then followed his rendering of Hugo's "Child at Play." One of the desires long cherished by Field was to write a little book to be entitled "On Reading in Bed." He talked to me frequently on this subject and outlined whole chapters of the work he had in mind. He afterward condensed his material into the chapter of "The Love Affairs of a Bibliomaniac" entitled "The Luxury of Reading in Bed." In earlier years he wrote delightfully on his favourite vice. Here, for example, is an article written at the time when he was regularly writing poems in bed after midnight—namely, in late February, 1889:

Our bibliomaniacs have made an interesting discovery. They find that as far back as that classic period when Latin was the polite tongue there was a word meaning "a bed," a similar word meaning "choice" and another similar word meaning "to read." Look in your Latin lexicons and you will find—

Lectus, adj., choice.

Lectus, sub., couch.

Lectus, p. p. of *legere*, to read.

The natural inference (and 'tis logical, too) is that these words were evolved from the same root originally. The theory among our wisest maniacs is that the original root must have been "leg," from which was derived the word "lex" or the law, which law, being published, was read; and then there came into use the verb *"legere,"* primarily meaning "doing or reading the law," and, subsequently, reading any printed matter. In due course of time the practice of reading in bed became so general among the ancients that the bed itself was called a lectus, signifying the machine designed for the pursuit of literary studies, and so engaging became this pursuit that presently was evolved the third word "lectus," signifying "choice" and implying that of all habits the habit of reading in bed was the most to be approved. And it is opined by our most sapient etymologists that our popular English word "delectable" had its origin from these three Latin derivatives—viz., "choice," "reading," "in bed."

That the habit of reading in bed is of great antiquity appears in the eloquent words of Cicero, who, in his oration for his old instructor, the poet Archias, said: *"Haec studia adolescentiam alunt, senectutem oblectant, secundas res ornant, adversis pefugium ac solatium praebent, delectant domi, non impediunt foris,* PERNOCTANT *nobiscum!"* Clearly, then, Cicero not only made a practice of reading in bed, but was proud to advertise that habit to the world.

But while our bibliomaniacs agree that reading in bed is a most delectable and edifying practice, they differ in opinion as to the kind of reading which should be done. Our clergymen, who are famous book hunters, insist that only literature of a pious tendency should be administered to the human mind when it is about to be consigned to the awful phenomenon of sleep; they recommend Young, Milton, Hervey, Mrs. Hannah More, Mrs. Hemans, Miss Edgeworth, Roe, *et id genus omne.* Yet it is a question whether this class of reading would indeed be beneficial to certain temperaments. If it is a soporific alone that is required, why not save time by taking an opiate?

Once upon a time we asked Henry Irving, the actor, if he was addicted to the practice of reading in bed and he answered: "Yes, and I always have been." Then when we asked him what kind of reading he preferred before going to sleep he replied with marked enthusiasm:

"Always something gruesome!" Yet 'twould be folly to recommend gruesome literature as a regular diet for the average reader, just as it would be sinful to feed an excitable child upon tales about witches and demons. . . .

It is generally conceded that reading which involves study should not be indulged before going to sleep; this, however, is not a rule that everybody needs to follow.   Nor is it any more reasonable to say that nobody should read exciting fiction before going to sleep.   A great many human beings never dream at all—poor creatures, how we pity them!   It is the man with the weak stomach and the disordered liver and who dreams of being chased by devils and falling over precipices who has our active sympathy and our earnest admiration; here we have a man who to the bettering of his intellectuals is required to exercise temperance, patience, fortitude, and every other cardinal Christian virtue. . . .

We have entered upon this subject with exceeding fear and trembling, for we are painfully aware that our temerity is like to bring about our heads the maledictions of the fair sex.   We say, without any mental reservation whatever, heaven bless the ladies!   and may heaven graciously put it into their heads to endure without recalcitration or complaint the peculiarly masculine habit of reading in bed. Consider, O ladies, how much more profitable it is for your husbands and your sons to be tucked up and propped up comfortably at home visiting with a proper book than it would be for them to be sailing around downtown amid the myriad temptations of after dark or to be abandoned to swinish sleep!

II

At another time Field quoted scornfully from William Davenport Adams' "Byways in Bookland" the arguments there advanced to discourage the practice of reading in bed.   Next he proceeded to demolish the enemy of his pet vice in the following fashion:

Then, urges this preposterous person, the difficulty of putting aside the book and extinguishing the light is so serious as to afford a good reason for not engaging in bed-reading.   Now who after hearing this objection will suspect that Mr. Adams knows anything of the practice of bed-reading or anything of the custom of lecto-bibliophiles?   Put aside the book indeed!   And extinguish the light!

Is not the book able to take care of itself?   Will it not, at just the proper instant, elude the fingers of the nodding reader and drop noiselessly upon the yielding down quilt with which the habitual lecto-bibliophile covers his couch? No fear of the book's being injured by the fall; nay, even though it should subsequently slip from the silken bed covering to the floor, no harm will befall it, for, before retiring, every prudent lecto-bibliophile invariably places a pillow beside his bed upon the floor to catch the precious volume when it escapes from the hand of the slumberer.

The confirmed, the simon-pure, the glorious bed-reader never extinguishes his light; 'twould strike him as a kind of profanation to turn from a feast with Horace or with Donne to the vulgar and debasing occupation of putting out gas or blowing down a lamp chimney or puffing at a candle. He lets the light blaze away, God bless him! and presently his wife patters in from a yonder chamber determined this time that she will wake him up and give him a round scolding for his heartless extravagance; but when the dear lady sees him slumbering so peacefully, his precious book just beyond his fingers, his face illuminated by the smile that accrues from saintly dreams—she relents, she extinguishes the blazing light herself, and, conscious of having done her duty as a wife and as an economist, she patters back again to that yonder chamber. There is no doubt or trouble about this; every wife will do it seven times a week, provided she has been caught young, well broken, and discreetly trained.

Field's dissertation upon cold feet and that sovereign remedy for the evil in question, the eiderdown quilt, deserves notice here, since so large a part of his literary product was the result of bed-reading and bed-writing. "It has long been our conviction," he asserted, "that the worst thing that can happen to a man is cold feet." And he went on solemnly to declare: "It appears from our investigations that the three classes of people to which cold feet are common are as follows: First, those who think; second, those who think they think; third, those who do not think." But there is for all such sufferers help and healing—the eiderdown quilt.

When spread upon a couch how persuasively does it address itself to the purpose for which it was devised! With what caloric tenderness its subtle influences steal upon the human system beneath, diffusing through every part thereof a grateful calidity!

It is important that this treasure be used with knowledge.

This quilt of which we speak is to cold feet what a genial book is to a hungry brain—a tonic, an invigorator, a food. It should be tucked in well at the foot of the bed and at one side thereof, but not on both sides, for bed-clothing that is tucked in on both sides binds the dormant body and induces restlessness and evil dreams. Care must be taken not to draw the quilt too far over the chest of the sleeper-elect, for the reason that the fine particles of down continually escaping from the quilt are in that event likely to be attracted by the inhalations of the sleeper and to be drawn into his lungs, producing immediate paroxysms by which the sleeper is awakened; or, collecting in the nostrils or in the throat, these particles are likely to aggravate divers rheums and distempers of grievous sort.

We count it occasion for joy that this grateful machine—this gracious engine—is within the reach of all. . . . The kind which we should recommend to those who suffer from cold feet is that which is made and trimmed in bright colors. There are certain shades of red which—as all intelligent folk know by experience—send of themselves a throb of warmth in at the eyes and through the entire corporal system of the beholder.

Field also luxuriated in a special garment to be worn in cold weather while reading in bed. It was a gift from a reader of his column. He wrote of it as follows:

We do not know that this estimable lady invented this ingenious and useful machine but we are none the less prepared and pleased to testify to its exceeding merit in that purpose for which it was designed. The device seems to be made of one piece of cloth and the cloth is of a soft, feathery material of a pink colour, although, as we are told and as we believe, the colour of the garment should be selected to match the complexion of the wearer, and almost any shade, hue, or tint will do for the average, so long as it be not of so bright a colour as to divert his attention from his book. And now that we come to think of it, we don't know that it wouldn't be better to have the colour of the garment match the reading, there being nothing so pleasing and so praiseworthy as consistency in all things. . . .

As to the name of this garment we are in doubt, since that is a confidence with which the fair maker has not yet honoured us. We know not whether to call it a mantle, pelisse, jacket, vest, corselet, jerkin, gabardine, bodice, waistcoat, pall manuta or camisole; but in the hope that some one more ingenious than we will relieve our anxiety we shall describe the vesture to the best of our limited ability. It is made so loose as not to bind the cervicle region, admitting of full freedom to the carotid artery and of the return of the venous blood from the cerebellum, without restraint, let, or hindrance. Constructed in such fashion as to lie loosely across the thorax, it must protect the interscapular space; the exposure of such space gives frequent rise to quinseys, asthmas, and phthisics, as all veteran bed-readers know full well. The length of this habiliment in front shall be of such a space that the lower hem or border thereof shall fall not more than the fourth part of a cubit below the manubrium, otherwise the xyphoid cartilage. The back, however, should not reach below the juncture of the dorsal and the lumbar vertebræ. The sleeves, describing a parabolic curve, should extend only to the distal third of the forearm, and they must be so spacious, ample, and uncircumscribed as to give unlimited license to the organs of prehension. More specific instructions we cannot give.

The offices of this goodly garment are as numerous as they are delectable. It seems eminently proper that he who pursues so ennobling a practice as that of reading in bed should wear about him while engaged in that pursuit some distinguishing mark, adornment, or favour; in this simple vestment we have that which protects the body from insidious temperatures and which at the same time becomes him in his present employment as fairly as ever a crown became a conqueror or a *toga virilis* a new-fledged Roman citizen. And a peculiar advantage which this article of raiment has over all other devices is that when one has no longer any need for its genial offices it can be slipped off over the head without ado, the ingenious abridgement of the reverse or posteriority thereof contributing felicitously thereunto.

III

On one occasion I was so signally favoured as to be permitted to see Field arrayed in the glory of his bed-reading regalia, and in the midst of his night labours. I think it was one evening early in 1889, when he was at the height of his infatuation for night composition, though it may have been somewhat later. I had taken dinner at Field's home and, when the evening was well advanced, I rose to depart. We had been talking of Field's habit of writing in bed, and suddenly Field conceived the idea that I must pass the night with him and so behold his method of working. He was so insistent that I stayed. At 11 o'clock or thereabouts we retired, I having been provided by Field with sleeping gear.   There was a small table at Field's side of the bed and upon it, within easy reach of his hand, were numerous books, ranging from fairy stories to substantial Bohns and including his favourite literal translation of Horace.   There were also pencil and paper. The gas flame above his head had been carefully adjusted to his liking, and it was furnished with convenient mechanisms for turning it on and off.   In these Field took particular pride.   So there he reclined with great satisfaction, his head in a glare of gas and his body propped high with pillows.

Field read a volume of fairy lore, pencil in hand and taking occasional notes.   It soon proved to me a decidedly dull show, because of my intense drowsiness.   Being young and in rugged health, I did not reflect upon the drain on Field's vitality due to those late hours of labour. I was, however, impressed with the discomfort attending such activities in the dead of night.   Accordingly, after a relatively brief survey of the poet as he busied himself with book and pencil, I turned ingloriously upon my pillow and went to sleep.

XVII

LITERARY FRIENDS ABROAD

I

FIELD'S last contribution to the *Daily News* before he sailed for Europe was published September 25, 1889. His next appeared on November 28th. It was "John Smith, U. S. A." A few poems were published in December, among them "Gosling Stew," which originally bore the title, "In Oberhausen." On Christmas day appeared "Yvytot," a poem on which he had worked desultorily for several years. He completed it at Llyandwreth. The voyage across the Atlantic had awakened ideas about flowing and wailing waters that enabled him to give his verses the mystic quality that he desired. In the months preceding his departure from Chicago he would frequently declaim fragments of the poem, particularly one line which does not appear in the completed verses:

> There was a king in Yvytot.

I believe that around that line, which long haunted him, the entire poem was constructed.

On December 26th was published "Bethlehem Town." For Field never could let Christmas go by without preparing either a Christmas story or a Christmas poem—if he did not prepare both a story and a poem in celebration of the festival which he held so dear. And just as inevitably he bestowed a Christmas remembrance upon each of his friends. Accordingly I received from him just before Christmas of that year a letter recounting in some

detail his European experiences.   Even the form of this
letter speaks eloquently of its writer's prowlings among
London's old bookshops.   Its first page is blank, except
that it is belted about the middle with two lettered lines,
carefully printed in gold ink by Field's pen, all the
capitals being elaborately ornamented.   This inscription
reads:

An "autograph letter, signed," from Eugene Field to Charles H.
Dennis.   It containeth an unique poem.   7/6.

The letter begins on its own page 3, with a gorgeous red
initial M.   Field wrote:

My dear Dennis:
If, at the time I left Chicago, any one had told me that so long a
period would elapse before I wrote to you, I should have chided and
rebuked him for one that lied in his throat.   Possibly you can understand how that one who, first of all, is beset of ill health, and, secondly,
is environed by a new atmosphere and by new friends, and, furthermore, is besieged by an army of new acquaintances—you can,
perhaps, understand how such a one becomes neglectful of his correspondents.   There has not, however, my dear boy, been a day that I
have not thought of you—I had almost said that there had not been a
day upon which I had not been reminded (willy nilly) of you by par-
oxysmal pains in the lumbar region.   [Here is the old backache joke
again.]   And I will add that my thoughts of you have at all times
been of the pleasantest nature.
You will be glad to know that in health (physical, moral, and spiritual) I have improved marvelously.   In fact, I am now feeling as well
as I ever did, and therefore I am really anxious to return to Chicago
and to my work.   But I am told by my friends here that it would be
foolish for me to go back to America so soon, since I may not be sure
that my stomach is really subdued, and, furthermore, since I may
never again have an opportunity of doing this part of the world.
London, vast though it be, does not give me the inspiration I thought
to find here.   I discover that I am simply incited to spend money,
for the chances in the way of old books and manuscripts are simply
prodigious; but, possessed of no money wherewith to buy, the condition of my soul is worse even than when indigestion had me for its
prey.
So far as my work is concerned, there would seem to be but little

fodder for me in London. I am yet to visit Canterbury and Chester, two charmingly quaint towns, and there I shall pick up, I fancy, much excellent material; but it was during my ten days in Germany and Holland that I found inspiration and material that will probably grind a good many verses out of me, sooner or later. Hanover is a particularly lovely spot—a pleasant commingling of ancient and modern; its old market place, with booths that made me fancy that a fair was in progress, appealed with peculiar force to me. In Amsterdam I had several lovely prowls, and I am anxious to go again. But there are other spots which I should visit—Paris, Antwerp, The Hague, Edinburgh, Berlin, and Cork. In the last-named city I shall seek for Prout relics, having secured the coöperation of a local priest, the Rev. Father Hegarty, who is upon terms of intimacy with Prout's nephews.

In London we live in lodgings, and our meals are served in our apartments. Every day I go upon a ramble, invariably through St. Martin's Lane (where Prout, Jerrold, Thackeray, and that coterie used to get convivial), down into the Strand or up byways into lanes and alleys where the musty book and print shops are. Still, I do little buying. In a social way I have done somewhat more. I have dined with Andrew Lang at his house, and there I met Mrs. Humphry Ward, accounted the most brilliant talker in England; Rider Haggard, who has a small head and a big nose and talks with all the enthusiasm of a boy; Lecky, the historian, loose-jointed as a hoop-snake and looking as if he had been "drawn by John Leech." With Irving I have supped twice—each time in the old Beefsteak Club rooms, in which (a hundred years ago) princes and noblemen used to get drunk and wallow upon the floor together. The second of these Irving suppers was in honour of Barnum, and there I met Clement Scott, Jos. Knight, J. L. Toole, Beerbohm Tree, Oakey Hall, Edmund Yates, Comyns Carr, Ed. Routledge and perhaps a dozen equally interesting people. I have lunched at the Century Club with J. R. Osgood, and a capital fellow he is—a typical New England rounder. One of my old Williams College classmates is here—Isaac Henderson, rich and cordial. He lives here and his handsome house is in a fashionable quarter. He is writing novels; you may have seen his "The Prelate" and "Agatha Page." I have not been agreeably disappointed in Lang; he is a typical Oxford graduate, cadaverous, sickly-looking, furtive-eyed and evidently very egotistical. Still, as I have seen him but twice, I should perhaps not flatter myself that I know him.

My children are in Hanover at school and are well and happy. Pinny is acquiring the German very rapidly. Mrs. Field is just at present absorbed in "Christmas purchases, or the secret art of making

£5 go into 20 shillings." I find that being poor costs a good deal of money. Yet why should I complain? Nay, I do not; I am grateful that I have compassed, wrought with, and subjugated the internal rebellion that threatened to undo me three months ago. As your favourite poet has sung, so I repeat with emphasis:

> "What care I for store of wealth
> So long as I am rich in health?
> The rosy cheek and fireful eye
> Are boons no sordid gold can buy,
> Nor is a Crœsus half as blest
> As he whose stomach can digest.
> Those boons I have in goodly store
> And, what is better, furthermore,
> I have a brain that's keen and strong
> And heart that's free from every wrong——
> The which (I'll add) is why this song.
> "E. F."

By the way, I would have you know that the foregoing is an "autograph poem with signature in initials, quite unpublished and unique"; to pursue the vernacular of the greedy, grasping trade, it is worth about seven shillings sixpence.

Well, now, if I have anything to add it is to give my compliments to your wife and to my sometime coparceners in crime in the *Daily News* office, and to express the hope that you will think—if not so often, at least as affectionately of me as I always think of you and yours.

EUGENE FIELD.

20 Alfred Place, Bedford Square, W. C.,
LONDON, DECEMBER THE 11TH, 1889.

II

During his later stay in London Field grew better acquainted with Lang and came to like him well. He also came to know more of Lang's very good friend, Rider Haggard, of whose books about that time, Lang said, to the scandal of literary London, that they showed their writer to be a greater genius than Robert Louis Stevenson. Field met Haggard again at a book publishers' dinner at the Holborn Restaurant. He wrote after that meeting:

Haggard has not a particularly prepossessing personality; he looks like a good-natured boy. His head is small and his nose is large; he has blue eyes and red cheeks; his manner is that of a loose-jointed, companionable fellow.

Field gave this description of Lang after he had become well acquainted with that writer:

He is unquestionably the foremost literary power in London at the present time. Among his associates he is simply revered as a being of superhuman genius. In person he is tall, spare, dark, with a noble forehead, dark, furtive eyes, and an ample lower jaw. He is as nervous as a cat and he gives the impression of being in delicate health. He has the Oxford drawl and a very nervous laugh. His hair is thick and beautifully frosted—Austin Dobson has called it "brindled."

The quotation is, of course, from Dobson's line:

Dear Andrew with the brindled hair.

Field greatly enjoyed discussing fairy lore with Lang, whose long succession of books of fairy tales had no more appreciative reader than the Chicago poet. In Lang's library Field roamed about with immense satisfaction. He wrote at the time:

Lang's home is most attractive. The best people are to be met there, and the Langs are charming entertainers. The house is full of beautiful things. Lang's library overflows with the rare, the curious, and the lovely, but Lang is careless in his treatment of his books; treasures are piled into cases and shelves in double rows, and the utmost diligence seems to have been observed in avoiding anything like a display of the rarities in which the large collection abounds.

Field asked Lang at one of their meetings whether he contemplated visiting America. Lang replied humorously: "Haggard and I have been talking about going to the States on a joint lecturing tour. At one time we had it all made up that I was to lecture upon the subject of

'Book Hunting' and Haggard was to follow with a lecture upon 'Rat Hunting.'" Haggard as an ardent country squire had been contributing papers to the agricultural press of England upon methods of exterminating rodent pests. At a later time Lang wrote in a light-hearted letter to Field: "As to visiting the States, I expect to lay my bones there as a literary hack." In another letter, written to Field after Field's return to Chicago, Lang thus expressed himself:

What a very funny poet Miss Dickinson must have been! I am adventuring myself in Sidney Lanier; perhaps he is a trifle too exotic. I hope you are well and flourishing and falling a victim, like me, alas! to books you ought not to buy—such as the first edition of Keats' first poems. Peccavi!

Field picked up somewhere a story of an old Scotchman at a New York dinner party who, when the talk took a literary turn, spoke of a nephew of his who had disappointed him greatly by becoming a writer.

"What is your nephew's name?" asked a fellow guest.

"His name is Andrew Lang. Did you ever hear of him?"

"Did I ever hear of Andrew Lang! Why, he is one of the greatest literary men in England to-day."

"Ah," sighed the old Scotchman, "'tis all verra weel to talk, but had he the grace o' God in his heart he would ha' made sic a gra-and meenister!"

III

One of the results of Field's stay in London was the renewal of his acquaintance with Oscar Wilde. The story of Field's prank in Denver when Wilde was to lecture there has been told in various ways. The day before Wilde's arrival Field attired himself in a Bunthorne costume and rode about the city in an open carriage, lan-

guishingly holding a lily in his hand and permitting the
beholders to think him Wilde. Field and Wilde met the
next day and Wilde took Field's joke in good part,
pronouncing it a bit of profitable publicity for his lecture.
Indeed, the two immediately took a liking to each other.
In London Field saw much of Wilde and was delighted
with his brilliant conversation. Field wrote:

Oscar Wilde is certainly the most charming conversationalist in all
England, and if he is particularly eloquent upon any one subject that
one subject is reading in bed. He says that for years he has been
addicted to this fascinating habit; that he reads himself to sleep and
that as soon as he wakes in the morning he reaches for his book.
"The habit grows on me. Often I find myself disposed to lie in bed
all day, reading. I read with amazing rapidity. When I was a boy at
school I was looked upon as a prodigy by my associates, because,
quite frequently, I would, for a wager, read a three-volume novel in
half an hour so closely as to be able to give an accurate résumé of the
plot of the story; by one hour's reading I was enabled to give a fair
narrative of the incidental scenes and the most pertinent dialogue."
Upon the mention of Andrew Lang's name, Mr. Wilde remarked
with the utmost gentleness and suavity: "Perhaps you do not know
it, but upon several occasions Lang has disembowelled me."

To Wilde Field was indebted for this story which interested him greatly:

Lady Wilde came into possession of a vast amount of fairy and folk
lore through the assistance of her husband, Sir William Wilde.
Most of the material for her "Fairy Legends of Ireland" and for her
"Ancient Charms and Cures of Ireland" was collected by Sir William
with the aid of his charity patients in the hospital of which he was the
head for many years. To that hospital came for treatment patients
from every part of Ireland. Being fond of all manner of quaint
Irish tales, Sir William would ask his patients if they knew anything
about fairies or other strange people or odd adventures. If they said
they did he would have an attendant write down the stories. Those
who could think of no old tale were asked to promise that when they
went home they would hunt up the legends of their neighbourhood
and then would have the parish priest write them out and transmit
them to Sir William. Thus was collected a most charming mass of
fairy stories and folk lore.

Field profited by his acquaintance with Father Hegarty, whom he mentioned in his letter to me, by extracting from him stories of Father Prout. Here is one, as Field told it afterward:

The Rev. Canon Hegarty, whose parish is at Glenmire, County Cork, within sound of Shandon bells, and only six miles distant from Watergrass Hill—this reverend gentleman is very properly an enthusiastic admirer of Father Prout, as all who have heard him discourse of Prout or have heard him sing "The Bells of Shandon" will cheerfully testify. Father Hegarty kindly gives me an anecdote of Prout which I do not remember to have seen in print. "My late bishop told me," says he, "that when he was completing his collegiate course (a brilliant one) old Father Prout invited him to come and stay with him at Watergrass Hill. He went, and, being in orders but not yet a priest, he was devoutly attending Mass within the sanctuary of Prout's church the Sabbath morning after his arrival in Cork. One of the congregation was a certain Captain Nagle, a Catholic magistrate or petty judge who was generally revered and was a most austere man. Old Prout duly faced the congregation and preached the word of God to them in *hic ipsissimus verbis:* "Ah, ye set of villains, I often told ye my heart was broke for ye! But I said I'd manage ye yet! There's Captain Nagle there and he couldn't angle ye. I couldn't do anything with ye, ye set! But d'ye see that young man there? I brought him all the way from Maynooth College for ye; he knows how to settle matters in this parish. He knows Hebraic and Chaldaic and Syriac and all the acts, and if he and Captain Nagle up there in the gallery can't manage ye I won't know what to do with ye at all!"

Field's remark in his Christmas letter to me that Mrs. Humphry Ward was "accounted the most brilliant talker in England" indicates that he had a proper regard for that noted lady's intellectual prowess. However, his gamesome method of conversing with her has been told in various ways. Field related the story to me in considerable detail and made it clear that neither clownishness nor impudence entered into his mood. His one desire was to make a telling protest against the superciliousness of culture as he found it in evidence about him and to align himself squarely with the people of his own community.

"Mr. Field," said Mrs. Ward—thus Field related the conversation to me—"do you not find the social atmosphere of Chicago exceedingly crude, furnishing one with little intellectual companionship?"

"Really, Mrs. Ward," responded the author of "Culture's Garland," "I do not consider myself competent to give an opinion on the matter. Please bear in mind that up to the time Barnum captured me and took me to Chicago to be civilized I had always lived in a tree in the wilds of Missouri."

Though Mrs. Ward may have been taken aback by this reply to her query, she could have been in no doubt as to its meaning. She must have been quick to realize that the Westerner was bristling in defence of his fellow townsmen, because he would not have it thought in London literary circles that he deemed himself better or more brilliant than the people back home. Barnum was then in London exhibiting his "greatest show on earth" and was one of the lions of the day among the novelty-loving smart folk of the British capital. Thus Field's claim that he was one of the mighty showman's jungle curiosities was particularly apt.

IV

Irving's dinner to Barnum in the Beefsteak Room of the Lyceum Theatre doubtless was in recognition not only of the famous circus owner but also of the old-time theatrical manager, the man of courage and vision who had made so great a success of Jenny Lind's American tour many years before. At that dinner Barnum made a felicitous speech which has been frequently quoted. It was in response to the toast, offered by Irving, "To my dear old friend, the showman." Barnum said in his speech that his old-time museum in New York had served as a training school for many who afterward became famous on the American stage. He had always been proud of his connection with the dramatic and operatic professions. He had written the story of his life twenty years earlier and had added a chapter every year since that time, so that the book had become twice as large as it was when first published. He had come to be an old man, past eighty years of age, and sometimes he suspected that he was doomed to live forever.

Field picked up the following anecdote at the dinner:

Near the farther end of the table sat an impressive-looking gentleman wearing a single eyeglass, In answer to my question as to who the gentleman was, Mr. Tree said, "Can it be possible that you do not recognize the great Bancroft?" And then Mr. Tree told me this story: Some years ago Mr. and Mrs. Bancroft made a marvellously beautiful production of "The Merchant of Venice" at their theatre (the Prince of Wales Theatre, as I recollect). Ellen Terry played Portia, the cast was a powerful one, and the piece was superbly mounted—yet it was a financial failure. Upon one occasion Tree met Bancroft and in all sincerity complimented him upon the grandeur of the production, and he sincerely deplored the circumstance that the public did not seem to appreciate the excellence of the work. "Alas!" said Bancroft in his most impressive basso tones, "there is another circumstance of which posterity will never become aware." "And what is that?" asked Tree. "It is the fact," answered Bancroft, "that I was the inventor of the single shirt stud for gentlemen's evening wear."

From his old college mate at Williams, Isaac Henderson, Field had this story at the time of their association in London:

In 1876, Henderson, then a young man, was assistant to his father, the publisher of the New York *Evening Post*. In the tense days following the national election, when the dispute as to whether Hayes or Tilden had been chosen President was at its height, William Cullen Bryant, then editor of the *Post*, authorized the sending of telegrams to the rival candidates, asking them to express their opinions of the electoral commission which had been appointed to decide the controversy.   No replies were received the first day, and there was not much expectation that either Hayes or Tilden would respond to the request.   So the younger Henderson as a joke prepared a bogus telegram and sent it up to the editorial department by a boy.   It read:

Editor *Evening Post*, New York City.   At this time it is for the people and not for the candidates to speak.

R. B. HAYES.

Soon Henderson discovered that great excitement prevailed in the office and that preparations for an extra edition were under way.   He saw that he must explain and be quick about it.   Hurrying up to the editorial department, he found almost the whole force in Mr. Bryant's room; the venerable chief himself sat in the centre of the circle of his associates, holding in his hand the identical telegram which Henderson had written.

"Come in, Henderson," called Mr. Bryant to the new arrival; "come in and hear the message we have just received from General Hayes."   Then he impressively read the telegram: "At this time it is for the people and not for the candidates to speak."   Turning to those about him, the aged poet-journalist said: "Gentleman, *that* is the utterance of a statesman."

Thereupon Henderson made his confession.   When he had done Mr. Bryant asked quietly: "So you wrote those lines, did you, Henderson?"

Henderson responded in the affirmative.

Mr. Bryant took up the paper and again read, even more slowly than before: "At this time it is for the people and not for the candidates to speak."   Then he turned to those around him.   "Gentlemen," he said, "upon reading these lines a second time and more carefully than before, I think we are all convinced that they express such a

commonplace as any one might have written.   They set
forth what any one might have said if in the position before
the country now held by the contestants for the presidency.   Let us say no more upon the subject, gentlemen."

Here are two pictures of literary London of his day
which were supplied by Field:

Mr. Walter Besant looks like a well-to-do business man; he is stout,
has a florid complexion, wears spectacles and a full beard, and his
address is cordial and earnest.   I should say that he would enjoy a
good dinner; that he was a prudent man in every way; that he had
great tenacity of purpose; that his views generally would be broad
rather than high; that he was a man with a mission involving the bet-
terment of his fellowmen.   I think that the most agreeable book
written by Mr. Besant is that entitled "The French Humorists."

R. D. Blackmore, known the world over as the author of "Lorna
Doone," continues to write with all his old-time assiduity and with
much of his old-time force.   He is a brisk old gentleman and as a sort
of avocation or amusement he cultivates grapes and fruits in his large
garden in one of the suburbs of London.   Some time ago he discovered
that one of his gardeners had purloined and sold twenty-five dollars'
worth of pears, and the old gentleman has been in a condition of great
mental perturbation ever since.   "Lorna Doone" has reached its
eighteenth edition!   And everybody who reads it wonders whether
it were possible for any man to be strong enough to pull the muscle out
of another man's arm.   Blackmore has received thousands of letters
on this subject.

His indefatigable searching for novelties in London's
old bookshops resulted in Field's obtaining a curious
glimpse into the character of a beloved woman poet.   Of
her he wrote:

Christina Rossetti, the sister of the poet, is a lovely, white-haired
woman now; she lives in Torrington Square, quite in that quarter
where the Americans find comfortable lodging houses.   Miss Rossetti has been very charitable; in fact, her charities have exceeded
her income to such an extent that she is in comparative poverty now.
She has been frightfully imposed upon from time to time; I have
picked up a number of her letters written to a certain imposter in
London who, pretending to want, wheedled this kindly lady out of

many a pound.   The letters of the amiable woman, inclosing money
to relieve the wretched beggar's alleged wants, are marvels of pathos,
for she speaks of her own poverty.

Field noted that copies of the first edition of Miss
Rossetti's early poems were then in demand among book
collectors at thirty-five dollars a copy.

V

One English writer with whom Field became well acquainted after his return to the United States he did not
meet while abroad.   That was Conan Doyle.   George
M. Millard said about the time of Field's death: "When I
was returning to this country last year Conan Doyle was
among the ship's passengers.   When he found out that I
was from Chicago he asked me about Field.   'We are
watching him very closely on the other side,' said Doctor
Doyle.   Later Doyle met Field in Chicago, and the
friendship which sprung up between them was warm."

The way that friendship began is a story in itself.   Before Field met Doyle, but after Doyle had begun his
American tour, Field published the following in his column:

Of all the unsightly, unserviceable trumpery now being put forth
as publications the Conan Doyle books are the most unsightly and
most unserviceable.   They are a libel upon the art of book-making,
badly printed, badly stitched, badly bound.   There ought to be a
law prohibiting the sale of such monstrosities.

In the interests of a better popular taste many of our native authors
are providing that their works shall be published in a dainty and
durable style.   Within the last five years book-making has had a
splendid impetus here, and recently some very beautiful specimens of
this art have been issued.   It is with a view of protecting this noble
industry that we protest against the cheap-john methods of Conan
Doyle's cheap-john publishers.

Observe that Field says—he wrote the words in 1894—
that the great advance in book-making in the United

States had come about "within the last five years." His "A Little Book of Western Verse" and his "A Little Book of Profitable Tales" had appeared exactly five years before. From the time of their appearance, because of their popularity and their physical beauty, Field had found himself in a position to lead a militant movement for the making of beautiful books. And the leadership he supplied was strong, unwavering, and effective. His personal friends stood by him in the movement, purchasing at high prices limited large-paper editions that paid for the plates from which later the popular editions were printed.

Not long after he had denounced the bad book-printing exemplified in Doyle's publications in this country Field met Doyle. Characteristically, Field had in his pocket the worst specimen of Doyle's badly printed and badly bound books that he could find. It was "At the Sign of the Four." With a countenance all innocence Field presented the volume to Doyle to be autographed. Doyle was equal to the occasion. Being a sufferer from American pirated editions of his works he wrote above his signature:

> This bloody pirate stole my sloop
> And holds her in his wicked ward.
> Lord send that, walking on my poop,
> I see him kick at my main-yard!

These lines delighted Field, and from that time forward he was a sworn friend of Doyle's. Six months or so later there appeared in an Atlanta newspaper a story concocted by some jester to the effect that a group of Atlanta police detectives, having been shown photographs of Doyle and Field, had pronounced them veritable portraits of a certain two well-known professional criminals. A copy of the newspaper containing the story was sent to Field. He in turn sent it to Doyle, who was then in Switzerland. Doyle, appreciating the joke, wrote in a letter to Field:

How extraordinary that the detectives should have got *you* so accurately and come to such grief over *me* !   I have read your last book to my little girl and you have sneak-thieved her heart away—so I can prove one conviction against you.

There was another vigorous young British author whom Field did not meet but whom he admired and for whom he demanded fair play in the midst of the general uproar produced in the United States by the young man's book of travel sketches, "From Sea to Sea."   Field wrote:

The truth would seem to be that Mr. Kipling is an unusually bright fellow, who enjoys a somewhat exaggerated opinion of his own brightness; it is quite natural that he should be somewhat swollen in vanity, for he has been flattered to an amazing degree since he woke up one morning to find himself famous.   We certainly should expect to find youth susceptible to the charms of compliment, and we are free to confess that we recognize a distinct loveliness in that freedom and confidence with which youth gives expression to those views which it invariably has upon all human things.   . . .

We hope that Mr. Kipling will go ahead with cracking his whip; he is young and lusty and full of fight, and these things help to keep other things moving.   We have much more respect for the sauciness of youth than we have for the hypocrisy of age; in other words, when we think of the absurd flatteries and lying arts which certain foreigners have employed to mulct us of our money and good opinion we are disposed to regard Mr. Kipling's combative pertness as refreshing and praiseworthy to a degree.

About the same period Field wrote:

Why not give Mr. Rudyard Kipling a rest?   The poor fellow has trouble enough in hand, now that Andrew Lang has got after him with a sharp stick.   Don't let us interrupt the fun, for—

There is no other thing in this life so delighting
As getting those critical British to fighting;
To the callous old Scot and the callow young stripling
We gleefully shout: "Go it, Lang!   Go it, Kipling!"

XVIII

DIVERSIONS OF A HOMESICK AMERICAN

I

WHILE Field was in London he was preparing the way for the widening of his fame in no inconsiderable degree by merely writing letters of advice and admonition to his children in school in Hanover. They were beautiful compositions in more ways than one. Experienced educators have pronounced them the best in existence for the stimulation of school children's interest in their studies and for the awakening of respect for their teachers, regard for their parents, and affection for one another. Published in a volume with carefully selected child poems by Field, the letters are widely used in the schools. If Field were to return to earth I believe nothing would give him greater happiness than the knowledge that he is thus influencing the minds and helping to develop the imaginations of many thousands of little folk. For Field frequently lamented the ruthless intellectual slaughter of the innocents that went on when the blessed gift of wondering was destroyed in child minds by a world of unimaginative grown-ups. He deplored the methods employed in stuffing children with facts, and making them dull and priggish and sophisticated. On one occasion he wrote:

It is pretty clear to us that we are not going to have any literature in this country of ours until our children are encouraged in the reading of fairy tales. For very many years we have been altogether too practical to deserve a decent literature. We give our boys bear stories to read and our girls are fed upon literature that treats of fashionable school life, of débuts, of love, etc., *ad nauseam*. Boys are taught "how to make money"; girls are taught "how to catch men."

The average juvenile magazine now patronized in America is just about as meretricious an instructor as ingenuity could devise. We read one of these fashionable stories the other day—just out of curiosity. It was all about two boys who used to rob orchards; their *modus operandi* was dwelt upon at hideous length. One of the boys was finally overcome by remorse, repented, reformed, and became a prosperous merchant; the other boy continued in his evil ways and died a felon. Pooh!

We are not going to have a fine American fiction until we have encouraged, trained, and cultivated in our children the God-gift, fancy. This gift first manifests itself in the trait which is vulgarly called lying, and all children have it to a degree. It is a beautiful inheritance; it may develop into an evil habit or it may redound gloriously to the advantage of humanity—it depends largely upon the discrimination and the care which the parents bestow upon its development. The trouble with parents in this country is that they consistently and incontinently set about killing the juvenile fancy as soon as it discovers itself; fancy is deemed impractical in these busy times of ours. Yet it was the fancy of Milton, of Dante, and of Bunyan that placed their names high on the scroll of immortality; yes, and fancy has made famous the best and brightest men and women literature has known.

II

Field was delighted with his experiences in Germany and Holland during his stay in Europe, and they furnished him with themes for many of his poems of that period. He acknowledged his peculiar indebtedness to "Studies in Folk Song," by Countess Montenegro-Cesaresco, a volume of essays on the folklore of Venice, Greece, Armenia, Sardinia, Corsica, and other lands. From this source he obtained the material which he wove into his "Corsican Lullaby," his "Telka," his "The Partridge" and his "The Brook and the Boy." I have the manuscript of the last-named poem. It bears Field's signature and the date line, London, January 10, 1890.

Field has left a record of his dippings into other collections of folk songs. For example, he wrote:

Very little comfort does a dyspeptic get out of Armenian folk poetry. I have just been reading the curious little volume printed at

Venice in 1867 by the monks of San Lazarus— "Armenian Popular Songs." This particular poem has amused me much; its title is, "On a Little Knife Lost":

> "My knife was very affectionate with me;
> When we went into the houses of others,
> When we saw the meat roasting or in broth,
> It did not let me take the curds," etc.

The favourite themes with Armenian poets seem to have been flowers, storks, cranes, partridges, and pancakes.

The many amusing poems written by Field on German themes reflect his high good humour with that country. He had one story to tell of a German joke of which he was the victim. A citizen of Hamburg with whom he became acquainted insisted to Field that Americans were lazy because they never walked and asserted that the average American did not walk a mile a day. Field retorted that on the contrary Americans were great walkers and thought nothing of starting out for a walk of five miles or more. Thereupon the German expressed the belief that Field was incapable of walking five miles. Field accepted the challenge and the test began forthwith. "I walked four mortal hours," said Field, "before my humorous friend casually told me that a German mile was equal to four and a half English miles and that therefore I was bound to walk twenty-two and a half English miles to fulfil my contract."

Dutch literature in all its branches Field found a disappointment. Dutch poetry, he complained, had "neither windmills nor wooden shoes in it." Failing to find in them any national characteristics, he declared that Dutch prose and Dutch verse alike had no interest for him. "Yet Holland itself," he said, "is marked and lovely in its individuality. It is hard to understand why there does not appear in its literature some symptom of the delicious personality that is everywhere to be seen and met with between the North Sea and the German boundary line."

And Field, of course, went shopping for wooden shoes in Holland. This is the way he told about it:

When I was in Amsterdam I searched for half a day before I found a place where I could buy a pair of wooden shoes. All around me were children and adults wearing wooden shoes, but none seemed to know where the article could be bought. One night about eight o'clock I was still hunting for wooden shoes. A gentleman and his wife thought I had lost my way—they spoke English and they accosted me. I unburdened my woe, and they told me that in a certain street, four blocks east and then two blocks to the left, I would be able to find what I wanted. The streets of Amsterdam run every way, round, diagonally, and cater-cornered. I kept on walking for an hour and might have been walking yet but that I wearied of the pursuit and abandoned it. Returning, however, to the Hotel Daelin, I had to pass through a narrow lane, and here I found a curious little dive filled with such homely wares as tallow candles, brooms, and wooden shoes. The shoes cost about twelve cents a pair. I bore a pair with me in triumph to the hotel, followed by a troop of clamorous gamins. The impudent little rapscallions wore wooden shoes themselves, yet you'd have thought by the way they followed me and hallooed at those shoes that they had never seen a pair of wooden shoes in all their lives.

III

By far the greater part of Field's fourteen months abroad was passed in London, where he was a prey to loneliness and dyspepsia. The number of complaints he made about English ways and English institutions is astonishing. Indeed, he was a militant American in every sense of the word, thanking God daily that his country was different, far different from the land of his exile. Many of the poems he wrote while in Europe are tinged with homesickness. Witness the verses on the Missouri coon in the Berlin zoo, "John Smith, U. S. A.," and various others. The fondness for Chicago shown by him on all occasions affords one more proof that his innumerable gibes at that city's pretensions to culture were so many efforts to spur it on to accomplish something worth while in the direction toward which it vaguely aspired. Field's habitually sunny nature did not prevent him from picking flaws unmercifully with English ways of doing things. A few of his observations at that time will illustrate his general mood.

English cigars he declared to be "notoriously just a little the worst cigars in all the world." "I think," he added, "that that must be the reason why most Englishmen prefer a pipe." He went on:

The popular cigar (if there be any) is one of home manufacture and it costs tu'pence (four cents!). The charge for one hundred is at the same rate, no reduction being made on a large order. A friend of mine here always buys his cigars by the thousand, and he pays a shilling apiece straight through; these cigars retail at a shilling apiece, and the dealers argue that my friend ought to pay more, rather than less, when he buys a quantity.

This curious policy obtains in Cuba to an embarrassing extent. A friend of mine, piloting a party over the island, applied to one of the railways for a dozen tickets. He was told that, as a special favour, he would be given the tickets at regular tariff rates—"but," continued the officer, "hereafter when you want to make the trip we shall have to charge you extra rates when you bring a party."

"Why so?" demanded my friend.

"Because," explained the officer, "so large a party necessitates our putting on another car."

Fred Berger, the dramatic manager, once applied for accommodations for eleven people at a Connecticut country boarding house.

"Our reg'lar rates is a dollar a day," said the old landlady, "but seein' there's so many ov ye we shall have to charge ye a dollar an' a quarter a day apiece."

Field complained of the weather in England, of the scarcity of bathtubs, of the fee for washing one's face in a public lavatory, of the tips taken by officials at the royal mews, of being perpetually cold. Writing in March, he said:

I have been in London since the middle of October and I have shivered nearly all the time. I go along the streets and I see the natives shivering, too—shivering with their hands in their trousers pockets, their shoulders humped up and their legs drawn up like a

thoroughbred terrier's.   But they affect to believe that their shivery
condition is healthful!

The grate fire is the popular instrument of artificial heat—not the
generous grate fire you might expect to find, but a ridiculous little hole
in the chimney, eighteen inches above the floor, with a capacity for
perhaps a quart of coals.   I use the word "coals" premeditatedly.
In the States we burn coal; here they burn coals.   We buy our coal by
the ton; here they buy it from day to day by the sack (of 100 pounds).
Purchased in driblets, coal becomes coals.

Women's shoes in England were pronounced by Field
"large and ill fitting."   He added: "The truth is that
English women have big feet—abnormally big feet."
That, however, was not all.   "Lacing is a vice that obtains very generally among women of this country; nowhere else are to be seen such slender waists as are to be
found here."   But there was worse to follow.

Another abominable practice that obtains among English women
is that of indulging in spiritous liquors.   Gin, rum, and Scotch
whisky are freely taken by women of every class here.   I suspect that
if English houses were better heated there would be a much smaller
demand for liquor.   As it is, everybody drinks more or less (generally
more) in order to keep warm.

Fortunately for English women, they did not smoke—
at least in public—in Field's day.

The ordinary American tourist who came within the
range of Field's vision did not impress him at all favourably.   He expressed himself on this subject in the following fashion:

Europe seems to be infested with two distinct classes of Americans
—the one quite as disagreeable as the other.   The first class is represented by the man who noisily asserts his Americanism on every
occasion.   The vulgar creature makes a practice of finding fault with
everybody and everything; as soon as he arrives he wishes he were
home again; he swaggers and bloviates, snarls and brags.   The second
class of disagreeable Americans is composed of those who not only
hear with seeming satisfaction but also indorse with emphasis every
disparaging remark passed upon the United States by foreigners.

IV

While he was in London Field wrote much of the old book-dealers whom he met, but not in a very cheerful vein, though he made numerous purchases from them, includ-ing many extremely interesting old play-bills. Appar-ently he did not particularly care for the tribe of London dealers. However, he was fascinated by "the truly great shop of the veteran E. W. Stibbs" in Oxford Street. Field pronounced Stibbs "a typical bookseller of the old school," who was then "nearly eighty years of age, in business fifty-one years, full of reminiscence and anecdote and carrying a stock of eighty thousand volumes."

Of Quaritch, Field wrote:

Quaritch is called the king of London booksellers, but he does not interest me half so much as Stibbs does. Quaritch runs to Latin folios and Arabic manuscripts, to the prayer books of defunct royalty and all that sort of thing—good enough, perhaps, for bibliopelts and freakomaniacs, but of little value to one in love with the English tongue as it has been written and immortalized.

Field set down the following reflections on the vicissi-tudes of a newly arrived book lover in London in his day:

There is, of course, a certain amount of experience which every visiting collector must undergo, and that experience costs money. For example, the bibliomaniac, upon reaching London, plunges head-long into Holywell Street, where Booksellers' Row is located, and where the descendants of the Forty Thieves made famous by the Ara-bian tale do business in their own peculiar, piratical way. The hap-less victim is quickly plucked; when he comes to his senses he taboos Smut lane as he would a robbers' roost or a charnel house.

That place of evil memory having been wiped out with the widening of the Strand, London is now so much the better. But some of the other abuses listed by Field still survive. Of the London practice of giving first rights to favoured customers, a practice which caused Field special annoyance, he had this to say:

Lady M. has her pick of the old china; my Lord B. is accorded the first inspection of swords and canes; Professor L. has the refusal of all new prints—and so the outrageous complication runs. Still, in the debris one is likely to find a vast lot of delightful stuff. Think of picking up a Paganini bill for twenty-five cents; a Charles Kemble for two cents; a Peg Woffington for one dollar; a Booth (Junius Brutus) for two cents; a Forrest for two cents; a Kean, a Buckstone, a Hacket, for four cents each!

Field set down also this complaint:

Nearly every book dealer in London is a publisher. Consequently if you seek a particular book it is hard to procure it at once unless you know the name and location of the publishing house. There are certain dealers—notably Hanchard in Piccadilly—who will get any book that is in print and can be got; but they require time. Go into any shop and ask for an item and the chances are nine to one that the answer will be: "No, we haven't it, but we can get it for you." In every little nine-by-four shop you hear talk about "our factory." "We shall have to send down to our factory" for this article or that. This sort of thing makes even strong men very weary.

Here is one more sample of the fruits of Field's observations in the old bookshops of London:

The chapbook has always fascinated me. Its quaintness, homeliness, simplicity and sincerity are qualities which would seem to appeal with special directness and force to the lover of the curious in literature, and the enormous prices that are paid for certain specimens indicate that not all these grotesque little prints are to be esteemed as mere trumpery. Some very pretty samples of Bewick's work are to be met with in chapbooks sold near the beginning of the present century, although as a rule chapbook illustrations are crude and coarse to a degree. The text is not always refined; in fact, the chapbook is particularly interesting to the student as reflecting the spirit of its time and as giving us a picture of prevailing customs and manners as well as acquainting us with contemporary literary taste. We must understand, however, that the chapbook was made for the lowly class of readers—that class of people which patronized the chapman, and bought not only their literature but their buttons, needles, pins, thread, jewelry, and miscellaneous gewgaws of him. The peddlers we encounter daily at our street corners, vending cheap kerchiefs and buttons and shoe-strings, are modernized, corrupted, degenerate evolutions of the ancient chapmen, those versatile geniuses who, by means of a song or a neatly executed jig, or of shrewd and kindly repartee, ingratiated themselves at once in the favour of hussifs and bartered their motley stock for those good dames' savings.

V

A frequent companion of Field's in his tours of the book-shops of London was a native of Vermont then residing in the English capital, one George Herrick.   For a consider-able time it had been a favourite joke of Field's to go into a bookshop and with an air of great solemnity ask the proprietor for an expurgated edition of the poems of Mrs. Felicia Hemans or of the works of Hannah More.   Herrick on some occasions had participated in this joke.   One day when he and Field were walking together he stopped in front of a bookshop and said: "I know the man who keeps this shop.   He is the most solemn of mortals and he never sees a joke.   Go in and ask him for an expurgated edition of Mrs. Hemans's poems.   He will fall over with astonish-ment.   I'll stay outside at first, for I once played a joke on him and he has never forgiven me.   If he sees me he will suspect that I put you up to making game of him. I'll just happen to appear in time to see the fun."

Field agreed to the plan.   He entered the shop and asked in his deepest bass tones whether he might obtain there an expurgated copy of the poems of Mrs. Felicia Hemans. The bookseller showed no astonishment at the question. "Yes, I have it," he said directly.   "But the book is very rare and costly.   Will you pay a fair price for it?"

Field thought to himself: "This fellow is a priceless numskull or else he thinks he can brazen it out.   He'll be great fun."   Aloud he said: "Of course I'll pay a fair price for it.   Bring it out.   I haven't very much time."

The bookseller placed a badly bound little volume in

Field's hands, saying: "Here it is. The price is one guinea."

Field hastily opened the book at its title page and read:

The Poems of Mrs. Felicia Hemans. Selected and Arranged, with all Objectionable Passages Excised, by George Herrick, Editor of "Isaac Watts for the Home," "The Fireside Hannah More," etc.

Silently paying down his money, Field took the book and departed. He found no Herrick awaiting him at the shop door. The next day he received a letter from his friend saying that Herrick had been called to Lambeth Palace to collaborate with the Bishop of London in preparing an edition of "The Pilgrim's Progress" that would give the youth of the land knowledge of the strength and the literary excellence of John Bunyan without bringing a blush to the cheek of modesty.

VI

One of Field's collecting triumphs consisted in inducing Gladstone to give him the ax with which that great man was wont to fell trees at Hawarden. That souvenir was perhaps Field's most highly prized possession among all the rarities that he managed to collect. It was always prominently displayed in his study. Having been a bit of a woodsman in my youth, whenever I beheld that ax the thought came to me that Gladstone must indeed have been a great man to be able to chop down trees with so clumsy an instrument. Indeed it seemed to me an ill-made, badly balanced tool that an American timber-man would have scorned. However, its possession made Field very happy, as did the possession of the scissors of Charles A. Dana, his favourite editorial hero.

Field recorded that he tried to procure a claymore at an antiquarian shop in Edinburgh, but the proprietor, aged eighty-five years, who had been in the business of buying and selling antiques for sixty years, could not tell him where one could be procured and asserted that he himself had seen but three claymores in his life. Some years before, when Melville E. Stone, after disposing of his interest in the *Daily News*, was about to sail for Europe for an extended pleasure trip, he asked Field: "What present shall I buy John Ballantyne?" "Buy him a claymore," said Field. "Any Scotchman would like to have one." So Stone searched Scotland for a claymore, but in vain. Doubtless Field had his brother-in-law in mind when he in his turn went shopping for a claymore. In announcing failure Field added triumphantly:

But I have and hold the curious old chair which Charles Kean is said to have used in his London performances of "Hamlet." It is a staunch, quaint bit of furniture, the red baize badly motheaten, the gilt badly tarnished and the paint badly cracked.

VII

The stay of Field and his family in Europe ended in sorrow. Melvin, the eldest son, named after Field's good friend and second father, Melvin L. Gray of St. Louis, died suddenly in Hanover. He was a quiet, obedient boy. Field told me once that an attack of scarlet fever had left Melvin a little slower mentally than his brothers. Now that the boy was taken from him Field grieved deeply. He wrote a beautiful, consoling letter to his son Eugene (Pinny) soon after Melvin's death, calling Eugene his elder son, his chief reliance, and saying:

Melvin knows all the great mysteries now. He sees us and loves us just as of old; perhaps, unseen, he will join you in your play. Who knows but that God will appoint him to be your guardian angel?

A few days before Christmas, 1890, Field, his wife, and their surviving children returned to Chicago and the body of the dead boy was buried there in its German coffin.

XIX

Years of Growing Fame

I

ON RETURNING to the United States after fourteen months in Europe Field found his publishers amiably ready to issue additional books of his as speedily as he could provide them. His royalties from those already published were adding materially to his income. He believed himself to be once more in fair physical condition. Despite the depression due to the death of his eldest son, he faced the future with hope and high courage. His friends and admirers had become legion, the products of his pen were in demand, and his opportunities to give public readings at remunerative prices were only too abundant. He resumed his work regularly on the *Daily News* and was generally cheerful and contented.

I recall particularly Field's gay demeanour at a luncheon given to Stedman at the Richelieu Hotel in Chicago late in April, 1891. The host was Francis M. Larned, formerly a member of the *Daily News* staff, who had been my successor as that newspaper's dramatic critic. Among the half-dozen persons at the luncheon was Melville E. Stone, then a banker. Another guest, Edward J. McPhelim, was the brilliant young dramatic critic of the Chicago *Tribune*. Field's high spirits forbade one to think him physically below par. The invalids of the party were Stedman and McPhelim, each of whom had recently suffered a serious illness, and the two compared their experiences as convalescents in some detail. Stedman had been delivering lectures on modern literature in two or three colleges for young women, and he humorously prescribed for McPhelim that particular form of human endeavour, asserting that the abounding health of his massed audiences of earnest girl undergraduates had had a tonic effect upon his languid frame.

Field meantime was making audacious sallies in all directions, but mainly they were aimed at his right-hand table comrade, Stone, whom he accused of having deserted the ranks of ordinary, red-blooded humanity for the society of those modern kobolds, the financiers. "You used to be genial and accommodating," said Field, "but now, whenever I go into your bank, I observe that the entire force from the cashier down—doubtless by your instructions—is not doing much except watching me." Stedman, a seasoned victim of Field's grotesque untruths, also came in for a liberal share of his raillery. The afternoon was far spent before the flow of Field's merriment slackened.

Stedman had come to Chicago to address the Twentieth Century Club of that city. Field, on learning of the proposed visit several weeks earlier, announced in his column that a stupendous welcome was being arranged for the New York poet. That welcome, as Field outlined it, would have been worth going miles to see. Not only were there to be brass bands and a guard of honour on horseback, but all members of the Twentieth Century Club were to appear in carriages, while members of the local Robert Browning Club were to ride in buses and the local Homer Clubs were to march, "preceded by a fife and drum corps and a real Greek philosopher attired in a tunic." There was also to be "a beautiful young woman playing a guitar, symbolizing Apollo and his lute, in a car drawn by nine milk-white stallions impersonating the muses," not to mention "two hundred Chicago poets afoot," the Blue Island Avenue Shelley Club, the city fire department, and other attractions. Stedman has recorded his trepidation when he got off the train at Chicago that fateful day, fearing that some fantastic parade actually had been organized under Field's inspiration, and his relief on finding no one to welcome him except two or three personal friends, including the broadly smiling Field, who bore him away to the luncheon at the Richelieu.

II

Near the end of 1891 Dr. Frank W. Reilly resigned as managing editor of the *Daily News* and I was made his successor. Years later I learned that while I was under consideration for the position Field was consulted by Mr. Lawson in regard to my qualifications or my lack of them. Field's verdict appears to have been favourable on the whole, judging by one remark of his that has been repeated to me. Field said, greatly to the amusement of Mr. Lawson: "Dennis is quite a fellow—he has a bank account."

It did not take much of a bank account to impress Field; a bank account of any sort was a marvel to him. In this fascinating world of bookshops and curio shops he was constitutionally unable to put away so much as a dollar against a day of need. In his view a rare book was a bargain at any price—provided he had the price—though years might pass before he would be able to prove it to the satisfaction of family grocers and other tradesmen who chronically suffered from lack of vision. Meanwhile, why should he make his actions conform to the narrow, not to say sordid, views of such persons?

Field, however, was entirely honourable in money matters. And he was generous to a fault. But he relied upon his devoted and very competent wife to run the affairs of the household.   In his own hands money's proper purpose was to give pleasure to himself or to another, and the best way to give pleasure was to present one's self or a friend with some amusing book or with a fantastic gimcrack that would produce merriment.   From his point of view, deliberately to save money for future use showed amazing self-control and might even be worthy of commendation, but the act seemed to put the person who performed it into a class with such curious beasts as squirrels and chipmunks, which also gathered hoards, rather than with normal members of the human race.

I have heard it asserted on one or two occasions by persons who had no more than a slight acquaintance with him that Field was tainted with parasitism because he accepted gifts from wealthy friends and admirers.   Yet such gifts—a set of rare and costly books, perhaps, or a beautiful piece of library furniture—doubtless bestowed even more pleasure upon the giver than upon the recipient. To have money that one can conveniently spare is common enough, but to have as a friend such a joyous spirit as was Field is one of the rarest of blessings.   Thus it was that the obligation remained on the side of the giver, as the giver fully recognized, if he was worthy of possessing the friendship of a man whose friendship was prized by many of the most intellectual men of his day.   Field talked to me at various times of this or that wealthy acquaintance who had asked his permission to give him an acceptable token of the prospective donor's regard.   Sometimes Field would keep a matter of this sort in abeyance for months.   Then if the friendship prospered and a suitable gift suggested itself to Field—it was nearly always a rare book or a set of rare books—he would make known his wish quite frankly as an earnest of his own good will.   He coveted no man's wealth.   "The worst possible use to which one can

put money is to talk about it," he said upon one occasion
when he had grown disgusted at the uproar made over
the marriage of two wealthy young persons.

III

One of the perplexing tasks that fell to me on becoming
managing editor of the *Daily News* was that of exercising
proper discrimination while choosing between the ad-
missible and the inadmissible products of Field's un-
trammelled imagination that were submitted daily by him
for publication in "Sharps and Flats." To draw the line
between a flagrant untruth that was both amusing and
harmless and a prevarication that might prove painful or
injurious to the unoffending victim sometimes proved
decidedly difficult. Occasionally I found myself compelled by my sense of duty to butcher Field's copy unmercifully. On such occasions Field proved himself a
good soldier despite the rueful countenance he turned
upon me now and again. To my satisfaction, Mr. Lawson required me to submit to him all paragraphs and
parts of paragraphs that I scissored from Field's copy.
Sometimes, of course, he overruled me and returned to me
for publication matter that I had held out. At other
times he expressed astonishment that Field should have
thought certain lucubrations within the limits of toler-
ance. But possibly in such instances Field had merely
resorted to his old trick of writing a few outrageous paragraphs especially for the editorial censor to kill in order
that the executioner might feel such a virtuous glow of
self-commendation over duty performed that he would
refrain from condemning other paragraphs the publication
of which Field particularly desired, paragraphs only a
shade less outrageous than the others. I recall one rather
extended article of Field's that dealt fantastically with a
religious topic. I held it out and it came back to me

from my superior bearing the pencilled comment: "This is literally a holy terror!"

As time passed and Field found himself more and more absorbed in preparing new books for the press he avoided visitors and—at least in theory—conserved his strength by doing his writing at home. However, he frequently dropped in at the office for a social chat or to arrange some business matter, always heralding his approach by agonized yelpings as he ambled down the long hall to my room. From 1892 onward he rarely did any writing elsewhere than in his own study.

I have preserved some of the numerous notes that came to me at various times along with Field's copy. The following are typical examples of the missives:

DEAR DENNIS:
   Please run "All Aloney" to-morrow and keep the other bits of verse in type to be run at the head of the column later on. I am confined to the house with bronchitis. I should like to see proof of the "Cradle Song" and "The Bottle Tree."
                                             Sincerely yours,
                                                 EUGENE FIELD.
   Buena Park, Oct, 15, 1893.

DEAR DENNIS:
   You can run these verses when you please. I should like them on the editorial page but I do not care to have them headed "Sharps and Flats." When the piece is set up, please send the copy to Joseph Jefferson, Esq., McVicker's Theatre. Ask the printers to be careful with the copy—particularly so with the fairies on the last sheet. Please call off this hyperborean weather and give me a season of tropical warmth.
                                             Sincerely yours,
                                                 EUGENE FIELD.
   Buena Park, Dec. 4, 1893.

The verses mentioned in the preceding note are "Lady Button-Eyes." They were inscribed by Field to his old friend Jefferson. The little golden fairies with which the author had adorned the manuscript illustrated this couplet:

> While upon the haunted green
> Fairies dance about their queen.

DEAR DENNIS:

Will you please read the proof very carefully upon the verses? As I have had them in tow nearly two years and have revised them over and over again, and as I regard them as my best work in this particular line, I am naturally solicitous that they should not be marred by typographical errors.

E. F.

Oct. 21, 1894.

The poem which Field had worked over so long and so painstakingly, as he testifies in the note above, is the tender and beautiful "The Dead Child," written in memory of his son Melvin.

DEAR DENNIS:

Will you send me an order for $5 for Mrs. Head, whom I got to shorthand some paragraphs for me to-day? I wanted to cover all possibilities and found I could not do it without help. You will probably be able to pick out a column from the lot of stuff I send.

E. F.

1033 *Evanston Avenue, Station X.*
Chicago, Nov. 6, 1894.

This, I think, is the only time in his life that Field either employed a stenographer or sent in typewritten copy. He was preparing to go out of the city to give one or more public readings and so provided some advance material for his column.

DEAR DENNIS:

The Foote collection of Americana will be sold in N. Y. City by Bangs & Co., on Friday Nov. 23. The sale will be so extraordinary that I think it might be well to have something from your New York correspondent on the subject. The address of Bangs & Co. is 739 Broadway.

Hastily,

EUGENE FIELD.

Chicago, Nov. 21, 1894.

Field kept close track of all sales of rare books and was always eager to learn whatever he could about purchasers and prices, he having made an avid study of the sales catalogues.

DEAR DENNIS:
I take the liberty of sending a number of old Christmas poems which you may or may not care to use as miscellany.   Please preserve copy of my Luther Hymn.   I have fooled away the whole day whipping it into shape to lead S. & F.   And please see that Bethlem is printed as I write it.   What is the street number of your residence?   I have forgotten it.

E. F.

(*Undated*.)

Manifestly Christmas was near at hand when the foregoing note was written.   Field later presented me with the manuscript of the Luther hymn, which throughout is carefully lettered by his pen.   The title is done in red ink and the initial letters at the beginning of the stanzas are, in their order, red, gold, purple, and red.   "Christ Child" in both the first and the second stanzas is in gold; "Bethlem" in the third stanza is in red and "God" and "Child" in the last stanza are respectively in gold and red. Holly leaves in green appear between the stanzas and at the end of the poem.

DEAR DENNIS:
I must have caught cold in my teeth yesterday, for I have had to send for a dentist and he is on his way here now to do what he can to fix me up.   So I shall have no copy to-day, but I shall be all right as soon as I get either some fillings or some cocaine into these stumps.
Sincerely yours,
Jan. 6, 1895.   EUGENE FIELD.

DEAR DENNIS:
Better use up the chicken feed that is on the galleys.   Sorry not to have found you when I called yesterday about 4.

E. F.

10th.   (Otherwise undated.)

Dear Dennis:
   I find upon investigation that Daisy lost my copy yesterday.   I
am very much disgusted, as I think I had an unusually bright lot of
paragraphs.

                                                              E. F.
   (*Undated.*)

                              IV

   In the years when these notes were written—the last
years of Field's life—there were two or three long interruptions in his newspaper work.   One of the interruptions
was due to a serious illness which Field suffered, followed
by a somewhat extended period of convalescence.   A
multiplicity of outside distractions was mainly responsible
for the others.   Not only was he naturally deeply absorbed in his new volumes when they were in process of
manufacture, but he was a prime favourite at dinners such
as were frequently given by the Fellowship Club of Chicago, dinners which were elaborately dramatized, if I may
use the term in this connection, being provided with plot
and incident mainly as a result of Field's unflagging ingenuity.   Further, there were constant calls from communities both near and far for readings from his poems.   He
appeared for a time as the platform companion of Bill Nye
and James Whitcomb Riley; then he and George W. Cable
formed a partnership and gave a considerable number of
readings, Field having succeeded Mark Twain as Cable's
associate.   His splendid voice and his fine sense of dramatic values, together with the attractive selections from
his poems presented to his audiences, made Field's readings markedly successful.   Though the fatigue of travel and
of platform work told severely upon his strength, he gave
occasional readings up to the time of his death.   He
cordially hated this form of activity, but it provided him
with a quick and sure way of making money, so he continued to engage in it.   Here is his own whimsical view of
the drudgery involved in roaming about and reading from

one's own works before audiences that had paid for entertainment and were entitled to their money's worth:

The business of appearing in public as a reader of one's own writings is not as pleasant as a misguided few might fancy. To us there seems to be no more graceless occupation. The inconveniences of travel, the changes of climate, the vicissitudes of weather, the different tastes of different publics—these are but the beginnings of the inevitable horrors that attend upon the career of him who takes to the platform.

The bards and minstrels of old had an easier time of it. They played fewer but longer engagements. There were no one-night stands in those good old times. The "talented and popular" minnesinger did not have to jump from Weeping Water, Nebraska, to West Brookfield, Massachusetts. He wasn't compelled to do "Western dialect" one week and Horatian paraphrases the next. There were no way freights in those days, landing a fellow at his destination at 3:08 A.M. When a minnesinger came to town he came to stay for a month of Sundays, and there was nothing too good for him. If the critics objected to his poems or objected to the way he touched his light guitar he was disembowelled or otherwise reproved. The poet had things all his own way; royalty housed and fed him and people considered it a great honour to be permitted to hear him drone out the poems which, as likely as not, he had cribbed from worthier poets in a far-distant country. There was some show for platform poets in those dim, majestic ages. True, there were no lecture bureaus then, nor any railways, but humanity was kind and the walking was good.

George W. Cable has told this story illustrating Field's way of leaving Cable, during the time of their association, to attend to the unpleasant duty of dealing with people who required to be vigorously handled for the good of their souls:

A young man speaking for a local management that had engaged Field to give a public reading jointly with another author, and which, after having secured a special concession in price, had managed things feebly, took him aside at the last moment and asked a further abatement. "My dear fellow," was Field's affectionate reply, "I'm neither the man nor the sort of man for you to come to. Go to my partner; his heart is marble."

Field's detestation for platform work caused him to rebel at times. Edward W. Bok has told how Field, when other devices failed, pleaded illness one night as an excuse for not appearing with Cable in Philadelphia, and then joyously hastened to the playhouse where Francis Wilson and his company were presenting a new piece.   George H. Yenowine of Milwaukee, so devoted a friend of Field's that he was always ready to serve him hand and foot, frequently accompanied Field on his public reading trips, looking after the business features for his very unpractical comrade.   In telling how great was Field's hatred of being lionized, Yenowine said:

Often when on his reading tours the people of the city where he stopped would give him a reception.   When it was half through Field would come around and say, "I'm bored with this."   And so he would slip away and let the reception go on without him.   At such times Field insisted on looking into all the old bookshops and pawnshops of the place, and if he saw anything he wanted he bought it regardless of the price.

Doubtless on such occasions he felt justified in indulging his favourite extravagance as a solace for the boredom of giving profitable public readings.

v

In the last column of "Sharps and Flats" published before his death Field dwelt upon the hardships of appearing on the public platform.   His old friend, Bill Nye, whom he, when managing editor of the Denver *Tribune*, practically discovered—Nye was then conducting an obscure Western sheet, the Laramie *Boomerang*—had offended an audience in Paterson, N. J., and had been pelted with missiles on his way to the train.   In defence of Nye Field wrote:

If there is anything more vexatious or more wearing than travelling about the country in all kinds of weather and at the mercy of railroad trains and lecture bureaus and hotel keepers, we do not know it.   We are ready to believe that overwork has induced a return of Nye's old trouble and that Nye is a sick man.   But we do not believe and we shall not believe upon the testimony so far presented that Nye has been guilty of an irregularity warranting a diminution of public confidence in him, and, least of all, justifying the unseemly outrage committed at Paterson.

It was in impromptu recitations from his own writings or in imitations of well-known actors that Field especially excelled. Julian Ralph briefly and vividly described Field's manner at such times:

Leaning upon the back of a chair, interspersing his recitations with sallies of wit and comic allusions to his listeners, he could keep the attention of a company riveted upon himself.   He had both mimetic and theatrical ability in great measure, and his strong, rugged, but very mobile face was made to fortify an actor's gifts.

At such times Field as an entertainer was inimitable. On the public platform he could not enjoy himself at the expense of his auditors as he especially delighted in doing when he was in a room full of personal friends.   Nor did he throw himself so completely into the characters of his child heroes when reciting his own poems before strangers as he did in a friend's parlour.   To hear him recite "Jest 'Fore Christmas" or "Seein' Things at Night" to a circle of acquaintances was to hear him at his best.

XX

FIELD AS A NEIGHBOUR

I

WHEN the World's Fair in Chicago was about to open its gates to the public in the spring of 1893 Field came to me for a season pass to that great spectacle which I had obtained for him. I explained that the pass must bear his photograph in order that the gate-keepers might readily identify him as its legitimate owner. Then I took him to the photographic department of the *Daily News* and stood him against a wall while a flashlight picture was taken of him. When a copy of the photograph was shown to Field a few minutes later he laughed heartily. Then he began to apostrophize his portrait.

"Prisoner at the bar," he said in his deepest tones, gazing with an awful frown at the offending picture which he held at arm's length, "prisoner at the bar, have you anything to say before sentence is passed upon you?"

Then came the reply of the condemned miscreant in a broken whine: "I am guilty—I confess it. But mercy, mercy, your honour!"

"Prisoner at the bar," responded the sonorous voice of the judge, "what mercy did you show your unhappy victims? You are here to receive justice, not mercy. You must look above for mercy. You are hereby condemned to hang by the neck until you are dead. And may God have mercy upon your soul."

That was Field's way of pronouncing the photograph awful. On two or three later occasions he drew his World's

Fair pass from his pocket in my presence, displayed the photograph, and sternly addressed it: "Prisoner at the bar have you anything to say——" and so on. At such times he would relate to me some of the adventures of the photograph, what this or that friend had said about it and what humorous World's Fair gate-keepers had remarked as they compared it with his veritable lineaments. Moses Handy and Fred Skiff and Julian Hawthorne and various other persons, he said, had been moved to merriment by that lamentable visage.

Field took great delight in the World's Fair and haunted it day by day until he fell seriously ill in the autumn. Through the spring and summer he and Julian Hawthorne not infrequently might be seen amid the bizarre surroundings of the Midway. Again, he might be found with Skiff and Handy taking liberties with dignified boards of management. The swarms of notable and interesting people from all over the world that visited the great exposition excited Field like strong drink. Having an unlimited license from the management of the *Daily News* to entertain distinguished visitors at its expense how and when he pleased, and being also a leading spirit in that indefatigable organization, the Fellowship Club, Field had much to do with the hospitality that attended the World's Fair.

A lady of my acquaintance tells this story:

As a young girl I heard Eugene Field speak at the World's Congress of the World's Fair. He was introduced by Benjamin Butterfield as "the well-known author of that beloved poem, 'An Old Sweetheart of Mine.'" Mr. Field winked at the audience in the most confiding and sympathetic way and did not correct Mr. Butterfield's mistake.

II

In my collection of Fieldiana are engraved announcements of two noteworthy events in the life of the poet that mark the early months of 1893. The first is as follows:

To Eugene and Julia Field
Born
March the 27th, 1893
a son
Roswell Francis Field.

Here is the other:

MR. AND MRS. EUGENE FIELD
have removed their place of residence
from 466 Fullerton Avenue
to 1033 Evanston Avenue,
Buena Park,
Chicago.

May, 1893.

Trotty, Pinny, and Daisy, the surviving children of the Field family previous to the birth of Roswell, as well as the three children who had died, were all born before Field and his family became residents of Chicago in 1883. The infant Roswell was duly nicknamed "Posie" by his father. In the last year of Field's life there came a daughter, Ruth. These two little ones were the direct inspiration of a number of Field's child poems. One day he said to me, happily, "They give me lots of ideas."

It may be mentioned here that "Seein' Things at Night" was written as a result of Field's having heard the young son of his friend Yenowine muttering in his sleep. The next morning he and the little boy had an edifying conversation about sleep-monsters, exchanging confidences on this important subject until they had exhausted it. Then Field sat down in a corner and wrote the famous verses, which he dedicated to his youthful collaborator.

Not until Field became a resident of Buena Park, an attractive district of homes near the lake shore in the northern part of Chicago, was he entirely satisfied with his surroundings, though he made friends whom he highly valued among his neighbours when he lived in

Fullerton Avenue, where he had settled his family soon after their return from Europe. But wherever the Fields resided their home was a place of hospitality and friendly associations. The Field living room in winter and the Field front steps in summer were for friends and neighbours gathering places of peculiar charm. Wherever Field was, in fact, merriment prevailed. The Field front steps on summer evenings constituted a sort of neighbourhood parliament of mirth. The informality of such assemblies may be illustrated by an incident that I recall. One evening I went with the Fields from their Fullerton Avenue home to visit the Ballantynes in Orchard Street. There the conversation on the front steps was animated. However, after a time the ladies of the party retired indoors somewhat abruptly. We men stolidly continued to talk, quite unmoved by the ladies' departure, until word presently was brought to us that Ballantyne was a father! When next I was in that friendly company Mrs. Ballantyne smilingly congratulated me on my narrow escape from being present at the accouchement.

III

The Field home in Fullerton Avenue was in the immediate vicinity of the McCormick Theological Seminary, a widely known institution for the training of young men for the Presbyterian ministry. While residing there, Field delighted to expatiate upon the saintliness of his surroundings. A number of his articles written at that time related to the sayings and doings, actual or imaginary, of his Presbyterian neighbours. One of them is such a report of a wedding as perhaps was never written before or since. I cannot refrain from quoting it.

In his learned treatise, "De Fullertonis Aveno," the Rev. Dr. Herrick Johnson says truly—we translate quite literally: "Amongst the women of this avenue called Fullerton there may be none that are not most fair to look upon and whose carriage in all things will not bear the most rigorous scrutiny. In short, it hath come to be a common saying that amongst all the women of earth there are none others that in such modest wise and to such an abundance comprehend and combine all the beauties of person and all the virtues of Presbyterianism." (Vol. II, page 316.)

The envied reputation for beauty and goodness which our Fullerton Avenue girls enjoy is largely the result of that jealous care which is exercised over those gentle creatures—a care participated in by the mature men and women of this delectable part of the city; for it is most fitting that we who have had experience with the world, who know the pitfalls and the snares therein, and who have learned that Satan lurks at every corner and upon every hand with evil intent—it is seemly, we say, that we should constitute ourselves the temporal guardians of the younger and unsophisticated representatives of our species.

When, therefore, it was observed, perhaps two years ago, that Mr. William Bleeker Read was paying attention to Miss Louise Chapin, there was a distinct flurry of consternation in Fullerton Avenue. Miss Louise was justly esteemed as one of the gentlest ornaments of that galaxy of fair maidens which constitutes the chief pride and glory of McCormick's Presbyterian addition to the city of Chicago, Section 39, Township of Lake View. Of Mr. Read nothing was known further than that he was of engaging appearance and address and that he was expert in the secular game called lawn tennis. An investigation conducted by one deacon and two laymen soon disclosed the further facts that the young man's habitation was upon the south side of town and that he was employed in the wholesale department of a large commercial house. This trustworthy committee was enjoined to pursue the investigations to the bitter end; the south side of town is regarded by Fullerton Avenue folk as a sort of land of Nod, wherefrom issueth little that is not vain and frivolous; so, therefore, it was determined to scrutinize and catechize this young man—to try him, so to speak, in the fire of McCormick Presbyterianism—and let him stand or fall according to the result of that righteous ordeal.

Well, Mr. Read has been upon probation two years, and in all that time naught has transpired to indicate his unworthiness of our fair young girl friend, whom he led last evening to the altar. Now that it is all over we shall confess that we trembled somewhat for him last spring while the Briggs excitement was at its height; for youth is full of impetuosity, and is too prone to be beguiled and seduced by the siren voices of heresies. But this excellent young man stood unfalteringly in the faith, heedless of the gilded sophistries of the iniqui-

tous Briggs and his fellow apostates. We shall confess furthermore
that at times we were pained by the seeming ease with which this
young man from the wicked south side walloped our theological
students at lawn tennis—but let bygones be bygones; Mr. Read is one
of us now—we call him Brother Read.

The wedding last evening was beautiful in its unostentation.   . . .
It was our intention to give a rather elaborate description of the toilets,
for when we were with the St. Joseph *Gazette* eighteen years ago we
were famous at that sort of thing and we were proposing to try our
hand at the old business on this occasion. But, having neglected
(in the natural excitement of the hour) to make the necessary notes,
we discover too late that our recollection of the gowns is too hazy to
be committed to print. One wore white and the other wore pink and
white and one wore a veil and the other did not, but whether it was the
bride or the maid of honour that wore the one or the other we cannot
now recall, and therefore we shall not say, for a wedding is too serious
an affair to be dealt with loosely. But this we do affirm, and this, too,
without fear of contradiction—the bride looked just the lovely girl she
is, and so did that maid of honour, and so did the bride's mother—
God bless 'em all!   . . .

And when it was all over and the last amen had been said the little
procession filed out to the Mendelssohn march played as only our
organist, Bradley, can play it at the wedding of a Fullerton Avenue
girl.   Mr. William Bleeker Read, the groom, marched down the aisle
as proud as a czar of all the Russias, with his bride upon his arm, and
Miss Louise—no, she was Mrs. William Bleeker Read now—she was, if
we may use the phrase, the incarnate apotheosis of modest feminine
felicity.   We prefer this phrase to that which we used habitually when
we were writing for the St. Joseph *Gazette*—viz., "the blushing bride."

But at the house—oh, you should have been at 472 Fullerton
Avenue last evening!   That is where Mr. and Mrs. Charles Henry
Chapin, the bride's parents, live, and of course they gave their
daughter and her husband a jubilee after the wedding ceremony.
There was no splurge, no formality, no caterer—no, nothing of that
kind—nothing but sincerity and cordiality and home cooking.   It
was the sort of send-off that obtained in the old time—perhaps at that
time in New England when Charles Henry Chapin and his bride
stood up before the minister at Chatham Corners and recorded the
tender, lovely vows which we are sure neither has ever regretted.
Mrs. Chapin has said nothing of it to us, but we suspect that the events
of the last week—or perhaps the last month—have recalled the old
time to her, and, all too probably, with the confusion and excitement
and happiness of the season preparatory to her daughter's new life,
there came the grace of that tender touch, the sense of bereavement

which only the mother heart can feel and of which the mother's lips
so seldom speak. But Mr. Chapin—you should have seen him! No
boy of nineteen could have been merrier; at one time we really thought
we should have to send him to bed without his supper, he was so
frolicsome and noisy.

And just to think, it was only last June that this same Charles
Henry Chapin sat out on his front steps one evening, his chin between
his hands and his elbows on his knees, grinding his teeth ruefully and
rolling his eyeballs wildly and vowing he would never smile again!
All because Blaine wasn't nominated. The neighbours pitied him
and in low tones spoke of him to one another as "one of them Blaine
yawpers." Mr. Chapin is of a mercurial temperament; his grief is
violent, but transitory. What recked he last evening of political
disappointments? Pshaw! So far as he was concerned, last June
and its happenings belonged to the paleozoic age. And he was right,
we say. At any rate he danced with the pretty girls and romped
with them and cut up all sorts of delightful but scandalizing didoes.
His good humour was infectious, and why not? Only the nearer
and dearer ones were there. So it was wholly within the limitations of
propriety that—that they all, young and old, danced and made merry
and heartily enjoyed themselves. . . .

After the bride and groom had gone and when all commotion had
quieted down Mr. Chapin confided to us a certain thing that seemed
to worry him. "Lib," said he—for though her name is Elizabeth he
always calls his wife Lib for short—"Lib hain't been herself to-day.
She has tried to act cheerful and happy, but I've caught her crying
softly to herself when she thought nobody was around. You see, it
is hard for a mother to give up her daughter. We men don't understand it."

But we do understand it. We understand fully how it is that the
mother, with the knife in her heart, assumes a gayety whose absence
might jar upon the happiness of her loved one. It is one of the di-
vinely pathetic beauties of humanity. We do understand it; it is
sacred and we revere it.

That story well illustrates the sort of neighbour Field
was. More: it illustrates the sort of human being Field
was at heart.

IV

Here is a Fullerton Avenue story of a different sort:

Mr. Wood used to keep a meat shop in Lincoln Avenue next to
Louis Ellsworth's drug store. He was one of the distinct characters

of that justly respected contingent of our community known as the Fullerton Avenue reservation.   . . .

Well, about ten days ago Mr. Wood's brother came to me to suggest what he surmised would prove a veritable boon not only to me and to mine but also to the whole neighbourhood. He knew where there was a burro to be had for little or nothing—a genuine imported Mexican burro, of proud pedigree, unusual intelligence, unimpeachable amiability, and exceptional training. He represented that a burro required but little food and still less attention. He reminded me that my boys were now reaching a time in life when it behooved them to eschew the frivolities of marbles and slingshots and peg-tops and sports of that kind that knee out their panties and jeopard all the windows in the vicinity and keep their mother forever darning stockings and sour their naturally sweet little tempers. He was not content to take advantage of my paternal love—no, Mr. Wood's brother artfully played upon my notorious passion for brute pets of every kind and for queer, strange things. "Your collection of curios is already large and valuable," said he, "but it lacks a burro; with a burro it will be complete and symmetrical; without it, it must forever lack concinnity."

The boys eagerly championed the cause of the burro; in fact, they were prepared to pay the price of the weird beast. Their mother seemed to favour the scheme, too; she recognized therein a surcease from the drudgery of darning and of patching. I had not been human had I stood out against the argument of Mr. Wood's brother, coupled as it was with the pleadings of my little boys and their mother. So we bought the burro—they bought it, the boys did, but I abetted the scheme; I am too just and too brave a man to seek to shirk my share of the responsibility of the affair.

The personal appearance of the burro impressed me favourably. He was somewhat larger than a premium Great Dane dog. He was shaggy and frowsy to the degree of Ruskinism or of Whitmanism; had he been two-legged instead of four-legged he would undoubtedly have been an original poet or an art critic. He had dark, sad eyes and expansive, mobile ears, and his movements were so languorous that they bespoke at once his tropical nativity. Yes, I conceived a fondness for the curious bird at once and I named him Don Cæsar de Bazin.

I noticed that his hind feet were not shod and I mentioned this neglect to Mr. Wood's brother. He opined that it would be safer to leave them so. I did not then understand the meaning of this ambiguous answer, but I found out later.

They put Don Cæsar in the barn; evening was coming on and we had no fodder. But Don Cæsar did not suffer. The Hawkes boys and Willie Chapin and Herbie Cheatam and Bert Grosse and Henny

Mara and little Addie Maxwell and Belle Guiney and Babe Cowan
and Joan Ballantyne and Hester Magee and perhaps thirty other girls
and boys (big and small) saw that Don Cæsar was provided for, and
while there are those who assert that a burro will subsist on old shoes
and tin pails, I am prepared to testify that he devours with seeming
zest pie and cake and sugar and cut flowers and other diet of that
sybaritic nature.   Next morning I sent out for a one-hundred-pound
bale of hay and a bale of straw and a bushel of oats and the same day
we got a currycomb and a brush and some other needful toilet articles
for Don Cæsar.   I never wish to see a brute suffer for the want of
the bare luxuries of life.   Somewhere that same day the boys resur-
rected an old saddle and, having begged the money from their
mother, they bought a bridle, and then everybody had a ride—every
one of the threescore boys and girls—and it was a delectable sight to
see.   Don Cæsar deported himself circumspectly; true, instinct kept
the children a respectful distance from Don Cæsar's unshod hind heels,
and it was no mere fun to lift those boys and girls on and off the burro's
back, but the children were so happy!

Along about three days after Don Cæsar's advent—yes, it was the
day we found the old blue hen mysteriously dead in the barn—a cart, a
beautiful pony cart, came as a gift to the boys from Mr. Stone, the
banker.   Oh, what a joyful time that was!   And of course we had to
send right off and buy a harness—a lovely russet harness fit for the
steed of an emperor!   But surely our Don Cæsar de Bazin was worthy
of it.

We hitched him up.   It took the neighbourhood to do it.   Major
Mars helped; he had been in the federal cavalry four years and what he
didn't know about horses wasn't worth knowing.   Ex-Alderman Maxwell and Uncle John Ballantyne and Mr. Hawkes helped, too, and the
men who ought to have been at work on the new flats yonder stopped
work to come over to watch and suggest.   Uncle John finally got into
the cart and took the reins and said "Get up!" and Don Cæsar moved
off, not rudely or impatiently, but with seemly dignity.   When I say
Don Cæsar moved I say the truth, the whole truth, and nothing but
the truth.   He moved as one moves when preoccupied by thought; it
was as if in his mind Don Cæsar revolved an all-absorbing sense of
degradation.   He moved, mechanically, automatically, grimly, deliberately; he moved, and that was all.   Uncle John tested the persuasive powers of the whip, but Don Cæsar paid no more heed thereunto than if that flagellation had been the pelting of roses.   He kept
moving and nothing more.

I thought Uncle John exceedingly unjust when, leaping at last from
the cart, he declared Don Cæsar was a plug; I wondered whether
Uncle John really supposed I intended to buy a race horse for the

children to dally with. Some men never can be reasonable, and of all men it does seem to me sometimes that Scotchmen are the most unreasonable!

I got into the cart myself; it was 10:30. Half an hour later we had gone two blocks, Don Cæsar moving all the time; but he moved so queerly—shuffled along and seemed inclined to stop and scrutinize people and things; wanted to get up on the sidewalk and examine fire-plugs and look at the scenery—never in all my life had I seen so inquisitive a beast. He did all this, and the whole austere Presbyterian community watching us, too! Oh, it was very trying!

In an outburst of charity I attributed these eccentricities to the circumstance of his having just come from a country where they don't have anything but alkali roads and naked folk and cactuses. It was cold, driving in this fashion. It involved several quinine capsules when I got home. But the little folks who took my place in the cart didn't complain. They had a way of getting greater speed out of Don Cæsar. While two of them rode in the cart half a dozen would pull Don Cæsar in front and half a dozen others would push the cart from behind. This secured a higher rate of speed and at the same time it divided the labour and the fun.

I think it was the next day that we had to have Jessie, our fox terrier, repaired. Jessie had always had pretty much her own way in the community and she did not fancy the idea of surrendering any of her rights or privileges to any mule from Mexico. Being of a sportive disposition, she fancied that there might be some amusement in separating Don Cæsar's tail from that suburb of his anatomy where nature had planted it. The consequences of this misdirected humour redounded to the pecuniary profit of a veterinarian who not inappropriately observed, as he put a few stitches through Jessie's pretty white pelt, that the burro was indeed the most treacherous of all animate things. So I began to distrust Don Cæsar and to dislike him. The burro that would harm so lovable a creature as Jessie must indeed be a reprobate. Moreover, I suspect it was Don Cæsar who made away with that blue hen and knocked our rat-trap into smithereens and bit an ear off our finest white rabbit.

Mr. Jenney tells me—and when it comes to a question of veracity between my conservative Presbyterian friend, Mr. Jenney, and an idolatrous Montezuman burro I shall discriminate in favour of the former—Mr. Jenney tells me that the burro is by nature a creature of the lowest cunning, so subtle and malicious that he will stay awake all night simply to practise diabolical tricks. What else, he asks, could you expect from a burro fresh from the most heathenish part of the world? This beast, born and reared amid the lowest class of humanity in barbarous Mexico, is perforce full of evil, and his sinfulness is all the more shocking when brought under the searching calcium glare of that singular piety which obtains on both sides of Fullerton Avenue beginning at the Reaper and Harvester Seminary and running westward to the car barns.

"I was off-colour myself," says Mr. Jenney, "when I moved up here into this neighbourhood last year, and it required several months to purge every vestige of the old Adam that was in me. As I figure it, your burro will become in time a proper burro, but it may take months, maybe years, to do it."

I am not an impatient man; I am willing to bide my time. I will endure even suffering if thereby I can reclaim a heathen burro from original sin. Still, the question arises: How long will I be able to stand the financial strain? I find that within a week this burro— this Don Cæsar de Bazin who was reputed to be able to subsist on "little or nothing"—has quietly got away with one hundred pounds of timothy hay (eighty cents), one peck of corn on the cob (fifteen cents), one bushel of oats (thirty-seven cents), three pies, one layer cake, one bag of cookies, a panful of stewed apples, one blue hen, one rabbit's ear, Bessie Chapin's parasol, one piece of Ben Hawkes' bird-dog and the self-respect of our little fox terrier Jessie. I make no account of the store of bread and butter, lump sugar, milk, string-beans, lettuce, pudding, and bouquets that has been surreptitiously conveyed by the children of the neighbourhood to that pampered beast in yonder barn.

When I see Mr. Wood's brother again I am not going to reproach or chide him for having interested me and mine in burros. I shall simply thank him for having suggested the propriety of not getting Don Cæsar's hind feet shod.

V

Surely it is not strange that Field knew the hearts of children, since he was in so many respects a child himself, as his sketch of Don Cæsar indicates. Don Cæsar, by the way, was the engaging beast to which Field, late at night, after returning from the theatre and perhaps a midnight supper with actor friends, was wont to address words of sympathy and endearment in his deepest, most lugubrious tones. "Dear old Don! Good old Don! Poor old Don!" spoken with proper emphasis and suitable mournfulness, sufficed to set the responsive burro to braying loudly and with heart-breaking melancholy in his stall night after night, by no means to the edification of Field's steady-going Presbyterian neighbours.

Madame Modjeska had an experience with Don Cæsar which she related in her "Memories and Impressions." Writing of Field she said:

He sent us a formal invitation to a party at his house "to meet a friend from abroad." But when we came there was no such friend, and as the evening went on the foreigner did not make his appearance. When we were on the point of leaving we heard a strange sound at the window. "At last!" exclaimed our host. Opening the window, he called out some name which I cannot remember. After a few seconds we saw the head of a donkey and a most frightful braying filled the room. Eugene Field stroked caressingly the long, soft ears, until the soothing effect of his hands stopped the musical entertainment and the introduction took place. "This is my belated friend! He is indeed a great donkey," remarked our host quite seriously.

It was a year or so earlier that the lively sons of Field had a goat for a playmate. The goat was required to submit to a good deal of handling while being harnessed to a soap box wagon and otherwise participating in the boyish pastimes. Consequently the well-defined aroma of goat that lingered about the boys when their mother called them to their meals was anything but pleasing to her. A family friend who sympathized with the boys in their dilemma gave them a bottle of perfume with which to anoint their hands after they had performed such ablutions as their mother prescribed when she found they had been caressing the goat. Believing in the policy of attacking an evil at its source, the boys, much to their father's delight, made haste to empty the bottle of its contents by pouring all the perfume on the goat!

The little fox terrier Jessie, mentioned by Field in his story of Don Cæsar, probably was Field's greatest favourite among all the many dogs owned by him from childhood on. Jessie was given to him by Will J. Davis, the theatrical manager, and Field named her after Jessie

Bartlett Davis, the opera singer, wife of the donor. Field became exceedingly fond of the pretty and intelligent little animal and was greatly vexed because of her frequent disappearances. On such occasions he would go to the drug store of which he made mention in his story of Don Cæsar and there would post up a notice describing Jessie and offering a reward for her return. "I think," said one of Field's neighbours to me, "that the boys around here take turns stealing that dog in order to get two dollars from Field every time they bring her back."

Finally, however, there came a time when Jessie disappeared and Field's posted offer of a reward failed to cause her to be returned. This was a blow to her owner. Field finally wrote of his loss in "Sharps and Flats." "We have tried our poems on Jessie and she always liked them," Field told his readers in making known the seriousness of his loss. "Some folk think that our poetry drove Jessie away from home, but we know better." He wrote further: "It is very lonesome without Jessie. Moreover, there are poems to be read for her approval before they can be printed; the great cause of literature waits upon Jessie."

Sad to relate, the cause of literature had to struggle along without the assistance of Field's pet, for Jessie did not return.

XXI

Producing Beautiful Books

I

FROM the time of his first success as an author of published books Field felt that he had a mission in throwing his influence strongly on the side of beautiful volumes and thus helping to put an end to the period of badly printed, cheap, paper-bound books, which were so common in his day, when authorship was in a sorry plight and the pirating of works by English authors was disgracefully common in the United States. At the same time, however, Field contended that only books of real merit should be richly bound by publishers or collectors. On this subject he wrote:

There has always been and there still is more elegance than taste in bindings. Many books are bought for their superb bindings; too often their purchasers, exhibiting an enthusiastic acquaintance with the kind and quality of leather used, the style of tooling adopted, and the character of paneling, etc., know absolutely nothing of the book itself, its history, its merits or demerits. How often, too, we walk into private libraries to find folios, quartos, octavos, and the rest bound uniformly—the rich and the poor met together in ostentatious garb, irrespective of age, worth or cost! To clothe a cheap, trashy book in tree calf or crushed levant is almost as atrocious an offense as it would be to parade the kitchen wench in the silks and satins of my lady. We can pardon him who, loving some particular little volume (for reasons perhaps wholly sentimental, which are not specially cogent in the opinion of others) chooses to array that particular friend in finery wholly unbecoming to its homely paper and what is printed thereon. So, too, we regard as a wholly pardonable offense the bad taste which parents sometimes exhibit in overdressing an ill-favoured child; nay, we respect that lovely feeling of affectionate devotion which shows itself even to the extent of absurdity. But to see a

whole family of freaks—the entire awkward squad, if you please—
rigged out in a splendour beseeming only the truly grand, why, that is
execrable.

The bibliophiles—and they are really bibliopelts or peltomaniacs
—agree that the dress of a book should partake invariably of the character of the book itself.   Gayety becomes the attire of a lively volume,
and gravity should enter into the garb of the severer tome.   That
artistic, that necessary consistency which the Venusian insists upon
is to be demanded in the bindings of books as well as in the treatment
of all other things.

The modern method of extra illustrating books seems to have developed quite as much vulgarity in taste and practice as has the modern craze for bindings.   We have yet to see—we say this deliberately
—we have yet to see a modern specimen of extra illustration that
should call from a man of judgment and taste an expression of approval.
Every sense of form and method, every requirement of order, tone,
and symmetry, and every instinct of appropriateness is outraged by
the bundling together of the archaic and the modern, the musty and
the savoury, the heroic and the miniature, the rare and the cheap, the
fine and the coarse—copperplates, wood cuts, and steel engravings,
higgledy-piggledy, *ad infin. ad naus.*   The octavo is marred with
black, gloomy portraits torn from old folios, and the florid landscape
with which those ineffable gift books of our grandsires were adorned
are once more called into service by the romantic loon who, ill content with the incomparable word paintings of the Wizard of the North,
seeks to illustrate with actual, tangible pictures the scenes Scott sung
and told of!   Bah!

II

What Field did in the cause of beautifully printed books
sometimes with the financial assistance of friends—
particularly of Francis Wilson and Melville E. Stone—is
indicated in a succession of paragraphs that appeared in
"Sharps and Flats."   The first of the series, published
January 11, 1892, was as follows:

The limited edition of Horace translations entitled "Echoes from
the Sabine Farm" and published by Mr. Francis Wilson has just been
issued by the University Press at Cambridge.   The edition of one
hundred numbered copies will not be put upon the market, but will be
distributed by Mr. Wilson among his friends and to certain libraries in
America and Europe.   Thirty of these copies are printed in red and
black on Japan paper; seventy upon hand-made white paper.   The

illustrations have been made by Mr. Edmund H. Garrett. A beautifully etched title-page is a particularly charming feature of the book.
It is probable that a second limited edition of "Echoes from the Sabine
Farm" will soon be published by A. C. McClurg & Co. In that event
the public will have a chance to see the book and pass upon its merits.

Because of his almost brotherly regard for Field and
also because of his love for rare and beautiful first editions,
Wilson not only looked after all details of the printing of
this book but accepted the financial responsibility for the
work. As Wilson explains in his preface to the popular
edition, the original plan was to print but fifty copies, but
so many of Field's friends clamoured for the book that it
was necessary to print one hundred, since Field was incapable of disappointing any one of whom he was fond.
Field's brother Roswell contributed somewhat less than
half the translations from and paraphrases of Horace
which make up the volume. Field's lines dedicating
the book to his old friend, M. L. Gray, and the epilogue,
also by Field and also addressed to Mr. Gray, are written
in the poet's most frolicsome mood. The original manuscript of the latter poem is in my possession. The popular
edition of his book, following the second limited edition
and printed from the plates made for the private edition
sponsored by Wilson, was issued about the time of Field's
death.

In a recent letter to me a representative of the University Press wrote:

The only letter which we have bearing on these [Field's] books, is
one from Mr. Francis Wilson, under date of December 23, 1891, which
we have in our library, framed with a picture of Mr. Wilson, which he
was pleased to present to us.

On March 2, 1892, Field published the following in his
column:

For the information of many who are vainly seeking to obtain copies
of Francis Wilson's edition de luxe of "Echoes from the Sabine Farm"

we would say that no copy of that book is or will be for sale, it being Mr. Wilson's determination to keep the book out of the market. The specimens he is giving away are so carefully placed as to render all likelihood of their finding their way into the hands of the trade exceedingly improbable. Messrs. A. C. McClurg & Co., of Chicago, will publish an edition of the work, limited to five hundred numbered copies and retaining virtually all the features of Mr. Wilson's charming edition, and in addition containing a brief narrative of the circumstances leading to and concerning Mr. Wilson's undertaking. These books will be ready for the trade, it is conjectured, by the first of next September. A considerable number of specimens of the proposed edition have already been bespoken by individual collectors in different parts of the country.

Field contributed the following to his column on September 28, 1892:

Answering numerous inquiries we will say that "A Second Book of Verse by Eugene Field" is now in press and will be issued in a first limited edition of three hundred copies on or about November 1st; a popular edition of the book will be issued immediately thereafter by Scribner's Sons of New York.

"With Trumpet and Drum," a collection of Mr. Field's verse for and about children, will shortly be published by Scribner's Sons in both limited and popular editions.

No subscriptions will be received for either of the publications named.

On August 10, 1894, Field's column announced:

A volume of verse entitled "Love Songs of Childhood," by Eugene Field, will be published in the autumn by Scribner's Sons of New York. The collection will be made up of the author's work hitherto unpublished in book form—forty pieces of verse in praise of child life. In addition to the popular edition a large paper edition, limited to one hundred copies, will be issued, and has already been bespoken. "Love Songs of Childhood" is dedicated to the author's only surviving aunt—Mrs. Belle Angier of West Swanzey, N. H.

Field's book-collecting friends snapped up the limited large paper editions of his various works and the popular editions when offered for sale went, as Field was wont to

express it, "like hot cakes." In these years he was happy
and busy, though in impaired health. While conscien-
tiously demonstrating how books ought to be manufactured in order that they might please by their appearance,
he continued his active campaign against badly printed
volumes. He had this to say on the subject on
September 20, 1894:

The first edition of DuMaurier's novel, "Trilby," consisted of
35,000 copies and it was exhausted by the booksellers' orders before it
was printed. It is so poorly made a book that we think the price demanded for it is extravagantly exorbitant. The publishers have, we
notice, a very reprehensible habit of not putting the date of publication
upon the title pages of their books. This practice tends to lessen the
value of the books to collectors.

III

Something of the methods employed by Field in trading
copies of new limited editions of his books for volumes
which he especially coveted is indicated in the following
verses, addressed to him by the Rev. Frank M. Bristol,
now Bishop Bristol of Chattanooga:

DECLINING AN OFFER TO SWAP

Your "Love Songs of Childhood's" exceedingly fine—
On Japanese paper it's quite in my line!
But I reckon I'd like to be seeing you come
To trade a whole cartload for "Trumpet and Drum."

Ah, no; though you're spoiling just now for a trade
With lots of old truck from a pin to a spade,
You need not expect with your humour so rum
To palm off the "Songs" for my "Trumpet and Drum."

I'll trade you my powder-horn, leggings, and gun—
A farm in Nebraska by Rattlesnake Run!
But, with oil in my cruse or ary a crumb,
I never will swap you my "Trumpet and Drum."

I'll dicker a section of cactus or more,
Throw in a few cyclones of double-twist bore,
But not a cent less than a Vanderbilt sum
Could get me to part with my "Trumpet and Drum."

So bring on your pewter and china and sich,
Your butterflies, axes, and snuff-boxes rich;
But don't you forget—you may talk till you're dumb
Before I will sell you my "Trumpet and Drum."

You'd ask me to trade on the smiles of my boys,
And barter the tears of their mother for toys!
'Twould make the whole household look gloomy and glum
To think of my trading my "Trumpet and Drum."

On Christmas, Thanksgiving and birthdays we read
The sweet little book that holds All-Children's creed;
And every dear boy's left the print of his thumb
On every dear page of my "Trumpet and Drum!"

No, no, you can't have it, my charming old friend—
It is neither for sale nor to trade nor to lend;
Of all my book-treasures now left here's the sum:
My Bible, my Shakespeare, my "Trumpet and Drum!"
    Evanston, Dec. 28, 1894.

These verses by Field throw further light on his swapping proclivities:

TO DE WITT MILLER

Dear Miller: you and I despise
    The cad who gathers books to sell 'em,
Be they but sixteen-mos in cloth
    Or stately folios garbed in vellum.

But when one fellow has a prize
    Another bibliophile is needing,
Why, then, a satisfactory trade
    Is quite a laudable proceeding.

There's precedent in Bristol's case,
    The great collector-preacher-farmer;
And in the case of that divine
    Who shrives the soul of P. D. Armour.

When from their sapient, saintly lips
    The words of wisdom are not dropping,
They turn to trade—that is to say,
    When they're not preaching they are swapping!

So to the flock doth it appear
    That this a most conspicuous fact is:
That which these godly pastors do
    Must surely be a proper practice.

Now, here's a pretty prize indeed,
    On which DeVinne's art is lavished;
Harkee! the bonny, dainty thing
    Is simply waiting to be ravished!

And you have that for which I pine
    As you should pine for this fair creature.
Come, now, suppose we make a trade—
    You take this gem and send me Beecher.

Surely these graceful, tender songs
    (In samite garb with lots of gilt on)
Are more to you than those dull tomes
    Her pastor gave to Lizzie Tilton!

IV

One of Field's characteristics was that he never would
send a manuscript to any publication on his own initiative.
Any contribution published outside of his column had
to be solicited, as he was determined never to subject himself to the indignity of a declination if he could prevent it.
And his references to the magazines of his day were nearly
always unfavourable.   In 1889 he wrote:

"Letting the Old Cat Die," was the title of a pretty dialect poem
published over James Whitcomb Riley's name in *Harper's Magazine*
last month.   The Harpers had that poem eight years before they
published it!   The price paid for it originally did not exceed ten
dollars.   We mention these facts for the simple purpose of showing
that the popularity which Mr. Riley justly enjoys has not in any way

been brought about by the patronage or the coöperation of the Harpers.

The *Century Magazine* did not recognize Riley until the popularity of his newspaper poems forced that recognition.

We should like to know this: Whether any American magazine has ever discovered a poet.

And this: Whether any American magazine has ever taken up a worthy poet until his reputation was established and the public clamoured for that poet's work.

And this: Whether American magazine literature of to-day is not of a poorer quality and is not obtained at less money cost than American newspaper literature.

We think that our American magazines are simply ponderous and inferior monthly supplements.

When Field in 1889 was writing his article on certain letters of Edgar Allan Poe's which came into his hands from the son of the man to whom they were addressed— Poe wrote them to Edwin Patterson, a hopeful young citizen of Oquawka, Illinois, who in 1848 was consumed by a desire to establish a magazine of national circulation in his own small town on the Mississippi—I urged him to submit the article to some Eastern magazine of standing. "No, I will not do that," Field replied. "If any of those Eastern magazines wants an article from me it can ask me to write one for it." I continued to insist that the curious, newly discovered letters by Poe ought to interest any magazine editor. Finally Field said: "Well, I'll not do anything more than let Gilder of the *Century* know what I've got."

Accordingly he wrote to Gilder that he was preparing an article on some unpublished letters by Poe, letters indicating that Poe was planning in the last year of his life to accept the editorship of a new magazine in Illinois and also setting forth Poe's views on ways to build up a profitable magazine circulation. Poe's expressed hope was, said Field, to obtain a list of 20,000 paying subscribers within five years. Wishing to know how this number compared with the circulation of leading magazines in 1889, Field asked Gilder for information on this subject.   Back came a courteously worded letter from Gilder giving Field the facts which he had requested, but disclosing not the slightest interest in the Poe letters or in the Field article. So Field turned over the latter to his friend Thompson for publication in *America*.

In commenting in the *Daily News* upon the article after its publication Field expressed himself strongly on contemporary critics of Poe.   He wrote:

The trouble with the Poe agitation has been, we think, that the jury (by which we mean the public) has been regaled too much with *ex parte* testimony.   Most of Poe's contemporaries seem to have been very small, narrow-minded creatures.   They were afraid of Poe while he lived; after he was dead some of them snarled at his memory and others exhibited their wretched cowardice by seeking to damn the dead genius with faint praise, with hypocritical "regrets," and with crocodile tears.   All appear to have been instigated by the ambition that fired the Ephesian dome.   R. W. Griswold fell out of theology into a "literary" mire, and there he wallowed—the mean little toad that he was!   The best answer to everything he has said would be simply to print his portrait.

John R. Thompson, editor of the *Southern Literary Messenger*, is quite forgotten now; yet he was a sort of influence forty years ago— when Willis was the fashion and when Lowell was vainly trying to catch on.   After Poe's death Thompson wrote a sanctimonious letter to Edwin Patterson, reviewing with alleged regret and ostensible pain his dead friend's dissolute career.   "I have not as yet recovered his trunk," writes Thompson, "so that I cannot tell you whether or no he left any unpublished manuscript.   The day before he went north from Richmond I advanced him a small sum of money for a prospective article which he probably never wrote."

Now, what was the exact sum advanced by Thompson to Poe? Five dollars!   Five paltry, greasy dollars!   Yet Thompson seeks to convey, under a veil of alleged modesty and alleged indifference, the impression that the sum loaned was actually worth talking about. Not a word does he say about what Poe gave him in exchange—a manuscript copy of his unpublished poem, "Annabel Lee"!   Nor has he a word to say of the numerous occasions upon which the *Southern Literary Messenger* had owed Poe money and couldn't pay.

It was Poe's misfortune to live at a time when such wretched, pettysouled creatures as John R. Thompson and R. W. Griswold stood forth and flourished in practical demonstration of the inscrutability of Providence!

V

From his scholarly father, an ardent student of the classics, Field inherited his passionate love of books. This inheritance was his great joy throughout his years of creative work. However, it was the droll or the unusual in books as in everything else that especially appealed to him, except in his more serious moods. He had a strain of melancholy, of mysticism, that ruled him at certain periods and that always tended to dominate his thoughts on the approach of Christmas. His many Christmas poems and Christmas stories were expressions of that mysticism. His friends were especially dear to him then, and Christmas remembrances had to go from him yearly to all of them.

In the autumn of 1888 Field became greatly interested in helping readers of his column choose appropriate books for Christmas gifts. I remember how he toiled over his lists, inviting suggestions from his fellow workers in regard to modern books, but readily supplying from his own knowledge a formidable array of fairy lore and works on quaint or unusual subjects. He began his advice by urging the purchase of well-bound books only. "There is not in all the world," he declared, "a more exasperating thing than a book that crackles and groans whensoever it is opened. This kind of book seems to be the triumph of the American binders' art." Here, then, was the opening gun of Field's long battle against badly manufactured books. The words were written when "Culture's Garland," Field's last paper-bound book, was selling at its moderate best. But already Field had determined that his name thenceforth should be associated only with beautiful volumes.

There is nothing remarkable in Field's lists of Christmas books for women, young or old.   Indeed, they are a bit perfunctory.   For men he made some novel suggestions. Then he wrote his real sentiments in these words:

Handsome editions and popular books are all very well, but the best way, after all, to buy a Christmas book is to snoop around for an old-timer; hunt for it, work for it, haggle for it; and when you get it, send it to a first-class binder and have its yellow leaves, that should always smell of the steerage, tucked warm and snug between compact and handsome covers.

In further proof of Field's enthusiasm for good printing I quote the following:

If there is anybody in Chicago who thinks that old Benjamin Franklin was not a first-class printer let him apply to the Rev. Frank M. Bristol for proof to the contrary.   Mr. Bristol has a "Cato Major" printed by Franklin in 1744, and it is as fine a specimen of typographical beauty as is to be met with anywhere. This book was printed at the time when Franklin used to trundle his "forms" in a wheelbarrow from his composition rooms to the building where his presses were set up.   No one can come from an inspection of this exquisite "Cato Major" without the conviction that as a printer old Ben Franklin knew and practised his trade to the highest degree of perfection.

On children's reading and books for children Field wrote most interestingly at that time.   Take the following by way of illustration:

Mr. Edmund Clarence Stedman once told the writer that it seemed to him to be useless to attempt to say what a child should or should not read; that the only thing to do was to give a child access to books and that he would quickly discover and devour the books he wanted— just as the human system assimilates what food it requires and does not assimilate what it does not require.   This theory, coming from so eminent an authority, impressed us very forcibly and we tried it on a small boy, aged twelve, who has been living in our family ever since he was born.   We bade him browse around in the library and read whatever he took a fancy to.   A week later we asked him about it; we were curious to know what pabulum his hungry mind assimilated.

He had found three books that seemed to please him very much; they were a "Lives of Highwaymen," a "Lives of Famous Pirates" (date of 1737), and Burton's "Arabian Nights." It is perhaps unnecessary to say that the work of assimilation came to a peremptory stop.

It is the duty of parents to discover the bent of the child's mind, to feed it, to encourage it and to educate it. If the boy is fond of tales of adventure let him have the best bear-story books to be had, and, heaven knows, the stores are full of this kind of literature. Sometimes the boy craves stories of the sea; if he does he should have them, and there are lots of good ones to be had. One day we fell into talk with a twelve-year-old boy who told us that he was very much troubled because his mother wanted him to be a minister when he grew up. He had earned five dollars by committing to memory the Ten Commandments and the Sermon on the Mount; with his five dollars he had bought a second-hand nickel-plated coffee tank (such as is used in restaurants), and this tank he had converted into a steam-engine— made and connected every bit of the machinery himself. His mother, instead of recognizing and encouraging his apparent genius, believed him to be possessed of the devil, and when one day she found that he had got hold of Beckman's "History of Invention" she spirited it away and set that twelve-year-old genius to reading Dick's "History of the Universe." A few months ago the boy fell sick of scarlet fever and died. It was better that he should die in childhood than live an unappreciated and perverted genius.

Field gave to parents this further advice:

While a child is being taught to read he should be taught how to use a book. He who does not respect books should not have books. It has always been our belief that Thomas De Quincey would never have been afflicted with the curse of opium had he not been so brutish in his misuse of books. Teach your boy and your girl these things: 1. Never to handle a book with soiled or moist hands. 2. Never to turn down the leaf of a book. 3. Never to leave a book open. 4. Never to stuff letters or leave a paper-cutter or a pencil between the leaves of a book. 5. Never to leave a book lopwise on a shelf. 6. Never to cut the leaves of a book with anything but a paper-cutter or a dull caseknife. (What a pig old Sam Johnson must have been; he used to pare an apple and cut book leaves at the same time with the same jack-knife!) And speaking of uncut leaves reminds us of a story we heard the other day. A certain wealthy Chicago man had upon his table a fine large-paper uncut copy of Barclay's "Schippe of Fooles." Quite recently a friend, admiring the book, picked up a paper-cutter and began separating the leaves in order that he might enjoy the quaint illustrations. Which seeing, "Hold on!" cried Porcus. "Don't cut any more of them leaves; there has been too many of 'em cut already!"

In one of these dissertations Field wrote, as truly as quaintly:

Books that make people cry are good books. So long as the heart has tears in it there can't be much room for evil. What oceans of tears must have been shed over Grace Greenwood's "History of My Pets"! By the way, what has become of that sweet little book? It seems to have dropped off the shelves.

The short list of his favourite books given in Field's "Auto-Analysis" includes John Bunyan's immortal work. I have seen the list criticized as mere foolery, in part because of this selection. Yet Field had written in sober earnest six years earlier:

Bunyan's "Pilgrim's Progress" is always a good present for a child or for a youth or for an adult. It is the one book, of all books, that appeals with equal force to all ages. Moreover, it is one of those books which are or ought to be part of everybody's education.

Field wrote at another time: "No properly constructed man can ever weary of Bunyan's wondrous fancy, pure English, and simple piety."

XXII

LORE OF BOOK-COLLECTING

I

IN ONE of his disquisitions on the use and care of books Field wrote in this interesting wise:

The disposition or arrangement of his books is one of the first problems that really vexes the collector. This is a vexation that not infrequently is never compassed, no man having as yet hit upon a plan or device whereby a large number of books may be so shelved as to be got at as soon as they are needed. It is quite as foolish and as impertinent to tell a man how he should arrange his books as it is to tell him what books he "ought to read." The fact is that a man ought to read what he is inclined to and wants to read. And different men have different methods both of thought and of practice; what is a system with one seems wild disorder to another. The bureau-drawer of the average man strikes the average woman as being chaos in miniature; yet the average man is seldom at a loss to find almost immediately in all that marvellous confusion whatsoever article he seeks. We have seen libraries that seem to have been set up in utter disregard of system; yet the owner, without being able to explain his system, evidently had one, for he knew instantaneously where to lay his hands upon the volume that was called for. Mr. Bristol, perhaps the most indefatigable and most intelligent of our collectors, says that he follows no set system in the arrangement of his books; he does not know exactly where many of his books are, but (he adds): "Let one of those books be spirited away and I find it out almost immediately."

Nearly every methodical collector—no matter how prim and precise he may be—is bothered now and again to determine where one class of literature ends and another class begins. The collector has secured, perhaps, a copy of Overbury's works (edition of 1730), with the autograph of Joshua Reynolds on the title page; where does this book belong? Hypocritus would say with the facetiæ; yet this book clearly is not one of that class, for is its tone not pure and moral and healthy throughout, and where shall you find a nobler poem than "The Wife"? But Overbury's works cannot properly be put into the de-

271

partment of poetry, for the reason that the majority of this remarkable man's writings are in prose. Does not the appearance of Joshua Reynolds's autograph on the title page warrant the owner in giving the volume a place among the Johnsonians—that splendid array of literature beginning with Boswell and ending with the love letters of the senile Mrs. Piozzi? Here is a book, we will say, that old Joshua gloated over; we can fancy that he regaled his visitors with snatches from it; the chances are that Sam and he discussed its beauties and the tragic circumstances of its ill-starred author's career time and again over their nocturnal brews of tea.   Clearly, this book—this particular volume, we mean—belongs with the Johnsonians. . . .

It is really interesting to study the ingenuity devised and practised by many men in smuggling contraband literature into their libraries. One of our acquaintances went to the trouble and expense of having his Balzac's "Contes Drolatiques" bound like his Macaulay's "History of England." He numbered it Volume IV and threw away the real fourth volume of the history. Another friend has had his Rabelais bound in a dull shade and entitled "Baxter's Saint's Rest." There is a quaint humour in all this deceit that is rather pleasing; nobody is harmed; the aged mother rejoices that her son's mind inclines to such godly reading and the wife is rather proud than otherwise that her husband's literary taste is of a serious nature. Therefore, if a friend should come to us and say that he had a Villon or a Scarron or a Poggio or a Joe Miller or a Karna Shastra which he wished to place in his library without running any risk of discovery, we should recommend him to have the same bound in sombre, forbidding style and labelled either: "The Remains of Henry Kirk White" or "Opie's Religious Tracts." Other felicitous fictitious titles are "Geological Surveys," "Patent Reports," "Catalogues," and "Essays." As facetious a volume of as lively old English ballads as we ever read we discovered on the shelf of a second-hand bookstore disguised as "Memoirs of the Rev. John Todd."

Still, if called upon to advise a collector we should certainly advise him to taboo as far as possible works of an erotic nature.   There are, of course, many books of an objectionable character which the scholar must have.   Suetonius' "Cæsars" is full of gross scandal, yet it is one of the necessary books. . . .

In the works of these ancients the holiest and purest-minded monks of mediæval times rejoiced, and these books, copied by hand upon parchment and beautifully illuminated, were loaned by one monastery to another, long processions of the *frères* conveying the precious folio from the one locality to the other. The monks, however, regarded this kind of reading as a very unworthy occupation.   It being an imperative rule never to engage in conversation in the apartment where the library was stored, the monks employed a system of signs whereby they informed the librarian what kind of book they wanted.   When a monk wished one of the erotics he scratched himself behind the ear, signifying by this gesture that he had debased himself to the condition of a dog, it being the practice of curs that are persecuted with fleas to scratch back of their ears with one of their hind legs raised at a convenient angle.

That the demoralizing effects of this literature were feared even in mediæval times appears from the chronicles that have come down to us, and through the medium of Thomas Hearne's diary there has been preserved a prayer against "evil speeche and uncleane thoughts" to this effect:

> "O Marie bricht, our moder hight,
>   Heed thou our pityse call;
>   We pray thee teach us seemlier speeche
>   And cleanlier deeds withal.
>   For evereche one before ye Throne
>   Must strict accounting give
>   For that he wrought or sayed or thought
>   Whiles that he ben on live.
>
> "Make thou us loathe to use an othe
>   Profayning God Hys name,
>   And make us speake full fair and meke
>   And do and think ye same.
>   Fill us with love to God above
>   And Charite to men—
>   So God us save beyond ye grave
>   For Chryste Hys sake.   Amen."

Hearne was a deeply religious man.   It was his practice to write out a prayer each night, and many of these have been preserved as models of devotional expression.   One of the most interesting of these is a prayer wherein, after returning thanks for God's invariable goodness to him, Hearne continues: "And I would fain give Thee thanks for Thy special goodness to me day before yesterday when Thou didst put in my way three rare old manuscripts. . . ."

Before you classify and shelve your books you must have shelves. In other words, "catch the rabbit before you heat the pot."   Referring to this ancient maxim, Doctor Wadd, in his "Comments on Corpulency," cites the old Scotch lady's recipe for making a porridge. "First of all," said she, "I wash my hands."   There are bookcases and bookcases, and most of them are unspeakably bad.   The bookcase question is a vexatious one, and it seems to be no nearer a solution than it was a hundred years ago. In his "Enemies of Books" Blades practically concedes that the styles of cases now in use do not answer the ends which a bookcase should answer. The open shelves admit dust and insects; the closed cases exclude the air. Books require fresh air; therefore the doors of a closed case should be opened at least once a day, to admit of the escape of the foul vapours generated by leather bindings and the inflow of the purifying atmosphere. Blades appears to favour a bookcase with doors not of glass but of lattice brass or wood; this lattice admits of constant currents of air, and the accumulation of dust is not harmful provided the book be taken out once a week and wiped carefully with a soft cloth.

A broom in the hands of a buxom servant is as malignant a foe as ever threatened a library. We have frequently seen incalculable damage done to rare and costly books by a three-dollar-a-week servant who, armed with a forty-cent broom, has been intrusted to sweep a fourteen-dollar carpet and this spectacle has always filled us with anguish. It were a thousand times better, we think, that the dirt should be knee-deep on that commonplace carpet than that inspired folios and beloved quartos should pale under the storm of dust which a healthy hired girl never fails to rasp out of a domestic three-ply. Collectors will agree with us that carpets are inventions of the devil— inventions which the devil, old Satan himself, invented for the special mortification and particular torment of bibliophiles. We therefore suggest that the floor of the library be tiled, or that it consist at least of hardwood appropriately stained. A painted floor will not do—that is another diabolical invention; painted floors have to be scrubbed too often. The only real security against the curse of dust that the collector can possess himself of is to be found in that character of floor which does away altogether with carpets and rugs and the broom. Provide your library with marble tiling and put the womenfolk under bonds to keep the peace and—there you are, friend bibliophile, fairly started upon a career of prosperity and bliss.

II

At a little later time Field took up again the subject of women as the bane of book collectors. He wrote:

All book collectors should have a little volume issued recently under the title of "The Enemies of Books." In this interesting work we are told very truly that women, as a class, are the enemies of books. We have a well-defined suspicion that women, as a class, are enemies of relics of any kind. We think that women care nothing for relics (as relics) except such as are genuine heirlooms—articles likely to testify to the antiquity or the honour of their own ancestry. In Grose's "Olio," which, by the way, was published after Grose's death, there is to be found an amusing letter from a woman who holds up to derision and scorn the follies of the pursuit of the antiquarian. The truth is that the hardest part of the work of a collector is sneaking his treasures into his own house. There is no delight in being confronted by an irate spouse who greets you with "More books, eh? More books with which to lumber up the house! And I suffering for months in the need of a new dress!"

But there are ways of evading—of eluding—that wifely vigilance which with feline shrewdness, not to say basilisk remorselessness, rivets its argus eyes upon the wayward husband. You can sneak your precious books into your house in the dead of night, after your wife has retired. This was the practice of that great and good man, Henry Ward Beecher, as he himself has borne witness. But there is nothing valorous in this practice. It is taking a mean, cowardly advantage of one's spouse. Another shrewd scheme is to write your father's name in your new book. We have several recent publications in which the name of the paternal ancestor has been penned, yet that father died (God rest his soul!) twenty years ago. The wife recognizes the father's name and, never thinking to look at the date of publication, is satisfied. Oh, who would destroy or weaken the confidence of a loving, trustful woman!

He, however, who would be truly bold and valorous will not content himself with these paltry artifices. He will take his newly acquired volumes under his arms, march bravely, ay, blusteringly, into the house, and exhibit the prizes to his wife with a certain assumed but fervent air of exultation.

"Did you buy them?" she will ask, perhaps coldly.

Then the varlet husband answers: "No, of course not." He will say that they are a gift from Jones or Brown or Smith. Invariably that will reconcile the wife; she will say "How nice!" or somewhat to that effect.

If perchance she asks why Jones or Brown or Smith should happen to make him so valuable a present, the culprit will answer that he put the donor under some sort of obligation—had rescued his favourite child from drowning or performed in his behalf some like prodigy of valour. By this means the wife is not only quieted but filled with most pleasing assurances of her husband's magnanimity, bravery, and popularity.

Another bold stroke is made by him who marches bravely into his house with an armful of books and says, "Wife, I have brought you a present; see, are they not beautiful?"

This will work occasionally; but it must not be tried too often—it should not be abused.   Other new books which are overhauled by the wife who has been lying in ambush can be hustled through under the plea that they are books which somebody else borrowed long ago and neglected to return.

The longer a man is engaged at collecting the more facile he becomes in the art of introducing new books into his house under the very eyes of his wife.   Some years ago we took home a fine set of Rabelais.   The divinity who directs temporal and spiritual affairs in that quiet home inquired: "More books?"   "Yes," we answered, "and just the books you've been wanting—Doctor Rabelais' works; it's a smart thing for us to save doctors' bills when we can."   This scheme worked smoothly enough for a month or two.   But one blustery night the baby began to bark with the croup, and then we knew that a crisis was at hand.   The spectacle of a woman sitting up in bed and nervously thumbing her way through the works of Dr. François Rabelais for a remedy for croup was but the awful calm which preceded a storm.   Oh, the——   But no; rather let us drop a curtain over that event, leaving it to the imagination of the reader to complete the sequel as he may please.   The next Christmas we got a very neat volume of "Opie on Lying" in our stocking.

Six years after this story of smuggling in Rabelais was written Field dressed it up in rhyme as it appears in his collected works.

III

The immediate result of the publication of the article describing women as the enemies of books was a flood of indignant protests from woman readers.   Consequently Field published, a few days later, an article on women as book collectors.   "While it is true," he wrote, "that bibliomania is no respecter of sex, it is commonly found among the male persuasion.   There are many things that stand in the way of a woman's becoming a confirmed book hunter."   He enumerated some of them:

In the first place, women have by nature and by education so high a regard for the value of money that they are incapacitated at once for entering upon a pursuit which requires that gold shall be esteemed simply as a sordid means of gratifying the bibliomanical passions.

Then again, most women have to get their money from husbands or fathers who seldom neglect to demand a bill of particulars as to the contemplated expenditure. Furthermore, women are, as a class, so neat and tidy as to have a supreme horror of dust and dirt; few of them could be tempted or hired to ferret around in the average second-hand bookshop—an occupation delightful to the maniac but involving ruin to the attire and a complete change of complexion. Still, when this madness seizes upon the woman, it rages even more violently than in man.

Field proceeded to give much sage advice to his woman readers on practical methods of smuggling books into their homes without the knowledge of their domestic tyrants, whether husbands or fathers. He told them:

If we were a bibliomaniacal wife, we should have no difficulty (we'll warrant you) in circumventing the husband. We should in the first place have it distinctly understood at the book-shops where we traded that under no circumstances whatsoever should our purchases be sent to our house. We should have these purchases sent to the grocer's or the dry-goods store or to the market or to the millinery shop and sent therefrom to the house in packages calculated to deceive the masculine eye. What sport it would be to smuggle in a Dibdin in a bushel basket under a goodly store of honest, mild-eyed potatoes! And what a calm satisfaction should we feel in taking from the under-done hands of the butcher-boy a ponderous package containing within its wealth of coarse brown paper not only the Sunday roast but a treasured little volume dressed in Bedford's best! What should prevent the laundress from toiling in of a Saturday night with her mighty basket well bottomed with books? What husband would think of plunging his profane hands into those billows of linen and lace in the expectation of resurrecting or expiscating contraband literature?

IV

Field once wrote the biography of a supposititious book collector into which he wove many fanciful details. It properly belongs here to round out this period of biblio-philic fantasy—a period about to be succeeded by the extraordinary time of poetic composition which I have tried to describe in an earlier chapter—a time when every day, or rather every midnight, produced its poem.

The details meticulously woven into the following sketch characteristically are of a sort well calculated to appeal to the credulity of the reader:

The death of Philo Baker removes from the midst of us one of our most respected townsmen. For twenty-five years he has lived in Chicago, and in that time he endeared himself to a multitude of acquaintances. At the time of his death Mr. Baker was seventy-three years of age; for some time he had been more or less of an invalid, never having fully recovered from the effects of an injury which he sustained in the summer of 1883 by falling from a ladder in a Dearborn Street book-shop. Occasionally, however, the old gentleman was to be seen upon the streets and in his old haunts. In spite of his crippled condition he was ever cheerful and cordial, and up to the close of his life he retained in all its original enthusiasm the ruling passion of his earlier years.

Mr. Baker was born in Dummerston, Vt., of well-to-do parents. His father had the largest farm in Windham County, and it was his boast that he owned more miles of stone fence than any other man in New England. Philo was an only child; at a tender age he exhibited a fondness for books, and this predilection caused his father much pain. It is narrated that when he was but seven years old the boy traded off his father's ox-yoke for a first edition of the New England Primer. When he was thirteen years of age he entered Middlebury College, and when he was graduated from that institution he was esteemed a prodigy in certain lines of learning.

It was while pursuing a collegiate course that young Baker wrote his two most famous essays, the first upon "A Theory That the Age and Value of Books May be Certainly Determined by the Olfactories," and the second being entitled "An Inquiry into the Personality of the Wandering Jew." The olfactory theory was subsequently taken up and demonstrated by a course of most ingenious practical experiments by Professor Philippe Guzman of the French Academy, and our own Doctor Hammond of New York City published (1858) a charming little volume on the subject; but the glory of the discovery belongs to Philo Baker, who, while yet a mere boy, provided the book-buyers of the world with a simple and sure guide to the purchase of their wares. The brochure on the Personality of the Wandering Jew was, however, the more ingenious work of the twain. It is in this essay that the author, after disposing satisfactorily of the legend touching the personality of the famous exile, advances the curious theory that the fable of the Wandering Jew is simply a pretty allegory (a fanciful creation—a Jew *d'esprit*, so to speak) originally intended to illustrate the fate of wretched jests or jokes. The author asserts that there is

no new joke under the sun, and that, ages and ages ago, the wretched
facetiæ which are used to torture mankind at the present time obtained
in all their original and native malignity.   These jokes were so bad
that offended nature decreed that they should never die; consequently
they have for tedious centuries gone maudlin and maundering up and
down the world, breaking out ever and anon in diverse literatures and
plaguing mankind in every condition of society.   Herodotus tells of
a Persian potentate who baited his hook with a frog and angled for
fish in the River Danthus; he sorely marvelled that, while others
around him caught many fish, he caught none.   At last his court jester
discovered the cause thereof.   "Canst thou not see, O king," he cried,
"that the frog wherewith thy hook is baited hath swum ashore and
doth squat on yonder stump with the hook still in his gills?"   Now,
this tale passed from Herodotus into the "Banquet" of Xenophon,
then appeared in the "Florida" of Apuleius, broke out in the facetiæ
of Poggio, invaded the tales of Boccaccio, was reproduced by La-
Fontaine, and "at this time," says the youthful essayist, "it is related
as an actual experience that hath befallen our president, Thomas
Jefferson, while he was afishing in the James River of Virginia."
Other jests are traced from their origin down through the lapse of
ages, and the reader is at a loss whether most to admire the erudition or
the ingenuity of the author.

In 1839 Mr. Baker married Prudence Higgins, only child of Moses
Higgins, professor of English literature in Middlebury College.   The
young woman's dowry consisted of one hundred dollars in cash and
a complete set of Lindley Murray's grammars, from the first edition
down to the year 1820.   The volumes were soon conveyed by the
happy bride to her husband, his heirs and his assigns forever.   Shortly
thereafter Baker's father died, leaving his son as the only heir, the
mother having died while the son was at college.   Selling the Dummerston farm, Mr. Baker invested all his money in Western securities.
These proved highly remunerative; at no time after his removal to
Chicago—in 1863—had Mr. Baker found it necessary to engage in
any business; nay, more, his abundant fortune enabled him to gratify
his uttermost inclination, his passion for collecting rare, curious, and
costly books.   And that book collecting was the ruling passion of
Philo Baker's life all who knew him well will testify.   His palatial
house in the south side of town is filled from cellar to attic with books
of every kind—the house overflows with books, and even the stable
has been converted into a receptacle for the insatiable bibliomaniac's
volumes.   It is estimated that Mr. Baker's collection numbers between 35,000 and 40,000 books.   In this collection every variety of
literature is represented, for Mr. Baker's madness was of a grand, a
universal breadth.   In his seventieth year, and after he had been crip-

pled by the fall from the bookshop ladder, he became possessed of a
mania for extra-illustration, and just before his decease he remarked
to a friend that he derived much spiritual consolation from the knowledge that during the last years of his life he had mutilated not less
than sixty tons of books in his capacity as an extra-illustrator!

Mr. Baker always had a curious fondness for figures and for sta-
tistics. He found pleasure during his last moments in calculating
certain arithmetical problems—such as the number of miles his books
would cover if they were laid end to end in a straight line. We recall
that on one occasion he told us that if they were so disposed his books
would extend as far as Hiawatha, Kansas, and he hoped to increase
the distance, before his demise, to the Colorado line. . . .

Our friend's last moments were full of touching incidents. Per-
ceiving his end near at hand, he asked that he be propped up in bed
and that a large number of his favourites be brought in and piled
about him, in order that, as he pathetically said, his dying eyes might
behold the friends which had been his delight and solace. Accordingly
thousands of volumes were brought into the chamber and piled up
and strewed about. Their presence seemed to soothe the aged sufferer.
He read with evident delight a number of hymns from his first edition
of Doctor Watts and then listened with vast earnestness to the chapter which his son Caxton read aloud from the original edition of
Baxter's "The Saints' Everlasting Rest," bound by Bedford. Doctor
Bridge assured us that the life of this amiable man was prolonged at
least a week by the satisfaction which he derived from the piles of rare
and costly books around him. "If," said the dying bibliomaniac one
morning, "if you doctors could only inject a Dibdin, or if I could but
take a draught of Bewick or of Finden, I should speedily be as well as
ever."

The end came at last. His wife noticed that there had stolen into
the aged sufferer's eyes a hungry, wistful look, and her heart gave a
great leap for joy when the dying man feebly motioned to her to come
to his side. For years she had pined for his love; for years had his
monstrous passion for books stood like a merciless giant in the path-
way of her happiness. She had hungered, she had thirsted, she had
yearned for his love—had this gentle, patient wife. And no wonder
that her heart should throb with joy when, with the hand of death
upon him and with the shadows closing round, he beckoned her to his
side to whisper into her ear the words of love she longed to hear.

The aged wife hastened to her husband, spurning with her feet the
precious volumes scattered upon the floor. She clasped his clammy
hands and bent over his pinched face.

"What is it, Philo, dear?" she asked tenderly. "What last word
has my darling to say to his beloved?"

Then the dying man gave a gentle sigh and murmured faintly: "Hand me that Elzevir yonder; I want to kiss it good-by before I pass away."

V

Out of his abundant experience with dealers in old and rare books Field, near the close of his life, set down the following observations:

The average bookseller knows that the hardest customer he has to deal with is the customer who assumes the air and tone of a man who doesn't want to buy anything. The attempt at deception is as plain as the nose on a man's face, for if there be one thing impossible it is the ability to disguise the passion which consumes the bibliomaniac when he is on the trail of coveted game. There is a hungry look in his eyes, a pinched look about his nose and mouth, his voice is hollow and unsteady, he assumes a gayety that is transparently fraudulent, his conversation wanders from one topic to another, assiduously avoiding that which concerns books in general and the object of his search in particular—in short, his appearance and his deportment betray to the practised eye of the bookseller that very condition which he would fain conceal. Yet the bookseller is polite enough and shrewd enough to humour his victim in this absurd dissimulation; he emulates the example of the crafty wife, who, while causing her husband to believe that he is having his own way in everything, actually leads him about as though she had him by a ring in the nose.

Mr. Benjamin H. Ticknor once took me into the labyrinthian bookstore under the Old South Meeting House in Boston and taught me "how to buy a book." I was after a first edition of one of Longfellow's books; not a rare book by any means, but then, you know, one likes a bargain whenever one can get it. We found the book, and Ticknor picked up four or five other volumes, saying: "The smart thing to do is to get these all priced in a bunch, for when the seller doesn't suspect you are after one particular book he'll be easy in his prices. Then, after you've got his price, you can pick out the volume you want and leave the rest. That's the way to fool him."

The plan seemed excellent, but when put into execution it did not operate as smoothly as had been expected. The books we did not want were priced at fifteen cents apiece, while the book we did want was $1.25. I bought it gleefully, only to learn a few hours later that the same thing was obtainable elsewhere for seventy-five cents. I have since been told by booksellers of every degree and quality that the practice into which my friend Ticknor initiated me is one with which the veriest tyro in the trade is acquainted, and is mentioned even in a letter upon the subject of petty popular deceptions written as long ago as the second century by Avunculus Scriblerius, a Roman bibliophile and a descendant of the Pliny family of blessed literary memory.

Pursuing his theme, Field analysed his friends the booksellers in this fashion:

Withal they are a gracious lot, these booksellers at home and abroad; great readers of human character and with minds and memories like sponges. How few of them have been readers, and yet how many of them are filled with a knowledge of (or should we say an acquaintance with?) books! You find them charming companions, for invariably they abound in reminiscence, and their narratives are invariably touched up just enough with fiction to be particularly fascinating. What a delightful compilation of reminiscences could be made by any of the older ones among our booksellers if only the enterprise could be directed by some other person competent to expurgate the solemn moralizing in which the bookseller too often indulges when he takes his pen in hand! As a rule, the very best people patronize the bookshops and stalls, the brightest people, the thinkers, the makers of opinion. They find in the book-shop that recreation that is most pleasant to them; they meet congenial people there, and it is there that they get suggestions and pabulum. Visiting a book-shop is a good deal like going fishing in the amiability of its purpose and the harmlessness of its consequences. At neither employment are conspiracies hatched or evils engendered. The higher spiritual faculties are involved; the sweets of communion and contemplation are wooed; the grosser considerations of life are temporarily forgotten.

In the last paragraph of this disquisition Field set down the true reason for the bibliomaniacal practices which so delighted him. The quaint, brooding philosophy of the proprietors of old bookshops was very pleasing to him, and his mirthful tricks at their expense were legion. And the friendship of rare spirits among his fellow prowlers whom he met among the musty stacks he cherished as he did the fruits of his continual search for odd things in literature. One of Field's special friends among dealers in old books was Frank M. Morris of Chicago. Upon one occasion Mr. Morris said of him:

Field had a peculiar liking for old books upon quaint subjects. Though he called such volumes "fool books," they gave him special delight.   A book on a subject like gastronomy he would gloat over, or it might be a book on "The Art of Contentment," or some other whimsical and little-discussed subject.   Whenever I got a book of that sort I always preserved it until Field came around, for I knew he would want to look it over.   Field also took delight in collecting odd and little-known portraits of celebrities.   He had so many friends that very often he had only to express the wish that he had a copy of a certain first edition or of a certain old volume to set a number of persons looking for it, and by and by the book would reach him as a gift from one of his friends.   Field often would come to my store late in the evening.   Then, with the doors closed, we would sit in the rear of the place and Field would put his feet on a table and sing old songs at the top of his voice.   As he had a very heavy voice he would make the whole room ring.

In a set of books presented by him to Mr. Morris, Field wrote:

To Mr. Frank M. Morris these books are presented with a keen sense of favours yet to come from him.

EUGENE FIELD.

VI

At the end of the Christmas holidays one year Field wrote:

The bibliomaniacs are just beginning to frequent their old haunts again.   During the Christmas season one doesn't see much of them for the reason that the booksellers get in little or no new stock during the Christmas season.   The veteran angler abides not where there are no fish; the bibliomaniac haunts no shop where there is no chance of his securing his beloved prey.

It was our good fortune to be present at a roundup of these curious people at McClurg's last Saturday afternoon; we esteem it good fortune because there is pleasure as well as profit in studying the characters and the characteristics of these people.   The bibliomaniac is *sui generis;* he is masculine in that he combines most of the evil passions of masculinity (such as jealousy, covetousness, envy, etc.) and he is feminine in so far that his character constantly presents some new phase or feature.   This hermaphroditic creature, therefore, doth by his quaint conceits, by his whimsical oddities, and by his strange carriages afford the student of human nature palatable food for reflection.

Among those bibliomaniacs that are husbands it is conceded that the time immediately preceding Christmas is of all seasons of the Christian year the most pleasant and profitable for the indulgence of this mania. For at that time the suspicions of that argus-eyed enemy of books— the wife—are strangely lulled, and the maniac is permitted to bring into his house every variety of package and no questions are asked. The theory is that the wife, upon seeing her husband stalking in with divers bundles in his arms, thinks to herself somewhat in this wise: "Dear man! He has been buying Christmas gifts for me and for our children.   Though I am dying to know what they are, it is better that we should be pleasantly surprised on Christmas morning."   Invariably the dear wife *is* surprised on Christmas morning; when she comes to inspect the scanty array of gifts provided by paterfamilias she begins to wonder what was in all those big bundles, those numerous and weighty packages, that paterfamilias smuggled into the house last week.   She doesn't get much satisfaction if she questions husband about it; husband's memory is painfully defective respecting the whole business.   "What packages?" or "What evening?" he asks, in a tone of dazed astonishment, and he really cannot recall any of the occasions to which his inquisitive spouse refers with distinct accuracy and unremitting pertinacity.

Yet who would have it otherwise?   Who would rob gentle womanhood of its reposeful confidence in man?   There are certain feminine characteristics that might be improved upon, but God knows we would not abate by one jot or tittle this sweet innocence and this beautiful trust which abound in the wifely nature.

Another circumstance that mystifies the bibliomaniac's wife is that upon Christmas her husband receives so many presents from people of whom she never heard before.   Of course these presents are always books, and they are always, too, the very books which the recipient had been wanting.   Not very long ago upon looking at the small but charming collection of our friend Wheatley's books we found that very many of the volumes had been "presented with the compliments of Archibald Smith."   We called Wheatley's attention to it and he answered with a significant closing of the lid of his dexter visual organ.   Subsequently he confessed to us that most of his books had been presented to him; that the donors were "Archibald Smith" and "H. J. Williams," lineal descendants of Sairey Gamp's friend Mrs. Harris.

Here, in embryo, is, of course, Field's later carefully wrought story, "Flail, Trask and Bisland."

At another time, writing on that favourite theme of
smuggling home one's purchases of books, Field gave this
sage advice:

There is but one kind of overcoat which the male book lover can
wear with any satisfaction at all, and that is the ulster. This garment is loose and spacious and is provided with numerous ample
pockets. Our admirable friend Doctor Poole tells us that when he
was a younger man and was suffering acute bibliomania he never wore
any overcoat at all; he wore a series of pockets which were attached
to slender bands of cloth buttoned in front. "This garment," said
Doctor Poole, "was called an ulster, but it was in reality only a system
of pockets."

Here it seems fitting to remark that Field invariably
wore an ulster if the weather permitted. Being gaunt and
thin-blooded, his tall frame throughout most of the year
was draped in that much-bepocketed and very ample garment. And its inner recesses frequently gave forth an
almost incredible number of books when Field brought his
spoils to the office after a good day's hunting in the old
bookshops. His desk not infrequently was stuffed with
prizes during periods when he was devising ways to bring
about their surreptitious transfer to his home.

The sale of a considerable part of Field's library at
auction in December, 1923, furnished me with amusing
evidence that Field practised what he preached on the
subject of taking home prized purchases under false
pretences. Whatever small gifts of books I may have
made to him at any time bore inscriptions in my handwriting, but at the sale appeared two volumes—"Lord
Chesterfield's Letters to His Son" and a book entitled
"Curious and Odd Characters"—in which Field had
written my name as the donor. One of the two bore the
date, "Christmas, 1888." And I am morally certain that
I gave him neither of them!

XXIII

With the "Saints and Sinners"

I

IN HIS joyous pilgrimages among the old bookshops of Chicago, Field had come to know some rare men— quaint characters, some of them, but all book lovers after his own heart.

The lovable old New Englander, William F. Poole, who for years had been the executive head of the Chicago Public Library, was one of these men. Poole stammered slightly, and Field himself at times had a barely perceptible impediment in his speech, a mere halting on a word now and then that was more a mannerism than an obstacle to free expression. Because Poole came from the vicinity of Salem, Massachusetts, Field would have it that his old friend was a believer in witchcraft and that Cotton Mather was his favourite hero. I think that Poole and the Reverend Frank M. Bristol were Field's especially beloved members of that imaginary aggregation, the occupants of the Saints' and Sinners' Corner, to which Field gave fame. On the founding of the Newberry Library in Chicago, Poole was chosen its librarian. He was already widely known for his "Poole's Index to Periodical Literature" and his other contributions to library science. The irreverent Field found in him an inexhaustible subject for sportively fictitious stories, all of which the amiable old gentleman took in good part.

Field wrote many articles purporting to describe edifying proceedings in the Saints' and Sinners' Corner at McClurg's bookstore. He bestowed the name on the section that was given over to old and rare volumes. George M. Millard, who had charge of that department and who was widely known among book collectors, was represented as the chairman or moderator of the alleged meetings. Many of the characters introduced by Field were somewhat shadowy; indeed, with the exception of the redoubtable Doctor Poole and the three so-called saints, the Reverend Mr. Bristol, the Reverend Doctor Gunsaulus, and the Reverend Doctor Stryker, the company was merely a sort of Greek chorus. The three brilliant young divines and the quaint old librarian were the paladins who had the high adventures in book-collecting and related activities recorded in Field's articles. At times these articles were published in rapid succession and again they were absent from Field's column for long periods. The series, begun in 1889, was continued until near the end of Field's life.

Doctor Poole was always represented as musing upon witches and witchcraft. Amazing feats of the Reverend Mr. Bristol in trading books or curios of no particular value for things infinitely more valuable were continually celebrated. Marvellous adventures of the Reverend Doctor Gunsaulus in Arizona, where he was alleged to own vast tracts of cactus, sagebrush, and sand, were described at length. The Reverend Doctor Stryker's supposed desire to have somebody burned for heresy was frequently dwelt upon. The distinguished careers of these clergymen afford proof that Field's admiration for them in their early manhood was not misplaced. Bishop Bristol of the Methodist Episcopal Church and Doctor Stryker, long president of Hamilton College, are eminent in their respective fields. Doctor Gunsaulus, now deceased, was for many years the beloved and eloquent pastor of the great Central Church organization in Chicago, serving also as president of Armour Institute, a technical school of high standing.

Early in 1889, before the doings and sayings of the Saints and Sinners had become celebrated, Field wrote:

The Reverend M. Woolsey Stryker is an able man; he is thoroughly in earnest, consequently in all he undertakes there is a distinct winning vigour. We like him so much as a companion and as a preacher that we are glad he has given the New York people a taste of his quality.

Then Field quoted with satisfaction the following from a sermon preached by Doctor Stryker a day or two previously:

There is unquestionably such a thing as sincere doubt, but being born blind is very different from deliberate blindness. To every serious man doubt is a thing which must be borne and suffered as a disease, with pain and humility. But to an insincere man doubt is a source of pride. When men flaunt their doubts, when they advertise them and sell them for two hundred dollars a night, they stamp themselves as insincere.

What memories Doctor Stryker cherishes of his dead friend are indicated in the following extract from a letter written to me by him not very long ago:

It is a pleasure to write a few lines concerning the warm-hearted and appealing personality of Eugene Field. It does not seem real that he has been gone this thirty years since. My memory of him is still vivid and most affectionate. I was not one of his intimates; but I did know him well and admiringly. He was genial indeed and with many differing persons. He was tender of sympathy and rang true on all the great matters. The quaint strain in his verse had a charm all its own. "Little Boy Blue" was just like him. "There burns a star in Bethlehem town" made a noble hymn of deep feeling.

But it is of himself I think. He made himself a welcome in every circle. He had the originality of a simple and cheerful mind. Something intensely human went away when he left us. Warm adjectives apply to him as to very few men. I am one who misses him.

In his preface to "Songs and Other Verse" in Field's collected works the Reverend Doctor Gunsaulus wrote beautifully of his poet friend, saying, for example:

Beneath and within all his exquisite wit and ludicrous raillery— so often directed against the shallow formalist, or the unctuous hypocrite—there were an aspiration toward the divine, and a desire for what is often slightingly called "religious conversation," as sincere as it was resistless within him.

II

It was on April 17, 1889, that Field first wrote of the Saints and Sinners' Corner. He then described the enthusiasm of the Reverend Doctor Gunsaulus in descanting to a group of book-collecting friends upon the glories of a newly acquired tract of land in Arizona. Having told of the vast sagebrush forests, the boundless fields of succulent cactus, the deep-voiced baying of the prairie dogs, he announced his own abandonment of book-collecting in order that he might devote all his time to the vital things of life. When his spirited tale was ended the ardent Gunsaulus was led aside by the mild-mannered Bristol. A little later Mr. Bristol, "looking like a picture of St. Agatha with a moustache," returned to the group and began to make inquiries as to the best works on irrigation, whereupon it was discovered that he had just traded an extra-illustrated life of Lincoln for the Gunsaulus tract in Arizona.

Not until he returned from his sojourn in Europe did Field make the doings of the Saints and Sinners a leading feature of his column. He then took an early opportunity to tell a wonderful tale about a red necktie belonging to the Reverend Doctor Gunsaulus. While in London, Field one day described a marvellous array of red neckties which he had beheld in a Regent Street haberdasher's window. Then he went on:

Doctor Gunsaulus once said to me: "I should like to wear a red necktie all the time; there is in a red necktie a certain harmless depravity which delights me beyond telling. I have one red necktie; I keep it at home. Whenever I am at the point of peril—when I think that I have done a particularly excellent deed or when I have a sort of pharisaical sense that I am better than my fellow men—I retire to my private chamber, lock the door, don that red necktie and look at myself in the mirror. Then I am overpowered by my sense of human weakness. 'No, Gunsaulus,' I say to my presentiment in the mirror, 'you are a vain and frivolous creature—you are an earthworm and good is not in you!' Now, if I were not a clergyman I should wear a red necktie all the time as a badge or token of my sinful, erring, and unregenerate nature. As it is, I can indulge my natural appetite in secret only."

When I saw that array of red neckties in Regent Street I plunged into the shop and inspected them. For the modest sum of two and six I purchased a particularly truculent one—a tie that seemed fairly to be instinct with and to breathe the mischievous folly of the old Adam. It is now on its way across the sea. It is pleasant to let the folk at home know that you remember them.

On his return to Chicago Field proceeded to describe the effects of that red necktie upon its recipient. Thus the tale began:

There is no other necktie in the world quite so red as the British red necktie; it is the consummation and apotheosis of redness. When Doctor Gunsaulus clapped eyes on that red necktie he was dazzled— nay, he was stunned by its terrific splendour. As quickly as he could he put it away. "I must not wear it," said he to himself. "It is too wicked for this part of the world. I will reserve it for Arizona."

According to the tale, as Gunsaulus was represented to have told it, the owner of the red necktie put it on the next time he found himself in the wild, free Southwest. On the train, the conductor, seeing the traveller's clergyman's ticket, was going to put him off as an impostor. However, Gunsaulus fortunately was able to establish his identity, whereupon the conductor thus admiringly addressed him:

"I've been livin' out here now for goin' on twenty-three years and I've seen every kind of human bein' from bonanza kings down to three-card-monte sharks, but I never seen a preacher with a red necktie afore! Say, pardner, yer a daisy, I'll bet! Although it's agin the rules, I don't mind lookin' at yer ef yer got yer bottle handy!"

At another time the elect were represented to be much interested in a genuine bookworm, the capture of which Field previously had thus described:

In a volume of "Hogarth Moralized," recently received from London, Mr. Millard, presiding genius of the Saints' and Sinners' Corner at McClurg's, found a genuine bookworm some days ago. The worm had evidently ended his travels, for he had begun to spin a web about himself when Mr. Millard captured him and clapped him incontinently into a vial of alcohol. This little fellow is about one third of an inch in length and he looks very much like the worm found in apples, peaches, and other fruits; he is tipped with black at both ends, differing in this particular from the bookworms Blades, author of "The Enemies of Books," met with. Doctor Blandinel of the Bodleian Library told Blades in 1858 that he frequently found bookworms and that they sometimes had black heads. Blades, repeating this information, adds: "I never heard of a black-headed bookworm before or since."

Mr. Andrew Lang remarked to the writer once upon a time that he had never seen a bookworm and that he had actually begun to doubt the existence of that pest; he seemed very much interested in hearing our description of one captured in Chicago—at Maxwell's bookstore, as we recall. It seems pretty well determined that the bookworm is not a native of America; the few specimens found here have been brought hither in English or other foreign books.

At a meeting of the Saints and Sinners the next day—according to Field—the captured bookworm brought on a warm discussion. Mr. Bristol insisted that it had been found in a copy of Doctor Gunsaulus's novel, "Monk and Knight," and that consequently when discovered it "cheerfully resigned itself to death."

REVEREND DOCTOR STRYKER.—That was what Mr. Millard told me and in commemoration of the event I dashed off this epigram impromptu:

> This bookworm once attacked a book
>   With ponderous learning stored;
> The book survived the worm's assault—
>   The worm it was was bored.

III

This further sample of Field's pleasant fooling in reporting a session of the Saints and Sinners may be taken as typical:

REVEREND DOCTOR GUNSAULUS.—I desire to serve notice that at our next meeting I shall read to the brethren a report of my bibliographical pilgrimage through Arizona.

REVEREND DOCTOR STRYKER.—Brother Gunsaulus will also please explain how so many of his relatives happen to be mixed up in that guerrilla warfare along the Mexican border. I read in the papers that about every other guerrilla is a Gonzales, which name is, as I learn upon application to the Banner of Heraldry, the original Spanish of Gunsaulus.

REVEREND DOCTOR GUNSAULUS.—The archbishop of the north side shall be duly informed. While I am not proud of my remote ancestry, I must admit that I am descended from an ancient Spanish family. Our name in the old country is Gonzales and "We come of a family that kill"! Don Miguel Roderigo Gonzales was a successful pirate on the ocean sea. A grandson named Pedro located in Arizona two centuries ago, and, contracting several lefthanded matrimonial alliances with the young lady natives in that arid country, instituted and perpetuated a bar sinister which (as you see, I blush to say) is almost as big as the original coat of arms of the Gonzaleses. At one time seventy per cent. of the natives of Arizona were Gonzaleses, but before the invasion of ruthless civilization this degenerate branch of the noble Castilian family has been slowly melting away. Still, there are several left, mostly halfbreeds. They call me Cousin Frank, and I suppose I am related to them through the dim and twinkling relationship which all men bear to one another as children of the old Adam. But out in Arizona the Indians interest me particularly. We are great friends. When I came away from there this last time they gave me a splendid bearskin robe and two beautiful beaded moccasins. They call me Wah-na-buk-sin, which means Young-Man-Afraid-of-Eugene.

MR. LARNED.—Is it true as reported that Phil Armour and you have preëmpted claims in Arizona to the extent of twenty thousand square miles?

REVEREND DOCTOR GUNSAULUS.—No, it isn't. We have some business interests in common, but by no means to that extent. I have a large acorn grove near Lost Soul water-tank which I intend to sell to Brother Armour for a swine pasture. We have a number of beautiful arid town sites which will undoubtedly become very valuable in due time. We have named these prospective towns after our friends—Pooleville, Bristol, Stone Landing, Gunther City, McCherryville, Higinbotham Heights, Strykerton, Peabody Junction, Wilson Corners, etc. Ultimately—mark the prediction—ultimately Arizona will blossom out into a veritable heaven upon earth.

REVEREND DOCTOR STRYKER.—You couldn't make Brother Herrick Johnson believe that. At a symposium of Presbyterian theologians the other evening Brother Johnson expressed the conviction that heaven was bounded on the north by Fullerton Avenue, on the east by Halsted Street, on the south by Belden Avenue, and on the west by the McCormick Seminary tennis lawn. Upon being hard pressed he admitted (though not without hesitation) that, by the manifestation of a special providence, 420 Fullerton Avenue might possibly be included probationally in this paradisiacal tract.

The somewhat restricted boundaries of heaven thus alleged to have been defined by the Reverend Doctor Herrick Johnson took in the buildings and the faculty residences of McCormick Theological Seminary, the one provisional addition to the glorified area being the residence of Field, on the other side of the street from the secure place of everlasting bliss.

IV

The following is part of a long report of another Saints' and Sinners' meeting:

Mr. Larned from the committee on foreign relations reported a resolution regretting the demented condition of Guy de Maupassant, the French novelist. Mr. Larned proceeded to state the unhappy man's symptoms and the causes of his malady, in French; for, as he explained, these were details which admitted of more discreetly delicate elucidation in the allusive language of the Gaul. Mr. Larned hoped that this resolution of sympathy would be adopted, and that engrossed copies of it would be sent to the families of the afflicted man.

DOCTOR POOLE.—I once bought one of Maupassant's novels to read, but I read only one paragraph. That was the first paragraph in the book and this was the way it went: "One day in the autumn of 186— M. Alphonse de Blasé was walking in the Rue Scribe. Suddenly he felt himself seized from behind. Shaking off the rude grasp of his assailant, he turned. There stood his friend, Jacques Jeune-Roué, trembling with emotion, the apotheosis of mental anguish. 'It is you!' cried Alphonse. 'Speak—something has happened. Do not kill me with suspense! Speak, I implore you!' 'Alphonse,' gasped the unhappy Jacques, 'Alphonse, my friend, I have made a fearful discovery! Justine, your wife, she is false to us!'"

The resolution went over.

Before the next Christmas meeting of the Saints and Sinners the Reverend Doctor Stryker had become president of Hamilton College and the Briggs heresy controversy was in full swing. So the meeting, which according to Field was simply drenched with the Christmas spirit, was said to have received a telegram from President Stryker reading: "Peace on earth, good will toward men— except Briggs!" And the good Doctor Poole, as a contribution to the general fund of kindliness and love, told how he had been taken in a few days before by a stranger who sold him a stake which the stranger said had been used of old time in the burning of witches. Indeed, it bore the letters "C. M.," supposed to have been carved on it by Cotton Mather himself. However, Doctor Poole's inquiry developed that the letters were actually the initials of one Cyrus Muggins, an Indiana farmer, who had used the stake in roasting an ox at a Democratic barbecue!

XXIV

Did Field Love Children?

I

SINGULARLY enough, this question has been raised: Did Field love children?

In his "Auto-Analysis" Field wrote: "I have tried to analyse my feelings toward children and I think I discover that I love them in so far as I can make pets of them." His pleasant enough, though somewhat cold, declaration seemingly marks an honest effort by Field to define his real sentiments toward children. Honesty of this sort by the children's poet in a world of make-believe is, it seems to me, worthy of honourable mention. Yet it is a superficial view that he thus expressed—disappointingly superficial considering all that this father of eight children had written so sweetly, so sympathetically, of childhood. After all, however, was it not enough for a man who habitually studied children and child life to say? He might have struck a literary pose and poured out rapturous phrases, but he preferred to make a plain confession, and it suffices.

In his biography of Field, Slason Thompson wrote:

This man, who could not have set his foot on a worm, who shrank from the sight of pain inflicted on any dumb animal, took almost as much delight in making a child cry, that he might study the little face in dismay or fright, as in making it laugh, that he might observe its method of manifesting pleasure. He read the construction of child nature in unreserved expressions of childish emotions as he provoked or evoked them.

In his "Fifty Years a Journalist," Melville E. Stone, writing of Field's deportment at the theatre, says:

Often if there was a child in the seat back of him Field would turn and make a face which would set the infant bawling. The mother, having no idea of the cause, would search in vain for an offending pin, while Field's sides were shaking with delight.

My long friendship with both Thompson and Stone, which extends over more than forty years, convinces me that the words of theirs which I have quoted were based on hearsay evidence, though both were intimately associated with Field. Surely neither of them would have permitted Field or any one else deliberately to frighten a little child in his presence without administering to the offender such a rebuke as would have deterred him from repeating the offence. Consequently I am not greatly impressed by their testimony on this point; for I, too, have heard grotesque yarns about Field's delight in frightening children. For my own part I can testify that I never saw Field conduct himself in the presence of children otherwise than in a manner to gladden their little hearts. He would tell them stories and enter into their games, a big and somewhat clumsy child among congenial playmates. And always, almost bashfully, he would attempt to win their confidence and affection.

F. Willis Rice, a long-time friend of Field's, said of him:

His love for children was a passion. Little babies especially he loved with inexpressible tenderness. When he called at a house where there was a baby, the baby was the host. He devoted himself exclusively to it and the adults of the household saw very little of him.

George W. Cable wrote:

Children went to his lap as promptly as to a garden swing.

If, however, hearsay testimony on this subject is permissible, I have a story to tell which may serve to explain the prevalence of the legend that Field loved to frighten children. The story was told me by an eye witness, a man who knew Field well. He was at Spirit Lake late one summer, when Field and his old friend, Melvin L. Gray, were there, Mr. Gray being the host. Field was the life of the place—so much so that the proprietor of the summer hotel kept it open some days beyond his regular closing time to accommodate the houseful of guests that remained to enjoy Field's delightful companionship. Of evenings in the hotel parlour Field recited poems, told stories, or gave imitations of actors for the pleasure of the guests. One morning Field and my informant were in conversation on the hotel veranda. A little child kept edging up to inspect at close range the man who recited verses for and about children. Field, becoming annoyed by these attentions, presently faced the small intruder and twisted his extremely flexible countenance into a grimace. The child ran away in terror.

That afternoon Field, at the request of the guests, recited some of his poems for the children at the hotel. Every mother was there with her brood. After the informal entertainment was over the mothers edged forward holding tiny hands in order that their respective darlings might meet the children's poet. It was all very beautiful; but in the midst of the greetings a tempest arose to mar the occasion. One little child suddenly burst into screams when her mother insisted upon dragging her forward to the kind Mr. Field. Her frantic kickings and unmeasured roarings won the day, and the scandalized mother carried her out with apologies for the incomprehensible conduct of her naughty offspring. In the midst of the uproar Field turned and surreptitiously winked at my informant, for both of them had recognized in the young rebel the child whom Field's sudden grimace had put to flight that morning.

This is the only specific instance of Field's intentionally
frightening a child that I ever heard of. I cannot think
that he got any pleasure out of the act; rather I fancy that
it was a thoughtless expedient intended as a bit of disci-
pline for a too inquisitive little one. And making grimaces
was second nature to Field's mummer's countenance.
However, the proof that children in general were fond of
this amusing playmate of theirs is overwhelming.

When Field and his two companions were on the point
of leaving Spirit Lake, Field went to the landlord and
asked for the bill for the three members of the party. As
usual, he had no money, but—also as usual—he scented
an opportunity to perpetrate a joke on his old friend
Gray, who was paying for the trip.

"There is no charge for you and your companions, Mr.
Field," said the grateful landlord. "Your presence here
has kept my hotel full of guests a week after the closing
time."

"You are very kind," said Field, now perfectly sure of
his joke. "When my friend Mr. Gray asks for his bill
please tell him that Mr. Field has settled for everything."

Mr. Gray in due time called for his account and, from
Field's point of view, showed a highly satisfactory degree
of amazement when told that Field had discharged the
debt. Knowing that the impecunious Field could not
have produced the necessary cash, Mr. Gray demanded
an explanation. On learning the truth he stormed at the
idea of being transformed into what he called a "dead-
head." The landlord, in order to appease him, made out
his individual bill and Mr. Gray paid it.

II

It always seemed to me that Field's attitude toward
children was very like the attitude of one child toward another. Like a child, he was a creature of impulse. He

had the free imagination of a child. He had the child's
gift of wondering and the child's delight in all things
strange or beautiful. He lived, as does a child, in a land
of dreams. He insisted that he believed in fairies and
hobgoblins and that he was given to "seein' things at
night." Spiritually Field never grew up. He loved
Christmas as a child loves Christmas, and the giving of
gifts for friendship's sake was to him almost a religion.
I have thought that the attitude of Field toward children
was the attitude of one dispossessed of a prized inheritance
toward those who were in full enjoyment of the privileges
denied to him. What would not Field have given, for
example, for the privilege of returning to his lost belief in
Santa Claus?

He proclaimed the doctrine that every child had a right
to be happy, to live in a land of illusion, to follow its own
devices. Of his little girl, Trotty, he would say: "Let
her sleep as late in the morning as she pleases and do what
she pleases so far as that is possible, for in a few years she
will be grown up and married, with cares enough and to
spare." He was always kind to his children but not always wise in his kindness. One day he brought his
small son Pinny to the office and thus introduced him to
at least one member of the staff: "Pinny, this is Mr. Hawkins. Go and strike him for a quarter." The joke was, of
course, on Mr. Hawkins, but the advice to the little boy
was scarcely edifying.

Field could supply at any time out of his fertile imagination an abundance of wonder tales to hold a group of
children breathless. He told his own children whole
cycles of marvellous stories of their own adventures while
riding a magic "stick-horse" which was able to carry them
anywhere. But mere story-telling did not satisfy him
when he was in the company of children. It was his desire not only to be accepted as a friend by any child with

whom he came in contact, but to establish confidential relations with that young comrade.

Field came to my house one day to walk with my two small sons and me through Lincoln Park. On several occasions while that otherwise uneventful excursion was in progress I observed my three companions apparently in close consultation. As their demeanour indicated that my participation in their counsels was not desired, I discreetly kept my distance. Not until years afterward did one of my sons confide to me that at each of these conferences Field transferred sundry small coins from his pockets to theirs, accompanying those transfers with solemn injunctions not to tell their father. The transactions were to remain a special bond between Field and them. Doubtless Field found enjoyment in studying the grave demeanour of those little boys when they were thus suddenly burdened with an inviolable secret.

On another visit to my home Field delighted my wife by begging for a sight of the bared feet of our infant daughter. He inspected them, measured them, and delivered himself of this verdict: "They have Trilby's beaten a mile."

III

Field unquestionably studied children with the purpose of expressing their ways and their emotions in his poems and stories. But I am sure he studied them sympathetically and, as a rule, with sentiments of tenderness. Two of his poems, "Hi-Spy" and "Humanity," were inspired by the sight of the children of a janitor who lived with his family on the top floor of a building just across the street from the *Daily News* office. In the twilight the two older children would play in the nearly deserted street, while "the big-eyed baby just across the way" would survey the universe from its mother's lap at a window opposite Field's window.

These and almost countless other evidences of Field's sympathy with, and understanding of, children which I might enumerate seem to me greatly to outweigh any testimony that has been presented tending to show on Field's part an elfish lack of regard for the child's delicate organism and its extreme sensitiveness to nervous shocks. However, the sweetening process that went on year by year in Field's nature was most marked. He had written for and about children almost from the beginning of his career and between his early work and the work of his last years there is a vast difference. Compare, for example, the heartless mirth of the "Tribune Primer" with the following closing sentences of a little story on the death of a child:

Children, laugh on, and sing and play, for, oh! this world of ours is beautiful with the glory and the tenderness of human love! Would to God the treble music of your play could awake that slumbering little friend of yours and mine!

Field's sympathy with the child's point of view is well illustrated by the following, written about a year before his death:

Four little people—mere children—living at Freeport, Illinois, were so infatuated with a peripatetic merry-go-round that they followed it all the way to Janesville, Wisconsin, where, upon advices from home, they were taken into custody by the police and subsequently sent back to their anxious parents.

It is not hard to understand why little children should be fascinated by the merry-go-round. We confess that, at an age when our thoughts should (according to the ascetics) be upon severer subjects, we take a rare delight in watching the flight of this gaudy machine with its cargo of gleeful little folk, and one of our sincerest sorrows is that we have not the stomach to engage in this exciting sport. The spirit indeed is willing, but the spot under the midriff is weak.

No other sight is more inspiring of gentle feelings than that of a lot of little girls and little boys seated in the coaches and upon the horses of a revolving merry-go-round. What noble horses they are! Was there ever a more extraordinary combination of attractive colours?

Can you estimate the joy of a child that is permitted to mount and ride a magnificent wooden horse, painted a brilliant red with jet-black ears, fiery blue eyes, a tail and mane of real green hair, and with a saddle and bridle of honest-Injun leather, beautifully embellished with gold and silver?   Or, if he prefer, the child can have a splendid black horse, with yellow eyes and a white tail, or a green horse with a pink tail, or a blue horse with a gold tail—in fact, there are many beautiful horses to choose from, and the most remarkable feature of all is that each horse is better than the others—if you doubt it just ask the little folk themselves.

The coaches, too, are charming affairs; maybe they call them chariots nowadays, and surely no oriental ancient vehicle was ever more sumptuously gotten up than is the merry-go-round's chariot, wherein it is for pretty little maidens to ride securely, with none of those dangers which confront one who rides sidesaddle and with none of the offense to feminine dignity that the divided skirt entails.   Can you fancy a prettier spectacle than that of a blonde little lady in a lovely blue chariot drawn by two prancing, milk-white steeds?   Or that of a dark little lady in a beautiful red chariot whirled along by a pair of untamed yellow horses?

The music, too, adds to the excitement and the charm.   It seems to come from an inner circle, a kind of holy-of-holies that is screened off in such wise that we have never been able to discover how the music is actually made, although we have distinct suspicions on that point.   Whether, however, this exhilarating concord of sweet sounds is emitted by a classic calliope (now, mind you, call it not cal-ly-o-py) or by a low hurdy-gurdy, its effect is provocative of enthusiasm and mirth.   It inspires not only the little women and the little men, but also the red horses and the blue horses and the other horses, and sometimes—yes, actually sometimes, while that merry-go-round went whirling and humming like a big, grand top, while the music behind the curtain went "ump-yah, ump-yah, ump-yah," oh, ever so sweetly! and while the boys and girls shouted and laughed and made other gleeful demonstrations, why, then—this is true what we tell you—we have heard those horses neigh and whinny with delight!

Now, if there is any pleasanter sight than this we have never seen it; if there is any other music sweeter than the laugh and shout of a joyous child we have never heard it.   So it is not so great a wonder after all that we love the merry-go-round, whose most endearing feature is those sympathetic associations with childhood which are precious to all good women and all good men.

The passions of youth do not altogether die with the years.   There are merry-go-rounds to amuse every age and every condition; and we all ride and enjoy the fun.   One prefers a red horse with a blue tail,

another a pink horse with a black tail, and still another a white horse
with a green tail, or, perchance, chooses a chariot painted yellow and
upholstered in Roman purple. There is a hobby for every one and
everybody rides, and the hidden music goes "ump-yah, ump-yah,
ump-yah" all the time. So much more reason have we to humour
the little folk in their innocent love for the merry-go-round.

IV

Field wrote in his "Auto-Analysis": "I am fond of the
companionship of women and I have no unconquerable
prejudice against feminine beauty. I recall with pride
that in twenty-two years of active journalism I have always written in reverential praise of womankind." And
indeed Field, whether in a serious or a humorous mood,
showed only respect for women, though he said uncom-
plimentary things occasionally of some members of the
sex. Take, for example, these observations on women in
London theatres:

The women wear conspicuous costumes. At the Criterion one evening I saw a scrofulous-red woman clad in a fiery red gown, the corsage
of which was actually plastered over with diamonds—not real diamonds, for very few ladies wear genuine diamonds to the theatres. In
fact, it seems to be quite the thing to blossom out in paste. I have
noticed that scrofulous-red females are all too common here in London;
the redder the face the redder the gown. Yet there may be philosophy
in this. I recollect that Madame Modjeska once told me: "Red worn
below the face deadens the complexion; worn above the face it height-
ens the complexion. If, therefore, a woman wishes to subdue the
colour of her cheeks she should wear a red gown or plenty of red rib-
bons about her throat; on the other hand, if she wishes to give her face
a certain touch of colour, let her wear a red hat or red flowers in her
hair."

Here is another bit of comment by Field on feminine
attire:

When a girl gets one of those impracticable, impossible flat hats
perched on the top of her coiffure she is unhappy until she gets aboard
an electric surface car and lets that impracticable, impossible flat hat
blow off into an adjacent township. Then all traffic must stop until

the precious noodle has recovered that egregious, preposterous and damnable flying-machine.

Far more in Field's usual manner, however, is the following, written in 1888, when Melville W. Fuller of Chicago was appointed Chief Justice of the United States Supreme Court by President Cleveland:

Mr. Fuller and his family will be a charming acquisition to Washington society.   He himself is a delightful companion and his wife is a most attractive lady.   Their sons are all daughters and there are eight of them—eight bright, beautiful girls!   One daughter is a godsend—a good many of us know that; but eight—eight lovely types of gentle, engaging womanhood clustering like posies around the domestic fireside—eight godsends!   That is a blessing which heaven bestows upon the favoured only.

So as a smart and good man, as a conscientious citizen, as the husband of a charming wife, and as the father of eight bouncing, bewitching, and bewildering girls, Mr. Fuller is clearly entitled to the preëminent honour for which he has been nominated.

Here is an example of Field's fondness for allying himself —in print, and to the confusion of his friends—with the cause of women:

To-night the Fellowship Club recognizes the potent and sweet influence of our good St. Valentine by giving a dinner to the ladies.   To this feast each member of the club bids his wife, and he is privileged to bring along, too, some other fellow and that other fellow's wife.   So the banquet hall will be crowded and there will be no end to the witty things and the complimentary things said and done.

We are heartily glad to know that the temper of the club has finally conformed to what we have urged for the last eighteen months— viz., that the ladies should be permitted to grace and to share in the occasional banquets.   This proposition was at first acrimoniously antagonized by Messrs. Scott, Rice, Handy, Selfridge, Kohlsaat, and Waller, and as these gentlemen constituted the directory we found it hard working the desired reform.   A breach in the opposition was first made when Major Handy went to New York to live, and this was widened by Mr. Kohlsaat's removal from Chicago.   Mr. M. E. Stone was elected to the directory in Handy's place, and, being a candidate for mayor, he sought to make political capital by declaring in favour of the ladies.   This brought Mr. Waller around into line, for he, too, wants to be mayor, and he didn't propose to be outwitted by any two-per-cent. money changer in the temple.   Meanwhile Secretary Rice and President Scott, having taken professional treatment of the Seven Southerland Sisters, began to think more kindly of the gentler sex, and so by an auspicious combination of haps and events the cause we originated and persistently agitated triumphed, as to-night's glorification will prove.

It is not our intention to exult over our victory.   On the contrary, forgiving and forgetting the past, we shall simply ask the proselytes to arise and join us in a health to our lovely, gracious guests whose presence is the noblest of dignities and the sweetest of delights.

One curious manuscript of Field's that is in my collection was written when President Harrison was about to form his cabinet at the beginning of his term—that is to say, in 1889.   It probably marks the earliest serious advocacy of a woman as a cabinet officer of an American President.   Field wrote:

Why not Mary Logan for a cabinet portfolio?   Is it not about time for the nation to recognize and to confer some handsome mark of distinction upon a representative of its womanhood?

Where is there to be found in all our land a nobler representative of our womanhood than Mary Logan?   Hers has been a remarkable experience, involving extraordinary toils, unusual hardships, extensive travel, and all those excitements incident to an uninterrupted and active participation in the career of her soldier-statesman husband.   With that unfaltering fidelity and that certain forceful wisdom akin to genius which all nobly great women have, she has been the inspiration of a camp, a distinct influence in statecraft, and a revered and beloved ornament both in the social and in the domestic circles.

From out of her years of heroic service has Mary Logan come, her noble character strengthened and quickened and beautified by chastening and by sorrow.   Why, in the honouring of such a woman, there would seem to be a wisdom, a justice—yes, a lofty pride, to which every manly heart must be keenly sensible.

V

With all his admiration for and courtesy to women, Field dearly loved to play practical jokes on them.   A favourite joke of his is thus described by William H. Crane:

One day when we were in Chicago, Field invited Mrs. Crane and me and Mr. and Mrs. Barnabee out to his house. He assured us solemnly that he would have no one else there and he said that the ladies were to come in their walking dresses. Imagine their chagrin when we arrived to find about fifty of the ladies of the neighbourhood assembled to meet Mrs. Crane and Mrs. Barnabee, all dressed elegantly in reception dresses!

Edward W. Bok describes a similar incident, Field having inveigled the ladies of Bok's party to his house in their travelling dresses a few hours before they were to take a train out of the city and there plunged them into a maelstrom of handsomely dressed women who had been invited by Field to meet them.

Attire was to Field a matter of complete indifference. He could scarcely realize that anybody cared about it, since he never did. On this point Julian Ralph wrote:

I once saw Field walk to an imposing house, to which he was invited for dinner, in his shirt sleeves, with his coat on his arm. This he did, not because the afternoon was warm, but because of the fun he found in that unusual mode of paying a visit.

XXV

Diversions of a Convalescent

I

IN THE green open spaces of Buena Park, whither Field removed with his family in the spring of 1893, he was particularly happy. Though that part of Chicago was somewhat sparsely inhabited then, it contained a number of beautiful homes and Field found his neighbours most congenial. Of the modest rented house in which Field established his family Hamlin Garland wrote:

His library was filled with all kinds of curious objects—worthless junk they seemed to me—clocks, snuffers, butterflies, and the like; but he also possessed many autographed books and photographs whose value I granted. His cottage, which was not large, swarmed with growing boys and noisy dogs; and Mrs. Field, a sweet and patient soul, seemed sadly out of key with her husband's habit of buying collections of rare moths, door-knockers, and candle-molds, with money which should have gone to buy chairs and carpets or trousers for the boys.

Of Field himself at that time Garland wrote this description:

A tall, thin-haired man with a New England face of the Scotch type, rugged, smoothly shaven and generally very solemn—suspiciously solemn in expression. His infrequent smile curled his wide expressive mouth in fantastic grimaces which seemed not to affect the steady gravity of his blue-gray eyes.

Indeed, the upward curve of the corners of the mouth, a curve that was in fact a bit of conscious mugging, commonly characterized Field's smile, which manifested itself only in the curiously flexible muscles of the lower part of his face. This localization of his expansive smile was one of the striking characteristics of that long, white, almost emaciated countenance.

Field's bedroom and study in the Buena Park cottage was on the second floor at the rear and its windows looked westward, directly out upon the broad vacant space which he made famous under the name of "the Waller lot." The owner of the lot was Field's good friend and amiable landlord, Robert A. Waller, the founder of Buena Park, where Waller's parents had been among the first settlers many years before. The tract is now built up solidly with apartment houses, but any one who wishes to identify it can readily do so by standing at Sheridan Road and Buena Avenue and facing northeast. The tall campanile of the Church of St. Mary of the Lake rises just across Sheridan Road from this playground of the children in Field's day. "The Delectable Ballad of the Waller Lot" and "The Ballad of the Taylor Pup," to mention no others, chronicled (and exaggerated) incidents that occurred under the poet's eyes as he sat at his writing table before his study window.

II

In the autumn of 1893 Field was stricken with typhoid pneumonia and for a time was desperately ill. As soon as he had progressed so far toward recovery that it was permissible to visit him I went to his house and was admitted to his room, where he lay in bed, weak but happy in the knowledge that he was making steady progress toward health. His bed was so placed that he could gaze out across the Waller lot and watch the children at their play. Displayed about the room were his collections of dolls and butterflies and pewter, his Gladstone ax and his

other treasures.   At the foot of the bed was a capacious
goldfish bowl with goldfish swimming about in it, and lying on a chair at Field's bedside was a small pole with
hook and line attached.   Field told me that by way of
amusing himself he sometimes sat up in bed, baited his
hook with a bit of food, and dropped it into the goldfish
bowl.   The accommodating fish, possibly by way of
relieving the monotony of their existence, bit at the bait
readily, so that after every cast Field speedily had one
of them swinging above his head.   The hook was barb-
less, and being caught upon it, Field contended, gave
the fish nothing more than a pleasurable thrill of adventure.   He insisted that if he were a goldfish he would
like to be entertained by an occasional experience of the
sort.

I did not encourage him to display his prowess as a
fisherman for my benefit, as fishing in a goldfish bowl
seemed to me too simple-Simonish even for a bedridden
poet.   However, another friend of Field's who called on
him about that time told me that while he was present
Field sat up in bed, dropped his hook into the bowl, and
promptly caught a goldfish, which the visitor as promptly
took off the hook and threw back into the bowl, the fish
apparently accepting the incident as quite in the natural
order of things.

Field told me that during the critical period of his illness he laboured continually under the delusion that
there were two of him lying side by side.   He was seriously distressed at the time by what he regarded as the
hard-heartedness of the physician and the nurse in ignoring one of him while lavishing attentions upon the other.
At the time of my visit he had just received from Stedman
a set of the latter's books which Field had purchased and
sent to their author to be autographed—a favourite
practice of Field's.   He selected a book from the lot and

read to me, with some emotion, the beautiful quatrain
that Stedman had written in it:

> Death thought to claim you in this year of years
> But Fancy cried—and raised her shield between—
> "Still let men weep, and smile amid their tears;
> Take any two beside, but spare Eugene!"

Field's first contributions to his column after his illness
were three pieces of verse—"Googly-Goo," "The Ride
to Bumpville," and "Cradle Song."

By Thanksgiving Field was up and about. He had
sent me a note inviting me to take Thanksgiving dinner
with him and his family. On his instruction I took a certain railroad train to Buena Park, there being no elevated
trains in that day. Field met me at the station, two or
three blocks from his house. As we walked eastward on
Buena Avenue he pointed to the vacant ground to the
north and said: "It may interest you to know that this is
the famous Waller lot."

"It does interest me," I replied, "for I had supposed
that the grounds about the old Waller homestead there
to the south were what you called the Waller lot."

"No," said Field. "Children are not allowed to play
in those grounds."

I have set down this conversation for the reason that
practically all writers on the subject have fallen into the
error from which Field delivered me during that short
walk. It is a natural error, for the old Waller mansion,
surrounded by its spacious grounds, was one of the land-
marks of that section of the city, whereas the Waller lot
celebrated by Field was a mere vacant tract quite devoid
of interest except to children or to some prospective in-
vestor in real estate. Still, the latter attractive building
site was free to the foot of any child, while the grounds
about the Waller mansion were carefully fenced in and
inaccessible to romping little folk.

At the time of my Thanksgiving visit to his home Field was preparing to start on a trip to California in the hope that its mild climate would aid him in recovering his health and strength. He departed for the Pacific Coast a few days later. Unfortunately he did not find the California climate beneficial to him. Months later he wrote a fantastic article on his experiences in the Golden West. I quote parts of it:

While we were in California Madame Modjeska urged us by letter to visit her ranch. This beatific spot is located about twelve miles from the line of the Southern California railway, among what are called the foothills. You get off the train at a platform named El Tauro and you drive over to the villa in a vehicle sent forward by the superintendent of the ranch. By dint of perseverance, ingenuity, taste, and a large expenditure of money, Madame Modjeska has transformed her ranch in the foothills into a veritable Eden, so they say.

We did not visit the embowered spot for the reason that we read in one of the Los Angeles papers one morning that, rendered desperate by cold and hunger, a number of mountain lions had descended from their snowy fastnesses and were enjoying the hospitality of the Modjeska ranch. They had carried off eighteen or twenty beeves and innumerable sheep, goats, and calves, and yet were not satisfied. Every evening they came down out of the woods and camped for the night on the front porch of the Modjeska mansion—waiting, evidently, for the appearance of somebody they were expecting.

So we didn't visit the Modjeska ranch, it being one of our constitutional idiosyncrasies that we cannot sleep at night while there are mountain lions purring around and whetting their fangs on the front porch. . . .

There are but two books read in California; one is Helen Hunt's "Ramona" and the other is the Whittier Birthday Book. You cannot go anywhere between Fresno and Tia Juana without having pointed out to you "*the* house where Ramona lived." There are no fewer than sixty of it.

We have made a special study of Ramona and her career, and we are satisfied that Mrs. Hunt drew very largely upon her imagination when she wrote that romance, and we think she ought to be turned over to the remorseless judgment of Hamlin Garland, who hath come to judge the quick and the dead.

We find that Alessandro (Ramona's first husband) was not murdered, as Mrs. Hunt alleges.   His last days were spent in San Juan Capistrano, and they were devoted to getting drunk—not wildly or hilariously, but just logily, soddenly drunk.   One time he secured a quart bottle of whisky at the hotel kept by old Mrs. Mendelssohn, and he went out into the climate and lay down under a palm tree.   In two hours he was just as dead as if he had taken prussic acid.   Judge Dick Egan held an inquest on the remains and rendered a verdict in accordance with the testimony afforded by the empty whisky bottle. By the way, this Mrs. Mendelssohn who keeps the hotel at San Juan Capistrano is quite a character.   It was she who originated the philosophical and memorable saying: "When you're in Rome do as Romeo does."

But as for Ramona, she still lives (as we are told and as we believe) at San Juan Capistrano.   We saw her as we journeyed to and from San Diego.   Upon the first occasion she came aboard the train, selling insect powder in small, brown-paper packages.   She was o'erburthened with the infirmities of age rather than with clothing and her appearance served as a most eloquent tribute to the propriety of the trade in which she was engaged.

When we came back from San Diego Ramona's house was pointed out to us as we pulled slowly through San Juan Capistrano, and we saw Ramona in the back yard, butchering a hog.

IV

After wandering disconsolately about California for some weeks, early in 1894 Field returned to Chicago.   By February 6th, however, he was in New Orleans and contributing "Lyrics of a Convalescent" to the *Daily News*. To this period belong "The Delectable Ballad of the Waller Lot," "The Humming Top," "The Drum," "Good Children Street" and "Dr. Sam."   Field took great delight in New Orleans.   Its balmy air, the quaintness of the French quarter, and the bargains in the curio shops made the city a joyous place for him.   About May 1st he returned to Chicago and on May 4th "The Peter Bird" appeared in the *Daily News*.   Three days later "Sharps and Flats" was restored to its place after an absence of more than half a year.   Field expressed his appreciation of the South and the Southern people in this fashion:

Let the average Yankee locate along the Gulf Coast, where he can't get any codfish and where baked beans are an unknown quantity; feed him on pompano and corn pone; what is the inevitable result?   The Yankee loses his shrillness of speech and he begins to drawl.   He finds himself losing interest in temporal affairs.   He awakens to a realization of the fact that money in itself is a vulgar, greasy commodity, and that the man who devotes himself to the accumulation thereof is practically a slave.   Then that Yankee buys a hammock and swings it between two trees in the piney woods and his eyes acquire a *dolce far niente* look, and the next thing we know that Yankee is voting the Democratic ticket and is bidding the Home Market Club of Boston go to thunder.

We defy anybody to live six weeks along the Gulf Coast and not fall victim to that inexpressibly delightful languor that is called Southern.   The sensation of not caring whether school keeps or not is particularly novel and peculiarly refreshing to Chicago people; in fact, we think the time is near at hand when the delightful country adjacent to the delta of the Mississippi will become the sanitarium—the vast health recruiting grounds—of overworked Chicagoans.   Neurasthenia is the *bête noir* of Chicagoans, and no other spot on earth is more congenial to the neurasthenic than is the country adjacent to New Orleans.   The climate is mild, inviting if not compelling outdoor life. There are sights to see and things to do; one is kept busy in a harmless, irresponsible way.   The people to be met with there are a soothing influence, they are so improvident and indifferent, so careless, so happy-go-lucky, so delightfully impossible.

v

During Field's illness of the previous autumn there blossomed forth on the editorial page of the *Daily News*, from which "Sharps and Flats" so long was conspicuously absent, a series of sparkling stories and sketches—all with appropriate illustrations—under the heading, "Stories of the Streets and of the Town."   To be exact, the first of these articles was published November 20, 1893, and they appeared daily thereafter for a considerable period of years. For a slender young man from Indiana, who for two years or more had been the star reporter of a staff of exceptionally able reporters, had won on merit the privilege of writing precisely what he chose to write and in the way that suited him best. After having written brilliant sketches about the World's Fair throughout the period of its existence, this young man—his name was George Ade—found himself back on the regular staff of reporters and unhappy in consequence because of the limitations placed on his opportunities to do good descriptive work and get it printed. So I gave him two columns on the editorial page and the coöperation of his bosom friend, John McCutcheon, then a member of the newspaper's art department and as modest as he was efficient, and told him to fill the space with stories and pictures to his own liking. Speedily the two ardent Indiana youths made a notable success of this daily feature, which they carried on together as long as Ade managed to resist the demand of syndicates, book publishers, and producers of plays that he cease his newspaper writing and earn a few thousand dollars a week by providing them with material such as he could produce. After the publishers awoke to the quality of the young writer's work they issued most of his newspaper sketches in book form. "Artie" proved so great a success when put between covers that "Doc. Horne," "Fables in Slang," "In Babel," and other volumes speedily followed.

While Field was recuperating in New Orleans in the spring of 1894 a young reporter of the *Daily News* staff was marching, at his own request, with "General" Coxey's army of hoboes and a miscellaneous throng of out-of-works from Massillon, Ohio, to the Capitol at Washington, writing the adventures of himself and his fellow marchers who, theoretically at least, were sufferers from the industrial depression of the time. That young reporter was Ray Stannard Baker, who since then has made two enviable reputations in the field of literature, one in his own name and one in the name of his admirable creation, the gentle philosopher, David Grayson. Of the march of this or a similar so-called army in that year of unrest Field wrote: "We look upon it as the biggest real estate transfer of the season." The comments of young Baker, with his instinct for studying the causes of social disquiet, were more sympathetic.

By this time the name of the morning edition of the *Daily News* had been changed to the *Record*, in order more sharply to differentiate it from the evening editions of the *Daily News*. It had come to be the most widely circulated morning newspaper west of New York, and the average high quality of its staff of writers has seldom been surpassed. I think the fame of Field had no small part in attracting to the *Record* many ardent young men who, almost without exception, afterward won high places for themselves in literature, in finance, or in journalism. Field was exceedingly fond of this bright coterie of aspiring youths and always spoke of them affectionately as "our boys."

VI

Field's own reputation by that time had become more than national and respect for his ability as a poet was expressed by intelligent people everywhere. Not many months later, when his earthly work was done, a discriminating critic wrote in the *Atlantic Monthly:*

If Mother Goose, wandering into the semicircle of light where Dante found the limbo of good poets, should sit at the feet of Shelley and learn the magic of his lyre, I fancy that her wizened, beatified old throat would break out sooner or later with much such a carol as "The Rock-a-By Lady from Hushaby Street" or "The Song of Luddy-Dud." It is no small thing to voice the joys and woes of one whole stage of the earthly journey, however short, especially when that stage is full of the most enormous little psychic adventures. This Field has done. He has written the Canterbury Pilgrimage of infancy. The great book of human interpretation is the poorer that the tale had to be left half told.

This same critic also wrote of Field:

It is not difficult to see that in the last years of his life his sense of the beauty and value of creative art rapidly deepened. He seems to have been conquered by the muse almost before he knew it, as one who should stop by an Athenian door-sill to chat with a lazy citizen, and go thence knowing Socrates and questioning the ultimate. Yet if this rare touch had never come to him he would still have been, from many points of view, an engaging and suggestive figure. He was one of those unusual men who continue to be profoundly typical of their time and environment at the same time that they retain the raciest of individualities.

To me this characterization of the man and his art ranks as the best of all that have come to my knowledge. Field was indeed typical of his time and of his environment; yet under no circumstances did he surrender any part of his unique and fascinating individuality. Whether swapping yarns with the lank, tobacco-stained, hickory-shirted denizens of the Missouri Valley or conversing with or playing jokes upon the literary and book-collecting friends of his latter years, he made no compromises with his soul. Pretense of any sort was to him at all times the unpardonable sin. And I cannot too strongly deny the injurious legend that he cultivated the rich in a sycophantic manner. Nothing could be further from the truth. Field chose his friends in an absolutely democratic spirit.

Something of what Field came to be to his fellow poets is shown by a letter which Stedman wrote to him a few months before Field's death, acknowledging the gift of a copy of "Love Songs of Childhood." Addressing the author of the book as "My Beloved Eugenio," Stedman said:

I have fallen so in love with your Dinkey-Bird singing in the Amfalula tree that I to-night have christened the Lear-Rands-Dodgson carols in my "Victorian Anthology" "The Land of Wonder-Wander" (quoted). I was at my wits' end for a title when I heard your Dinkey-Bird.

There have been lamentations by writers in recent years because none of Field's friends and associates "had the Boswellian talent" to take down and preserve his drollery and his wit. One writer has said:

In truth, Field's hand of "summer lightning, which illuminated what it touched," was too swift, too fine, to be caught and put into cold type. He who attempted it would have found himself in the position of the child who tries to catch the glistening dewdrops in the morning grass and carry them home to his mother. Only a few flashes of Field's lightning-like wit, which played here and there on kindred souls, have been caught and held fast—the rest have disappeared like all other electric flashes.

And it is true that Field's merry talk and his innumerable jests would have been difficult to preserve. However, the essence of his humour has not been lost, as I think readers of the quotations from his pen which are contained in this volume will testify.

XXVI

LAST SCENE OF ALL

I

THE last springtime that he was to know on earth Field hailed with special delight. He wrote, late in April, 1895:

More beautiful spring weather than that with which Chicago has been favoured for the last week can hardly be imagined. Vegetation has made a rapid advance; the trees are getting ready to burst into leaf, the shrubbery is budding out, and the grass is just green enough to invite the demonstrative caresses of the little folk. With another week of this persuasive sunshine we should certainly have Nature in her freshest and most gracious loveliness. . . .

Let us content ourselves with the pleasures of the present, with the cheery aspect which Nature presents at this season, and with those employments which either the sincerity or the gayety of our revived beings may suggest. The muses are in the midst of us. Pan has come out of his hiding, and from their hollow trees and secret caves the satyrs and nymphs do issue. Upon the greensward, all in the mysterious light of the virgin moon, doth Venus lead the dance, and hither come the Graces and unbelted Laughter and Mercury and the others of that precious company. Can you not, O Sextus, hear the music, and doth it not awaken pleasing echoes in your soul? Come then, let us out of doors whither a thousand endearing voices call; it is the time to devote to those gracious allurements which bring gods and humankind together in the companionship of song and mirth.

That particular month of that particular year was indeed delightful to Field, for early in that month he and his wife bought "The Sabine Farm."

Buena Park and its people were beloved of Field. His merry stories about his neighbours, his ballads celebrating the alleged adventures of his own and his neighbours'

318

children, his joyous chance conversations on street corners
or on doorsteps whenever he happened to meet acquaintances in his strolls—these indicated his great fondness for
his home surroundings. He wanted to live there the rest
of his life, and he wanted a home of his own to live in.
At dinners of his much-prized Fellowship Club, where
Field was always a prime favourite because of his abounding mirth, he was accustomed to speak of his good friend
and fellow member, Bob Waller, as his "grasping landlord." On one occasion Field described in detail for the
edification of his fellow diners Waller's alleged merciless
methods of collecting the rent and the consequent sufferings of himself and his hapless family. Waller, thereupon,
with equal enjoyment, rose to confess the truth of Field's
accusations and, after adding further harrowing details,
remarked that his heartless oppression was so efficacious
that Field's payments at that time were only three months
in arrears! Probably Field might have had the house
rent-free for all that the big-hearted Waller cared.

Field, however, wanted a home that he could call his
own. So he searched persistently for a house in the
neighbourhood that he might purchase at relatively small
cost and on easy terms. His growing family required
more room than the rented cottage provided and Field was
extremely eager to possess a spacious library wherein his
books might be properly disposed; he also wanted a place
where he might display his various collections of curios.
In one of my walks with him he took me to see a vacant lot
near his home which he especially desired to possess in
order that he might build a house upon it. It proved to
be a large, triangular piece of ground at the intersection
of Sheridan Road and Broadway, as those streets are now
called, on which stand to-day the Buena Memorial Presbyterian Church and its parish house. Field was oblivious
to the heavy costs that would have been imposed upon

him by the excessive street frontage and he took no account of the noise of the tides of traffic flowing by on three streets. He only saw the pleasant wooded place as it then existed, with its wild birds and its green grass, and he longed mightily to possess it, though its price was far beyond his means.

II

At last one day Field told me with manifest excitement that he and Mrs. Field had purchased a house and that it was precisely what they wanted—or it would be after they had reconstructed it. Fortunately the aged couple who had owned and occupied the house for many years had consented to accept a very small sum of money to bind the bargain, since that particular sum was all Field could raise on short notice. He showed special pride in Mrs. Field's bargaining powers, to which he gave chief credit for the outcome. Now the important question was whether his indulgent friend Mr. Gray would furnish him with the necessary money not only to complete the purchase but so to reconstruct the house as to make it suitable for the needs of himself and his family.

The subject of purchasing a home had been broached by Field to Mr. Gray a year and a half earlier, and some sort of tentative understanding had been reached between them in the intervening period. However, when Field now communicated with Mr. Gray he awaited that good man's reply with anxiety. When it came the reply was favourable. It was speedily arranged that Field was to pay back the money in weekly installments and that Mr. Gray was to be consulted on his financial affairs while the debt remained uncancelled. So Field entered delightedly upon the task of putting the house in habitable condition. It was a frame structure that had been built many years before amid the sand dunes bordering Lake Michigan.

Clarenden Avenue later had been extended past it, but at a distance of two hundred feet or more. There were great willows and maples in the front yard and there was sand everywhere, the lake, upon which the house fronted, being only a few hundred yards away. Newer residences had been constructed on neighbouring cross streets, but this pioneer residence turned its shoulder coldly upon them. Such rooms as there were in the house were fairly large, but there was a painful lack of modern conveniences and the structure needed paint from end to end.

In the succeeding weeks Field added two rooms, extended the porch, put in plumbing, gas, a modern heating plant, and hardwood floors. Thus was the old settler's substantial house transformed into a commodious and comfortable home. As the weeks passed and the work went on, with the usual—and some unusual—vicissitudes, Field wrote amusingly and sometimes even truthfully of his experiences with workmen and contractors. He had hoped to move his family into the new home late in May, but it was July before he was able to vacate the rented house a few blocks away and go to live in the Clarenden Avenue house—his own!

III

Even amid the tumult of getting his family settled in the new quarters, where painters and other workers still swarmed, Field was eager to display its beauties to his friends. I had been ill for some weeks, but as soon as I was able to do so I responded to Field's invitation to "come and see the new house." Already it had been named by its master "The Sabine Farm," as a mild Horatian jest. Field's articles in his column on the cares that afflict the man who undertakes to remodel an old dwelling had amused and interested me, so that I was particularly glad to behold the nearly finished product of all his and Mrs. Field's planning. As Field showed me through the house I thought the work upon it had been carried out with admirable judgment. Apparently it was well suited to the needs of the Field family. And at last Field possessed a large and beautiful library where his books and other treasures might be suitably disposed.

The afternoon was exceedingly hot and there was no breath of air. While Field was showing me his prized north room with its mirror-like hardwood floor, in which he took special pride, he opened a door leading to the porch in an effort to discover and let in a breeze. A few minutes later we retired to the library, where we took off our coats because of the stifling heat and sat down for a talk. Our conversation lasted two or three hours. While we talked a storm came up and there was a terrific downpour which brought a breeze and the house became delightfully cool.

Oblivious to the uproar of the storm, we continued to discuss Field's new surroundings, his literary prospects, and certain concrete plans of his for the future. The demand for his writings had become so great that he was recasting all his ideas regarding his career. He was deeply interested in planning his "Love Affairs of a Bibliomaniac," which he was then beginning, and he was also pondering a book based on his boyhood recollections of New England in the years of the Civil War. "Now that I am here in my own house I shall do better work than ever before," he said more than once during the course of our talk. Field showed me with pride his new built-in bookcases and his beautiful library table, which had just arrived, the gift of a friend. He had been assembling and arranging his books on the shelves and in my presence he opened a package of books which had come that day by express. It contained a set of the works of Richard Henry Stoddard, which Field had got together and sent to

Stoddard for autographed inscriptions. He took up the books one by one and read to me what his old friend had written in each. Field also read me a letter from W. D. Howells, written in response to Field's request that he place his autograph in each one of a set of Howells's books which Field had sent him for that purpose. Howells promised speedy compliance and further assured Field that his typewritten reply was a true autograph letter since he himself had typed it.

IV

Thus was Field carefully and lovingly placing upon his shelves the books which meant so much to him and which he had gathered together with such enjoyment. There most of them remained for twenty-eight years, until the poet's widow shipped them to New York for sale late in 1923, though I think the choice volumes of the collection previously had been disposed of at private sale.

For a long time while Field and I talked on that summer day the rain poured and the thunder bellowed. Not, how-ever, until I read in Field's column a few days later, in a new installment of "The House," rueful mention of the dire results of our having left that north door open to the storm, did I realize how careless had been the poet and his guest that day. This is what I read—it appears in Chapter XXIV of the published volume:

The fixtures came late, too late for the big storm. There being no bolt or any other fastening to the north porch door, the wind blew that door open and the rain descended in torrents upon the hardwood floor of the guest chamber. Next day it was apparent that the floor was practically ruined. The carpenters agreed that it would have to be scraped and that it was very likely to swell and spring out of place on account of the soaking it had suffered.

It was, as I knew, an agency other than the wind that opened the north porch door to the storm, and neither

324 EUGENE FIELD'S CREATIVE YEARS

Field nor I had remembered that open door amid the sluicing of the rain and the bellowing of the thunder.

The storm finally spent itself. Before the rain entirely ceased a cold wind swept through the house. We had begun our talk in the breathless heat that had preceded the tempest; now, coatless, we found ourselves shivering. Putting on my coat, I prepared to depart. Though I was planning a health trip of a few weeks across the Atlantic, I expected to see Field again before I left Chicago. Field went out with me to his newly constructed front lawn. There lay a garden hose busily spouting water into a sizable puddle, as evidently it had spouted all through the tremendous downpour. Field laughed at the double soaking which his young grass had received and waded through the puddle to turn the nozzle of the hose in a new direction.

As I pursued my way to the street under Field's dripping willows and maples, I called back to him that as a militant citizen I should have to tell the first policeman I met that the proprietor of the Sabine Farm was violating a city ordinance by watering his lawn at a forbidden hour. Field shouted a merry reply and went on sprinkling his lawn. I never saw him again.

v

While returning home on a street car I suffered a severe chill. Being weak from my recent illness, I had a relapse and was confined to my bed for some days. As soon as I was able to get out again I left Chicago for Europe. Early in November I was back in New York Harbour after my brief trip abroad. From letters delivered to me on shipboard I learned that Field had died suddenly while I was on the Atlantic and that his funeral was set for that very day.

He had been happy and busy until the last. He had continued writing "The House" and he had begun and all but finished "The Love Affairs of a Bibliomaniac." Amid his other tasks he had written a few poems, notably "The Dream-Ship." Mr. Gray had stood staunchly by him, supplying more and more money to complete all the necessary improvements on the house. However, Melville Stone had volunteered to pay for the painting of its exterior. This circumstance adds point to a bit of humour that appeared in Field's column less than a month before his death. "Dr. Norman Bridge," the article began, "arrived from Los Angeles day before yesterday. He said: 'I came because I learned that Mel Stone had fallen off a coach and hurt himself.'" Field, proceeding with his story, quoted the doctor as having used a ludicrous medley of medical terms, ostensibly descriptive of Stone's hurts, which included a damaged right hand. "Does this injury," the anxious inquirer interrupted, "prevent Mr. Stone from signing checks for his old friends who happen to seek his aid in their temporary financial embarrassment?" This question brought another extraordinary flood of medical terms which ceased only when the inquirer interrupted to ask:

"Is it probable that Mel will never be able to sign any more checks with that hand?"

"Alas, that, I fear, is too probable," answered the kind physician.

"In that event," said the interviewer, "his duty would seem to be clear enough; Mel should learn to write with his left hand."

Further proof of the degree to which Field's thoughts were wrapped up in his new house is furnished in a letter, dated "The Sabine Farm, 24 Aug.," addressed by him to the editor of the *Critic*, who for some reason had written to a large number of American authors to discover whether or not they rode bicycles, those machines being then in great vogue. Field replied:

Last Christmas a friend gave me a bicycle and I thought then that I should surely become an expert wheelman as soon as the spring came with its beautiful weather and inviting roads. But here it is nearly autumn again and I am no more of an expert wheelman than I was a year ago. I do not ride and I do not seem able to muster up any ambition to ride. Maybe this is because I do not belong to the New Woman school.

But I *am* an expert at pulling weeds. My wife bought an old-fashioned house last May, with a half-acre of lawn around it, and I have busied myself for the last four months fighting weeds. I am death on plantain, dandelions, pusley, and pigweed. No gallivanting over the boulevards and turnpikes for *me* until I have put my own house in order!

VI

Though I have tried to show from his own pen what kind of man was this "many-sided Field"—the term is Julian Ralph's—I am glad to present a few estimates of him by persons well qualified intelligently to appraise his qualities. Ralph wrote:

He was to his wife a tender lover; with his children almost a child; in one Chicago circle a working journalist; to the world at large a poet, minstrel, and story-teller; to some acquaintances a clever mimic and raconteur, to others a scholar, a book-lover, a collector; to everyone a practical joker and to very many a sympathetic, kindly, hearty friend. Once I even heard him called a worshiper of success, with no heart left for the humble and the unfortunate. It may be so, but I never noticed any trace of this in his talk or his conduct.

Field had detractors, as Ralph intimates, but they were men whose knowledge of him was slight or wholly non-existent, men who were mentally and morally incapable of measuring his rare qualities of mind and heart. And certainly Field did not worship success, and he did most earnestly sympathize with the humble and the unfortunate. Only his intimate friends, for example, knew of an aspect of Field's mind that has been set forth in a few words by George Millard:

Soon after I met him ten years ago I became aware that under his apparent hilarity there was a vast amount of sentiment. I was walking with him one Christmas Eve when the crowds were going home with armfuls of gifts. He turned to me and said: "I always feel like shedding tears when I see all these people going home with their little gifts for the babies. I can't help crying. It overwhelms me."

The many tender Christmas poems and Christmas stories which Field wrote in themselves afford ample proof of his love for the sentiments which inspire Christmas giving. And the Reverend Frank M. Bristol said when the poet of childhood lay dead:

While Field was genial and whole-souled, affable and hail-fellow-well-met with all, yet there was a tender, serious minor strain running through all his best verse that appealed to the sympathies of the world. He was a classic scholar. Horace was his ideal among the classic writers. He was fond of pure, simple English. He read Bunyan's "Pilgrim's Progress" and Walton's "Angler," Charles Lamb and Father Prout, and was particularly fond of books written for little children, even of the old New England Primer. He believed in God and a future life, but he would never talk theology. He had a creed, but thought every man ought to be allowed to have one of his own. He would do battle for anyone who was down. If one chanced to speak hard of anybody Field would always try to say some pleasant thing in his behalf. He wouldn't enter into any controversy about the person's merits, but would simply say: "Oh, well, the battle is hard enough for all of us. No use making it any harder." I think Eugene Field's poems contain more comfort for parents whose hearts have been wrung by the loss of little ones than do all the sermons ever preached.

At the time of Field's death Hamlin Garland said:

Eugene Field was inexpressibly dear to me. I knew him intimately, loved him profoundly, and admired him greatly as a man and as a writer. Only a week ago I was with him and we talked long of his work and of his hopes. At that time I told him I felt that he was entering upon a period which would see him produce his best and greatest work. Great as his work was, I am convinced that he had it in him to do much greater.

VII

Field died in his sleep shortly before dawn on Monday morning, November 4, 1895. In the *Record* of the preceding Saturday his column had appeared as usual. How Field died and his surroundings as he lay dead were described in the *Record* by the capable pen of the young man who years later conceived and wrote the beautiful books of David Grayson. Here is part of what the young man wrote:

While he slept, early yesterday morning, death crept in and touched Eugene Field gently. And the children of the land mourn their laureate.

On Sunday he looked out from the wide window of his library where the dry leaves whipped about in the sunshine.

"This is the dying time of year," he said, only half seriously. Then he laughed again as heartily as any of them.

In the evening he was ailing. The doctor came and said that it was nothing, that with a night's rest he would be better. And so the family parted. An hour or two before daybreak, while the house was still dark and quiet, the poet turned in his bed and groaned. His young son, who lay beside him, called to his father, but there was no answer. Then he reached out and touched him, but there was still no response. Terrified, the boy crept from the bed and alarmed the household. When lights were brought it was found that Eugene Field had passed from the quiet sleep of life and health to the deeper slumber of death. He had died as he had often wished to die—in the midst of his work, at the zenith of his strength. . . .

The body lay in the upper room where death had entered. It is a long, high room, the most wonderful room in all the city. From floor to ceiling it is covered with a thousand and one relics that the poet had picked up in various parts of the world since he had been a collector. And it is cluttered up with heaps of his favourite books and hung with ancient pictures and photographs. At one end stood the table where Mr. Field did his writing. It also was covered with piles of manuscript in the poet's microscopic hand.

On the corner of the table lay a number of packages addressed to some of Mr. Field's friends. One of them bore the name of General Nelson A. Miles and another that of George M. Millard. The poet's life was one long exhibition of generosity and friendliness that was bounded only by his means. When he saw a book or a print that he thought a friend would prize he purchased and sent it.

At this table also Mr. Field had written the last chapter of "The Love Affairs of a Bibliomaniac" on Sunday afternoon and he had delivered it to his little son "Daisy" to be taken to the office of the *Record*.

The poet was not a conventional collector. Nor did he have any fads. What his fancy chose he bought and kept. And thus it happens that the bookcase at the side of his wonderful den contained a "thumb" Bible and the smallest dictionary in the world, and the stand next to it held a collection of odd and curious canes, and the shelves across the room were loaded with bottles of a hundred different shapes and sizes and all unusual and wonderful. And there also was Gladstone's famous ax presented to Mr. Field by the great premier himself, and Charles A. Dana's scissors framed and hung above the bed. Mr. Field was a great lover of mechanical toys and small images and he had hundreds of them about his den, together with strange pewter dishes picked up in some out-of-the-way place across seas. Old blue china almost as delicate and fragile as cobweb there was, too, and rare old prints, and the most complete collection of works on Horace in the world. All these thousands of things were jumbled up together. Their very catalogue would make a big book, and yet there was a history of each of them lost with the death of the poet. In all of them he took an almost boyish delight, and it was this characteristic of youthfulness that gave him such a charm with children and that has made him the supreme master in the realm of child verse.

But his antiques were not all in his little den, for the reason that it could not possibly hold them. He loved old clocks, and clocks therefore stand at every turn in the house. In the front hallway there is a tall, old-fashioned New England clock with a pictured face, and there is an old clock on the stairs. And there are little clocks that tick very loud and big round clocks that tock sonorously. Yesterday their tongues made noisy clamour in the desolate house. Other hands will have to wind them now.

Of books there is no end. Mr. Field possessed one of the rarest libraries in the West, and it is made up of every description of book, both bad and good. From the time that he went abroad as a boy with an inherited fortune and came back penniless, with heaps of books and curiosities, to his death his passion for books never flagged. And he loved odd arrangements. Here are the books that stand in a row in one nook of the big, airy library, with its built-in cases: "Statesmen's Dishes and How to Cook Them"; a copy of the works of Pliny; Austin Dobson's "At the Sign of the Lyre"; several volumes of a rare edition of DeFoe's works; "What I Know about Farming," by Horace Greeley, and "Why Priests Should Wed."

All about the library are other curiosities and the walls are covered with autograph letters, autographs from every one, from Robert Browning to Lily Langtry. In another room is an old Napoleon dresser. In its drawers are bits of rare fabric, the robe of a Japanese priest, and other wonderful things.   There is also a collection of dolls of curious makes and shapes.

When I first read this article in the files of the *Record* more than a quarter of a century after it was written—for it was published while I was on the ocean—I had no difficulty in deciding that only one reporter on the newspaper's staff at that time could have written it.   There, for example, was the sentence about the "little clocks that tick very loud and the big round clocks that tock sonorously."   But to make sure beyond question I wrote him for confirmation and received this letter in reply:

Amherst, Mass., October 2, 1923.

DEAR MR. DENNIS:

Yes, I wrote that story of the death of Eugene Field.   I remember how deeply I was impressed; but I also remember that the city editor cut out some of the things I liked best!

Did you know that Field was brought up here in Amherst?   We lived for a couple of years in his boyhood home when we came to Amherst.   His uncle, Mr. Jones, left a fortune to found a library here and the librarian has been getting together quite a number of Field mementoes—which you may like to see when you come this way, as I hope you will sometime be able to do.

Cordially yours,

RAY STANNARD BAKER.

VIII

Field, according to his family physician, died from heart failure, probably induced by sudden intense pain.   His death, so untimely, so unexpected, brought expressions of sorrow from thousands who had known and loved him. At his funeral, two days after his death, a great throng was in attendance.   His own "Singing in God's Acre" was sung and in the sermon, delivered by the Reverend Frank Bristol, the minister said:

Some day, out in God's acre, where angels sing their "Sleep, oh, sleep," a monument shall mark the resting place of our gentle poet.

And let it be built, as was Daniel DeFoe's in the city of London, by the loving, grateful contributions of the children of the many.

That monument now stands in Lincoln Park, Chicago, though Field's earthly remains lie in Graceland Cemetery in that city. The monument was paid for in considerable part by the small contributions of thousands of children. It shows a slim and smiling spirit, instinct with grace and beauty, and poised on butterfly wings, that bends lovingly over two drowsy little children upon whom her slender hand drops poppies. Is she the Rock-a-By Lady from Hushaby Street who

> Bringeth her poppies to you, my sweet,
> When she findeth you sleeping?

This charming group in bronze rests upon a granite pedestal rising from a spacious granite platform, upon the floor of which appears in bronze letters: "To Eugene Field." Chiselled in low relief upon the pedestal appear the magic boat of Wynken, Blynken and Nod; the wonderful Sugar-Plum Tree, with glad children gathering the fruit; the Flyaway Horse with its intrepid rider, and the unhappy hero of "Seein' Things at Night." The whole is admirably conceived and delicately wrought. It is continually surrounded by admiring throngs, particularly children. On any sunny day one may see parents bringing their little ones to be photographed with the little sleepers in bronze and the dream-spirit in the background.

When, on a chilly afternoon in late autumn of 1922, this lovely memorial was dedicated in the presence of many of Field's old friends and associates, the widow of the poet was there and so were all the children who survived him—"Trotty" and "Pinny" and "Daisy" and the two who were babes when their father died—Roswell ("Posie") and Ruth ("Sister Girl"). At the appointed moment the little son of Roswell and the little daughter of Ruth unveiled the monument.

IX

After Field's death I was able to be of some slight assistance to Mrs. Field in getting off promptly to the publishers the copy for "The Love Affairs of a Bibliomaniac." It lacked but the final chapter which Field had planned to write, and because of this lack the ending was abrupt. I have frequently regretted that I did not suggest to Mrs. Field a simple transposition that would have made the present Chapter XII the last chapter. The transposition, it seems to me, would have provided a most fitting ending to the book, the writing of which closed the life work of its author. For that chapter ends in this wise:

That was in the springtime, Captivity Waite; anon came summer with all its exuberant glory, and presently the cheery autumn stole upon me. And now it is winter time and under the snow lies buried many a sweet, fair thing I cherished once. I am aweary and will rest a little while; lie thou there, my pen; for a dream—a pleasant dream—calleth me away. I shall see those distant hills again, and the homestead under the elms; the old associations and the old influences shall be round about me, and a child shall lead me and we shall go together through green pastures and by still waters. And, O my pen, it will be springtime again!

No words, I think, could more fittingly serve as colophon to the writings of the children's poet, who so gently "fell on sleep."

THE END

INDEX

INDEX

Stryker, Rev. M. Woolsey, a subscriber to Field's volumes of poems and stories, 184; "member of Saints and Sinners," 287.

"Studies in Folk Song," Countess Montenegro-Cesaresco's book, source of several of Field's poems, 223.

"Swapping" of books, Field's proclivities for, 262.

"Telka," source of the material for the poem, 223.

Terry, Ellen, friendship with, 67.

"Than you O valued friend of mine," writing of, 170.

"The Bibliomaniac's Prayer," writing of poem, 169.

"The Bibliomaniac's Bride," writing of poem, 171.

"The Brook and the Boy," source of material for the poem, 223.

"The Conversazzyony," writing of poem, 171.

"The Cyclopeedy," writing of the story, 169.

"The Dead Child," written in memory of Field's son, 239.

"The Death of Robin Hood," writing of the poem, 176; first draft of, 178.

"The Delectable Ballad of the Waller Lot," when written, 312.

"The Dream Ship," writing of, 325.

"The Drum," when written, 312.

"The Happy Isles," writing of poem, 171, 176; first draft of, 177.

"The Humming Top," when written, 312.

"The Little Peach," enormous popularity of the poem, 31.

"The Little Yaller Baby," story of its writing, 146,161.

"The Luxury of Reading in Bed," Field's essay on his favourite vice, 200.

"The Old Homestead," Field's appreciation of, 63.

"The Partridge," source of material for the poem, 223.

"The Peter Bird," when written, 312.

"The Ride to Bumpville," when written, 310.

"The Symbol and the Saint," publication of, 157.

"The Twenty-Third Psalm," the poem, 170.

"The Wanderer," writing of the poem, 38.

"The Wooing of the Southland," writing of poem, 171.

"There fell a star from realms above," writing of poem, 169.

"Thirty-Nine," Field's birthday poem, 179.

Thomas, Theodore, Field's description of orchestra of, 36.

Thompson, Denman, Field's appreciation of "The Old Homestead" 63.

Thompson, Slason, friendship with, 48; joins staff of Chicago Daily News, 69; Field's favourite companion, 72; resigns from Daily News staff to assume editorship of America, 115; on arrangement of matter in "Culture's Garland," 150; assists in subscription work for Field's volumes of poems and stories, 182; publishes Field's article on newly discovered letters of Edgar Allan Poe, 266; on Field's attitude toward children, 295.

Ticknor, Benjamin H., publisher of "Culture's Garland," 10; requests material for publication of a book, 148; entertains Field in Boston, 158; gives instructions on buying books, 281.

Ticknor, Miss Caroline, makes public Field's

letter to her father regarding publication of "Culture's Garland," 149.

"'Tis spring! The boats bound to the sea," writing of poem, 170.

"To My Old Coast," writing of, 171.

Toole, J. L. anecdote on, 58; meeting with, in London, 209.

"Three Cavaliers," writing of poem, 170.

Tree, Beerbohm, meeting with, in London, 209.

"Tribune Primer," in many editions, 37; publication of, 156.

"Trilby," a badly printed book, 262.

Trogden, Howell, incident of his flag in the anarchist parade, 75, 76.

Tufts, Rev. James, Field attends boarding school of, 15.

University of Missouri, Field's attendance at, 19.

"Venus, dear Cnidian-Paphian queen," writing of poem, 171.

Waller, Bob, as the "grasping landlord," 319.

Waller lot, its location, 308, 310.

Ward, Mrs. Humphry, meeting with, in England, 209, 214.

Warner, Charles Dudley, purposely confused with patent medicine maker, 97 et seq.

Washington, George, comments on his red nose, 89.

Way, Washington I., publishes the "Florence Bardsley" history, 92.

"What perfumed, posie-dizened sirrah," writing of poem, 170.

"When, Lydia, you (once fond and true)," writing of poem, 168.

"When you were mine in Auld Lang Syne," writing of poem, 169.

White, Henry Ten Eyck, author of "Lakeside Musings," etc., 152.

"Widow or Daughter," writing of poems, 171.

Wilde, Oscar, renewal of acquaintance with in London, 212.

Williams College, Field's attendance at, 16.

Wilson, Francis, makes use of "The Little Peach," 32; Field's friendship with, 57; his versatile legs, 59; a confirmed book collector, 110; a subscriber to Field's volumes of poems and stories, 184; finances publication of de luxe edition of "Echoes from the Sabine Farm," 259.

Wilson & Son, John, publish Field's volumes of poems and stories, 182.

"With Trumpet and Drum," publication of, 261.

Wood, Eugene, "discovered" by Henry Ten Eyck White, 152.

Women, the bane of book collectors, 274; observations on, 303 et seq.

Women, English, Field's impressions of, 227.

World's Fair, Chicago, Field's delight in, 246.

Writing in bed, the habit of, 4, 75, 174, 200 et seq.

"Wynken, Blynken, and Nod," writing of, 170; parody on, 172.

"Wynken, Blynken, and Nod," first reading of, 174.

Yates, Edmund, meeting with, in London, 209.

Yenowine, George H., or Field's hatred of being lionized, 243.

"Yorick," Stedman's name for Field, 1, 316.

"Yvytot," writing of poem, 185; first publication of, 207.